"We live in a time in which we are inundated with quick-fix resources. This book is not one of them. David Young invites individuals and congregations into a disciplined and thoughtful process of awakening to God's presence in our midst. It is an invitation to participate in life transformed through Christ."
—*Stanley J. Noffsinger, Church of the Brethren*

"David Young's latest book bears the title of the thorough-going program he has developed for transforming congregations, *Springs of Living Water*. Young has drawn upon his extensive experience as a pastor and as a teacher, and upon his impressive work with congregations and clusters of churches, to produce a comprehensive and timely resource for those who are serious about church renewal. The program he describes is biblically based and theologically sound, and his personal illustrations reinforce its spiritual integrity. That the author is himself a man of God is evident throughout the book. He knows whereof he speaks, for he himself has drunk deep from the springs of living water. He has invited countless pastors and church members to do the same, and his book will help many more to taste and see that the Lord is good."
—*Richard Stoll Armstrong, Princeton Theological Seminary*

"I encourage all pastors and church leaders to consider David Young's *Springs of Living Water* initiative. Its practical, Bible-based, Spirit-led approach to individual and church renewal begins where change is most necessary—in the human heart. *Springs* was well-received by our churches and is bringing new life within and among them."
—*John Ballinger, Church of the Brethren, Northern Ohio District*

"Unlike many books on the subject of church revitalization, David Young's book on *Springs of Living Water* is not a packaged product that will guarantee the success of renewal. Rather, Young promotes renewal as a spiritual journey that builds on what is right rather than what is wrong with the church. Renewal is not

seen as a "done deal," rather David sees it as an ongoing process that can be enhanced through the process prescribed in *Springs of Living Water*. An interesting twist found in this book is the connection of church renewal with servant leadership. This is not surprising when one realizes that the author's whole approach to ministry is focused on a servant leadership style. Young's book will not remain on a pastor's shelf collecting dust. It will be a handbook kept within easy reach for the ongoing ministry of the local church."
—*Louis A. George, American Baptist Churches of Vermont and New Hampshire*

"David Young skillfully lays out the necessity for Christian formation, vision and a definitive plan for mission. In doing so he also describes the kind of leadership that produces the fruits of the Spirit."
—*Claude E. Payne, Episcopal Bishop of Texas*

"David Young's refreshing gift to the church and its leaders is his vision to reconnect the oft-severed cord between individual spiritual renewal, the reawakening of the local fellowship of believers, and the soul transformation of the whole body of Christ for the sake of the world. This dynamic process, if embraced by a people of the cross, will no doubt result in the emergence of that mark of renewal toward which David Young points us—a Christ-centered people in mission with God."
—*Phil Wagler, Mennonite Church Eastern Canada*

SPRINGS OF
LIVING WATER

SPRINGS OF
LIVING WATER
Christ-Centered Church Renewal

David S. Young
FOREWORD BY RICHARD FOSTER

Herald Press
Scottdale, Pennsylvania
Waterloo, Ontario

Library of Congress Cataloging-in-Publication Data

Young, David S. (David Samuel), 1944-
  Springs of living water : Christ-centered church renewal / by
David S. Young.
      p. cm.
  Includes bibliographical references and index.
  ISBN 978-0-8361-9411-1 (pbk.)
  1. Church renewal. I. Title.
  BV600.3.Y68 2008
  269–dc22
                                      2008017751

For scripture acknowledgments see page 17.

To Joan, spiritual companion
Jonathan, faith visionary
Andrew, joyful missionary

Contents

Foreword

Springs of Living Water is not only the title of this book, it is also
the name for the congregational renewal effort David S. Young
has brought into being to help churches everywhere experience
new life. Springs is a spiritual renewal process for congregations.
Please note that I say "process" rather than "program." To be sure,
there are numerous programmatic elements here, but at its heart
this is a spiritual renewal process. This is an emphasis I like very
much. As David's son, Jonathan, said to him, "Dad, this is a book
about the soul transformation of the church!" And so it is.

David himself is deeply rooted in the Church of the Brethren,
one of the historic Anabaptist denominations, and some of his
most salient ideas for congregational renewal flow out of this tradition. These ideas, of course, should never be confined to any
one group, for all of the great spiritual treasures are "loanable."
Indeed, David has worked with any number of denominational
groups around the country in congregational renewal efforts. He
is also in intimate conversation with many traditions from Jesuit
to Reformed to Baptist to Quaker. With this book David is
engaging in the catholicity of sharing.

Springs of Living Water takes the great themes of spiritual formation and seeks to flesh them out in the context of congregational renewal. David writes, "Congregational spiritual formation
is the most promising option for creating vibrant churches." This
is no whistling in the dark: a congregation that enters into a spiritual renewal covenant with Springs is committing to a three- to
four-year process. Throughout this process ample space is given
for retreat and solitude, both individually and congregationally.

Because rest is integral to renewal, attention is given to personal and congregational Sabbath as a key element of renewal.

11

There are times for "sleeping in" and "physical restoration," even "mental restoration." The point here is that spiritual renewal is never viewed as a crash program, but rather as a process of character growth for the long haul.

Spiritual disciplines are at the heart of this renewal process. David began by asking what would happen to a church that seriously undertakes a regular diet of spiritual disciplines? Well, he found out. Each congregation that enters this renewal process engages in intensive times of practicing the spiritual disciplines. This involves an extensive process of preaching and teaching, study and praxis. I have yet to find a renewal effort that takes engagement with the spiritual disciplines as seriously as Springs.

Oh, and prayer. In the chapters on prayer and spiritual disciplines, David tells the story of his habitual practice, some twenty years running, of using Saturday mornings for developing a pattern of personal retreat, prayer, and solitude. The character formation and insights that have flowed out of this extended, lively experiment is astonishing.

Most important of all, it has placed the life of prayer at the center of this congregational renewal process. Some of the finest lines in the book are these:

> The role of prayer in the renewal of the church cannot be overstated. Aligned with prayer, a church has new energy. Aligned with prayer, servant leadership is strengthened. Aligned with prayer, leaders discern the movements of God. Aligned with prayer, people invite new people to the church. Aligned with prayer, leaders balance people needs and program needs. As a church becomes aligned with a life of prayer, prayer turns into action. In other words, a congregation infused with prayer brings people and churches to fresh encounters with Jesus.

The mention here of Jesus prompts me to note the deeply Christocentric nature of this entire renewal process. David calls it "resurrection theology." Every part of the renewal process— from the signing of a renewal covenant to the development of a spiritual disciplines folder to establishing a renewal team to identifying the core values of the congregation to learning the skills of servant leadership to identifying a biblical passage as the guiding text for the entire process to discerning a biblical vision and a three-year plan to implement the plan with practical expressions of service—is intended to bring individuals and congregations into encounter with the living Christ. The stories here are genuinely encouraging. In fact, every chapter opens with one such story, and this pattern never feels contrived.

One of the guiding principles throughout the Springs renewal process is to focus on the strengths of the congregation rather than its weaknesses. Rather than finding out what is wrong in a congregation and trying to fix it, the approach is instead to find out what is right and build on it. This accent on strengths as the building blocks for spiritual renewal is genuinely uplifting.

Another thing I like is David's willingness to work not only with individual churches but also with clusters of congregations. This involves anywhere from two to six congregations working together for three to four years on spiritual renewal. The great value I see in this approach is that it encourages congregations in a given community to cease thinking of each other as competitors and instead to see how they can cooperate and support one another.

Servant leadership is a strong emphasis in this book and is one of the great spiritual treasures of the Brethren heritage. David makes good use of the image and practice of foot washing, a Brethren practice that contains multiple applications. Churches of the West, with their ingrained CEO mentality, would do well to listen prayerfully to the insights into this particular approach to spiritual leadership. Servant leadership is part of David's DNA, and he models it better than just about anyone I know.

Perhaps my favorite chapters are on spiritual discernment and its applications for discerning the spiritual movements of renewal in a congregation. Here David draws from the writings of Ignatius of Loyola and applies them to congregational renewal. He observes,

"Spiritual discernment will take longer than you wish, but not as long as you fear, and the outcome will be more right than you could ever know."

Throughout the discerning process David encourages us to watch for surprises. "To enter discernment," he writes, "be ready to entertain the unexpected." One such unexpected outcome concerns a Church of the Brethren congregation that had worshiped for some sixty years next to a Native American community in genuine peace and reconciliation. Through their discernment process this congregation realized that, growing out of their witness for peace, one of their great strengths was a ministry of reconciliation with groups of diverse backgrounds.

David and his wife, Joan, have two children, Jonathan and Andrew. I have met them both and they are a delight to be around. Andrew is language impaired. Even so, he has found ways to communicate that are exceedingly effective. David writes, "With his neurological makeup, Andrew lets us know by his actions what is happening in a church. When things are together, he settles more easily in the seat. When there is conflict, he is restless." Andrew's serenity suggests a congregation filled with relational harmony. Conversely, his agitation indicates a church with a high level of unresolved conflict. David adds that for Andrew externals of a church facility mean nothing. No, what Andrew picks up on in the various congregations David works with is their sense of "welcoming space."

These are telling observations. Over the years I have watched the sensitivity and care with which David and Joan work with their children. And I am convinced that these experiences—hard as they surely have been at times—have made them more sensitive than most of us to the special needs and handicaps of the congregations to which they minister. All of this helps to explain the insights of *Springs of Living Water* into the human equation.

—Richard J. Foster

Acknowledgments

This resource is written with great gratitude for the countless people who have been instrumental in making it possible. Provisions were often made for renewal even before we knew of apparent needs.

My own thirst for renewal began as I walked over the threshold of my first church, Bush Creek Church of the Brethren in Monrovia, Maryland. I wish to thank the courageous lot there who faced the fear that their church would close its doors. The originators of a doctor of ministry in church renewal at Bethany Theological Seminary provided such help to us. The writing project still stands and helped in the writing of this book.

Then there are all the people and the many churches I have worked with over the years. I wish to express gratitude to each individual, congregation, pastor, executive, and denomination noted in this book. Each story tells of those whose lives were changed and who devoted time, talent, and energy to the renewal of their churches.

I thank the advisory group of the Springs of Living Water! initiative in church renewal: Lou George, church executive of the American Baptist Churches from Concord, New Hampshire; Glenda Machia, CEO of Assets in Lancaster, Pennsylvania; Jonas Beiler of The Family Center of Gap, Pennsylvania; Michelle Armster, pastor and from the office on conciliation at Mennonite Central Committee in Akron, Pennsylvania; and Donald Miller, founder of the Bethany doctorate of ministry program in church renewal now of Richmond, Indiana.

Others give regular support, providing a balanced view of the local church, helping in interpretative training events, and going out to other districts, telling others of what has happened in their local church. That team includes Bob and Lisa Smith, Glenn O'Donnell, and Rod O'Donnell from Green Tree Church of the Brethren. I also thank the extensive prayer team that lifts up each step of the renewal initiatives.

Deepest thanks go to the readers who gave advice: Lou George; Steven Ott; Center for Career Development near Boston; Donald Miller; Michelle Armster; Glenn O'Donnell and Guy Wampler.

Others gave invaluable feedback: Emilie Griffin of Renovaré in Alexandria, Louisiana; Stan Noffsinger, general secretary of the Church of the Brethren, Elgin, Illinois; and renewal teams across the nation who paved the way. The team at First Church of the Brethren in Harrisburg, Pennsylvania, tried out summaries of the text found in the appendices and used them in renewal team training.

Thank you to my writing mentor, Tom Mullen, from Earlham School of Religion; Cindy Snodderly, member of Emmanuel Mennonite Church, Reinholds, Pennsylvania, who edited drafts; and Sarah Kehrberg of Herald Press, who picked up the spirit of the book and has done a wonderful job making the text more readable. Thank you to Peggy Fajardo of Nueva Vida Norristown New Life for translating the disciplines folder into Spanish.

I express deepest gratitude to Richard J. Foster for the spiritual depth in his writings and his heartfelt support of *Springs of Living Water*. Richard's work with Renovaré and coming to the Elizabethtown Conference for a regional meeting made *Celebration of Discipline* come alive. I also thank him for graciously writing the foreword to this book.

Thank you to the students, pastors, and church leaders who were not only a delight to teach in seminaries, seminars, and local churches, but who significantly impacted the process. I appreciate the pastors at Eastern Seminary, who said, "Put your spiritual stuff first," which led to the process of having spiritual growth throughout the Springs process and the use of a biblical passage concept.

This book could not have been written without the help of

Herald Press. Levi Miller, Michael Degan, Patricia Weaver, and the people who do artwork and cover design have demonstrated servant leadership throughout the publication process.

I also thank my family. My sons Jonathan and Andrew offered both perceptive feedback and practical illustrations in the work of church renewal. My wife, Joan, is a soul companion in the work of church renewal. She read the drafts of this book and said, "Keep it practical." Just hearing her talk about these churches guarantees excitement.

Finally and foremost I am grateful for the help of Jesus Christ. God has sustained this author and renewal servant. All honor and praise to Christ, who has given living water to sustain us through the efforts of church renewal praying, pastoring in renewal, starting up a renewal initiative, holding renewal training events, and writing this resource.

Only through Christ and the living God could any of this work have been accomplished. The book has been prayed through, and the themes came in times of spiritual discernment. May you and your congregation feel invited to receive and share life-giving water!

—David S. Young

Bantam, Doubleday, Dell Publishing Group, Inc. Reprinted by permission. Scripture taken from *The Message* is Copyright © by Eugene H. Peterson, 1993, 1994, 1995. Used by permission of NavPress Publishing Group. Scripture marked TEV is from *Today's English Version*—Old Testament: Copyright © American Bible Society 1976; New Testament: Copyright © American Bible Society 1966, 1971, 1976. Scripture marked CEV is from the *Contemporary English Version* and is Copyright © American Bible Society 1995. Scripture marked KJV is from the *King James (Authorized) Version of the Holy Bible*.

Introduction

Jesus Shows Us the Way

"The water that I will give will become in them a spring of water gushing up to eternal life" (John 4:14 NRSV). What a wonderful promise! What a wonderful message! Not cistern water, stale and contaminated, but living water, springs bubbling up, refreshingly pure—quenching the parched soul. Would you like to partake of living water?

These life-giving words of Jesus to the woman at the well are not just for individuals but also for congregations. This message is God's positive invitation for the spiritual renewal of the church today. Out of this invitation comes a very practical process for the ongoing revitalization of the church—your church.

Let us draw a little closer to this text and come to the well. Can we picture Jesus sitting on the edge of the well that belonged to Jacob, a great person in the lineage of faith? A Samaritan woman comes to draw water. The story to follow reveals a journey of faith that is inspirational and instructional for us.

Looking at this old, old story, we find four dynamics of renewal: thirst, encounter, transformation, and mission. Dynamics are life-giving, vibrant forces of the gospel.

Thirst

Thirst is the first dynamic of renewal that arises from the biblical text. The encounter of Jesus with this woman at the well happens at an unusual hour, in an unusual situation, because of different needs.

Driven by her thirst, the woman comes at high noon. The other women of the town would have filled their water pots the night before in cooler temperatures. However, because this woman had compromised her faith through her lifestyle, she would have been ostracized if she had gone to the well to socialize with the rest of the women. Now she is faced with getting water in the worst heat of the day.

As we come to this text, can't we all identify in one way or another with this woman? We thirst. We may not have compromised our values of faith directly, but have we come up short in faith and faithfulness?

We can feel left out, spiritually dry, facing an impossible challenge. Sometimes that thirst is in our churches, where we feel God is inviting us to more. What do we do? Where do we turn?

Is it possible that thirst is a good thing? In the body, thirst indicates the need for hydration. Spiritually, thirst leads the faithful to seek more. We need restoration to gain a fresh perspective.

Sometimes our churches thirst for more. We sense more is possible. We have a spiritual thirst that we feel can be filled, albeit with effort. We need a living faith. We need a vibrant church!

As we come to this Scripture in John, we acknowledge our thirst, our powerlessness, even our desperation. In the midst of this challenge, we listen to this inner voice: something more is possible.

In the fourth Beatitude Jesus speaks of thirst in this positive way: "Blessed are those who hunger and thirst for righteousness, for they will be filled" (Matthew 5:6).

Encounter

If thirst is the first dynamic of renewal, then encounter follows. In the biblical text the woman encounters Jesus, who offers life-giving water in a grace-filled manner. Jesus comes to us at the point of our deepest need and greatest anguish. In the story we can find ourselves by this same well with Jesus.

It is interesting in this story that Jesus is also thirsty, but for a different reason—travel. What an unusual meeting because two people were thirsty. Jesus identifies with our need for vitality and validates our thirst and anguish even in the church. More is possible.

If you turn back to the verse that precedes this story, John records that Jesus "had to go through Samaria." But the Master did not have to take this route through Samaria. Like other religious officials, he could have gone around that region.

The phrase "had to go through" conveys Jesus' sense that God's will or plan was involved in his ministry.[1] Under the divine MapQuest of God, Jesus came by Jacob's well to meet this woman. In the same way, he meets us.

What if Jesus *had* to pass by our church? Can we imagine the divine MapQuest of God sending Jesus our way—to our church? Imagine what it means for God to take the initiative right in the midst of our struggles.

Rather than telling this woman what to do, Jesus initiated *dialogue* with her. He reached over barriers of religion, race, and gender, and did the unbelievable. As a servant, he lifted her status by asking her for a drink.

Is Jesus asking *our church* for a drink? What do we have to offer? Our individual selves? Our church? Our district? Our denomination?

This style of conversation leads to dialogue, a process we use in church renewal, which invites a response. The woman at the well took liberty and amusingly observed, "Sir, you have no bucket, and the well is deep" (John 4:15 NRSV).

Our thirst, our challenge, can lead us to encounter Jesus in new ways. To think we are called on to offer Jesus a drink! Any church that believes it has something to offer is taking the next step in renewal. If a church responds to its thirst and encounters Jesus, transformation soon follows.

Transformation

Transformation is the third dynamic of renewal. This Samaritan woman was transformed in her encounter with Jesus. Again, he used dialogue as a servant, not condemning her, but revealing the obvious. She had had multiple husbands, and her current man was not her husband. Her relationships had been void of meaning.

The power of dialogue deepened as the woman explored whether this man was a prophet. This led to a discussion of worship. Did worship happen in this location or that? Of course, Jesus told her about the real meaning of worship—that it had to be done in spirit and truth.

Jesus led her deeper and deeper into spiritual realities, revealing who he was. "I who speak to you am he" (John 4:26). This is the great "I am" in John's Gospel, where Jesus is the divine reality. Jesus offers life-giving water—"spring water."[2] Partaking of this water transforms and renews life.

Personally I find it helpful to go to this well. My own life has been powerfully affected by a Saturday-morning prayer discipline I've had for over twenty years. This is how the renewal process called Springs of Living Water emerged. During my weekly time at the well, I do four things. First, I release all to God and attempt to feel God's love. Then I read and meditate on a Scripture and pray for God's help to follow that Scripture. Then I read a short portion of a devotional classic. Finally, I spend time listening and being with God.

During this period of quietness I discover the movements of God and, as I like to say, spiritual discernment finds me. Looking at something one way provides peace, another way, anxiety. Solutions come to unresolved problems I did not realize were on my mind. Creative ideas come to mind. Sensitivity toward people comes. God's love enters. I rest. Right here at the well!

In this retreat time, I prayed through how transformation of churches often happens. I felt led to John 4 and the woman at the well because it lifts up the gentle but effervescent way in which I have witnessed transformation in congregations.

Mission

If we have thirst, encounter Jesus, and are transformed, mission is soon to follow. Why does John record that the woman at the well left her water pots behind? Checking with biblical scholars, I learned that every word counts in John's Gospel.

So why does John note this detail? She was going to need a water pot later. Was it a symbol she associated with her past? Or was it because she became so committed to living water that she wholeheartedly gave herself to her mission?

Notice where she went with her mission—to her hometown! Think how hard it would have been for her to take that step. In light of all that had happened in her life, that took courage. Her mission called her to draw on the strength God gave with the call.

And when she went home, she used the same engaging method of dialogue that Jesus had used with her. Rather than telling them what they should believe, she invited them: "Come, see a man who told me everything I ever did" (John 4:29). Could he be the Messiah? She let them decide for themselves.

Is our mission as a congregation right in our own hometown? Is it to open the home missions department of our churches? The outcome of the Springs process of renewal, described throughout this book, is heartening—churches are filled with new life, energy, faith, and unity. God is at work mightily!

When we partake of living water, we go on a mission to tell others. We see the courage this takes. We have a compelling witness to bear of what Jesus has done in our lives. We invite others to go and see who this Jesus is for themselves.

Many Samaritans believed in Jesus because of the woman's testimony. When they came to him, they asked Jesus to stay with them. Just think of the risk and the trust this represented. Upon their request, Jesus stayed not just overnight, but for two days. Many more Samaritans put their trust in Jesus.

They believed not because of what the woman told them, but because they heard and saw it themselves. They answered the question in their own mind about the Messiah when they said, "We no longer believe because of what you told us; we have heard him ourselves and we know that he really is the savior of the world" (John 4:42 Jerusalem Bible).

We hear Jesus inviting us on a spiritual journey of renewal of the local church using servant leadership to build healthy churches with an urgent Christ-centered mission. Out of the invitation of this Scripture from John comes a renewal process known as Springs of Living Water, which can assist you and your church to find the life-giving water of new vitality and mission.

∽

Many people in the pulpit and pew are thirsting for new life in the church. I have witnessed their thirst as people enter the renewal process. Churches that have used Springs have discovered new life and continue to find new vitality. At no time have I experienced such interest in a spiritually oriented, servant-led process yielding revitalization of churches. Even before decline sets in, a church can take up a renewed mission to which God is inviting it. I stand back in awe and observe that this new life is more than a process. This new life is of God.

The Mark of a Renewing Church

Let us define renewal. In 2 Corinthians 4:16 the apostle Paul says, "So we do not lose heart. Even though our nature is wasting away, our inner nature is being renewed day by day." Fresh faith is a grace gift each day. When he writes Paul uses the passive voice saying how he is renewed day by day. God does the renewing continually giving the gift of new life.

The word *renewal* is used in this book to describe new life in the church. Rather than a "once done, forever done" program, renewal is an ongoing process by which churches discover the living presence of Christ. Within renewal is transformation, revival, and reconciliation. Such new life is never just for the church itself; rather, it transforms the church into a mission in God's kingdom.

In the end, the mark of a renewing church is that it becomes Christ-centered. Christ becomes more known, more influential, and more central in the life of the church. Christ is lifted up, becomes preeminent, and rises above programs, styles, and tastes. Renewal is a vibrant faith journey of individuals and congregations. The outcome is changed lives, active witness, and service to Jesus Christ. Soul transformation happens in churches that gather by the well, encounter Jesus, drink life-giving water, and enter into mission.

A Renewal Manual

This resource is a manual of sorts. The pages are crafted to help church leaders move step by step through a journey to assist their church in discovering and sustaining new life. It can be used by pastors, church leaders, and church executives. At the same time it is for renewal teams and individuals in training for ministry or for study by an entire congregation that feels a thirst for new life. Questions at the end of chapters prompt discussion, as do the resources in the notes and appendices.

Springs of Living Water can also be used with a cluster of churches walking side-by-side in renewal. Renewal teams from each church meet for leadership training and to encourage one another. Each church adds its experience and wisdom. Coming at a crucial time of denominational revitalization, this resource helps churches do together what is harder to accomplish alone. Church clusters have a ripple effect of new life in regions and denominations. The spiritual journey becomes a movement, God's movement.

My hope is that the reader can work with a team from his or her church to respond to God's invitation to renewal and can move step by step. This book is not a program, but a process that can be creatively adapted according to the spiritual discernment of the church. Throughout this book you will read of people just like you who felt the thirst and began to respond.

This book invites you to bring your knowledge and experience to the process. You may wish to read the entire book through and then return chapter by chapter for implementation. A reviewer of a previous book of mine said it was like a spiritual companion. I hope this new resource can serve this purpose as well.[3]

Outline of the Book

The message of John 4 provides the inspiration for this book and gives its outline. There are four major sections, each covering a renewal dynamic: thirst, encounter, transformation, and mission. Each dynamic is explored in four chapters with a lead story, interpretation, and practical tools for the spiritual journey of renewal. The appendices provide tools for application.

Each section guides the reader to explore where God is inviting new life. If you are working with a renewal team, you will want to read the appropriate section ahead of a meeting. Since topics are sometimes introduced and further details are filled in later, use the index to find additional information on any given topic. My hope is that you have an exciting faith journey of renewal.

Is Jesus inviting your church to give him a drink? We resoundingly affirm, "Yes!"

Yes, come all who are thirsty.

For Reflection and Discussion

1. Are you able to picture Jesus at the well with you and your church, entering into dialogue with you? What thoughts come to your mind of such a meeting?

2. Do the four dynamics of renewal—thirst, encounter, transformation, and mission—describe experiences you've had as you've grown in faith? Can you envision a faith journey for renewal of a church?

3. By the divine MapQuest of God, is Jesus asking you and your church for a drink?

4. In the biblical story, mission rises right out of the text. Can you see how mission is integrally tied to the process of renewal of a church?

5. What are your thoughts about a church needing an ongoing renewal process in order to continue to grow in vitality? What next steps do you feel invited to take?

Part 1

Thirst

But he had to go through Samaria. So he came to a Samaritan city called Sychar, near the plot of ground that Jacob had given to his son Joseph. Jacob's well was there, and Jesus, tired out by his journey, was sitting by the well. It was about noon.

A Samaritan woman came to draw water, and Jesus said to her, "Give me a drink." (His disciples had gone to the city to buy food.) The Samaritan woman said to him, "How is that you, a Jew, ask a drink of me, a woman of Samaria?"

—John 4:4-9 NRSV

1

Getting to the Well

Charlotte White, pastor of New Zion African Methodist Episcopal Church in Delaware, said she needed to be "boosted up." Charlotte attended an intensive course on church renewal that I taught at Eastern Seminary in Philadelphia. She was troubled because her church could not pull together a building project. That week Charlotte learned a church renewal process that begins with entering a more intentional spiritual journey and then moves to involve the entire congregation. In those five days of classes she felt God renewing her spirit. She said the closing communion service tied it all together.

For the communion service we modified an observance of the Lord's Supper that would normally include an agape meal, foot washing, and eucharist. Instead of foot washing, we received and gave verbal affirmations of care, dramatizing being served and serving in the name of Christ. Instead of the agape meal, we shared refreshments, symbolizing our love in the bond of Christ. For the eucharist, we broke from a common loaf, representing Christ's body broken for us, and drank from large glasses of juice, symbolizing the bounty of God's grace. Charlotte said she wept. She said she had never experienced God that way; she felt so humble.

Later that summer, Charlotte was excited to share her discovery. "Oh those disciplines," she said, referring to spiritual disciplines. "They have changed my life!" She had begun to practice spiritual disciplines as described in Richard J. Foster's book *Celebration of Discipline: The Path to Spiritual Growth*.[1] Disciplines such as regular Bible reading, prayer, meditation, and fasting help people go deeper in their spiritual journey.

In a follow-up letter several months later she told how the intensive course helped her regain focus in her ministry. She discovered God's goodness and was able to help her congregation. She began to listen to the Lord for direction. Renewal had begun. Having experienced the rewards of practicing spiritual disciplines herself, Charlotte preached a series of sermons on the disciplines. She started with the discipline of prayer and then worship. She discovered "people were not dead; they just needed to be fed."

As the months unfolded, people began to read the Bible and devotional literature and make entries in a journal. Some began fasting. They learned how to listen to God and began to see their lives from a different perspective. Tithing took hold and there was money again. People reported it was "more fun to be around one another at church." Charlotte began to realize that the church that needed building was not a physical structure, but within the hearts of people. The renewal process she had learned was touching not only her own life but also the life of her church.

The Dynamic of Thirst

Thirst is the first dynamic of renewal in John 4. Like the woman at the well, our thirst is the indicator to go deeper spiritually. In this chapter let us look at thirst and how it connects with the renewal process.

In renewal endeavors, pastors and church leaders feel an inward desire for more. At that point, such a longing is a vague concept. In churches, people say they really don't know what that "more" means, but they do feel more is possible in their church. This is like a physical thirst you would respond to by getting a drink. Thirst can be a good thing—pointing us to God.

In a time of thirst we learn we are no longer in control. We realize that it is best to live in a receptive role in which God is the initiator. Then we understand the depth of the redemptive work of Jesus and come to a new experience of God's love.

Renewal is responding to divine nudging and leading. Our openness, our yieldedness, our obedience is crucial. Back in 1906, Rufus Jones called this the double search.[2] God does the renewing and is reaching out. On the other hand, churches are thirsting and are reaching out too. Each is trying to connect with the other.

Renewal entails growing in absolute dependence on God, who reaches out to us. Some people talk about this as entering the desert. Carlo Carretto, a modern-day desert father, describes going to live with the Little Brothers of Jesus in the Sahara: "Put yourself in front of Jesus as a poor man: not with any big ideas, but with living faith. Remain motionless in an act of love before the Father. Don't try to reach God with your understanding; that is impossible. Reach him in love; that is possible."[3] In the desert we learn absolute dependence on God. In this position, renewal occurs.

The importance of prayer. In such a position, prayer becomes serious business. All the church renewal endeavors I've been a part of have led to an increased prayer life for individuals and for congregations. In the Springs process, a prayer group prays for each training event and for the churches as they take up renewal. This is not prayer as a must or prayer as a routine but an honest, heartfelt contact with God. Thirst can lead us out into our own wilderness to cry out to God.

Sometimes we don't know how to pray. What do we pray for? What do we cover in prayer, especially in terms of the church? Many questions may come into our minds. Our thirst is so great; will our prayers be sufficient? In this book we delve into prayer, spiritual discernment, the movements of God in renewal, spiritual guidance, and growth in the faith journey as the means by which renewal is achieved. All church renewal is surrounded by prayer.

The importance of action. Just as important as prayer is action. In fact, in prayer we are prompted to action and are given sensitivity to know what to do. Sometimes churches have a sense that something needs to be done. Often they are willing to act; they just don't know what to do. Once presented with a simple, understandable path, they feel ready to enter the process. Responsive action is done in the framework of tending to the thirst. Rather than go out on our own, we follow God's leading. We go in prayer. We go serving.

In an unusual twist, St. Ignatius of Loyola summed up how faith and action go hand in hand: "Work as if all depended upon God; pray as if all depended on you." Renewal is labor intensive. It takes a lot of hard work to see a church renewed. It entails the investment of hours, the sacrifice of self, the hard work of reconciliation, and the hard work of shaping a new ministry in a ministry plan. Much devotion is needed, but as you will soon see, devotion is a willing work of love. The outcome is that people feel they have gained much more than they have given.

The Promise of Living Water

The good news is that there is living water to quench our thirst. A Samaritan woman meets Jesus by the well, seeking water—living water. As she comes thirsting on one level, Jesus recognizes within her the need for a source of living water on another level. In the dialogue, Jesus offers her a spring of living water within herself that will save her life.[4] Unlike cistern water, stale, murky, and of limited supply, living water is pure and never-ending, "a spring of water gushing up to eternal life" (John 4:14 NRSV). Not bound by time, living water is for eternity.

At the heart of living water is life. In Scriptures life is breathed in by God. In meeting this woman, Jesus is offering her the very source of life: "The water I give will be an artesian spring within, gushing fountains of endless life" (John 4:14 The Message). So, what she seeks externally on one level, Jesus offers to her internally and eternally on another level. In a similar manner, churches may seek new life in externals, but the gift of God of renewal is internal and more than we even imagined. Life, eternal life, is what people discover personally and as churches. As humans we share in God's life.[5]

A resurrection theology. While it takes just one person to start a renewal process, one person cannot do it in his or her own strength. In John's Gospel, at the well, the resurrection is a reality. All church renewal is built on a resurrection theology. While it might seem a giant leap from the restoration of Israel to the resurrection of Jesus, we can affirm that God is raising up a church to new life. God wishes for healthy congregations.

As in the raising of Lazarus, God can bring new life and new hope. The basis of renewal is to have this hope on our hearts. Our effectiveness in renewal is based on the surging power of the resurrection: "Unbind him, and let him go" (John 11:44 NRSV). No wonder Jesus proclaimed, "I am the resurrection and the life" (v. 25)! God's invitation is one of grace and joy. Renewal is the power of the gospel at work. Throughout this book we build on biblical promises of hope.[6] We build on a resurrection theology.

Entering a Renewal Process

The story of Charlotte represents what a pastor is able to do by tending to thirst. Though, she came empty to the course in church renewal, she had taken the important step of going to a class to learn how to fill that emptiness. As a congregation identifies this thirst, it knows God is inviting renewal. In the midst of Christ inviting a church to give him a drink, it discovers it has something to offer. The congregants realize that Christ is offering them living water, and they become involved in the next step of a faith journey.

Choosing a renewal path. Churches soon discover that the design of a renewal process is important. Some alternatives are quick fixes. Such programs yield less than hoped-for results. There are no short-cuts in renewal. Just fixing what is wrong won't work. Just adopting this or that program has limited results. Raising expectations, like setting goals, without the energy or way to implement them can be more harmful than helpful. A church needs to discern where God is leading. The spiritual journey aligns with God's will and desire.

The Springs approach is for a church to adopt and carry out the renewal process. There is flexibility to honor the unique nature and call of each church. People are given practical handles on what will lie ahead and how to move forward. And mostly, Springs functions from a spiritual center, where spiritual renewal comes first and then leads to mission and outreach.

Springs is not a management or programmatic model. In Springs, you will learn how organizations work and use concepts like the life cycle of a church to alert you to the dynamics of growth and decline. But we know that a program does not in and of itself bring renewal. Using servant leadership, churches understand the spiritual needs of people and learn to connect people's hearts with their ministry. Servant leadership affirms that motivation stems from the heart.

The role of leaders. The challenge in leadership is not just to be out ahead leading the way, but also to be with people as they respond to the thirst. Servants do that. They go to the springs together with people.

In this renewal process, leaders build on the strengths of their church. Rather than focusing on the weaknesses, you will learn to discover the identity of your church—its unique strengths— and from there to shape a vision and implement a plan.

When caught in the snags of weaknesses and hit by setbacks, leaders help the church tend to spiritual thirst. Rather than be defeated when things don't turn out as hoped, leaders work to discover the path through the valley. The church is shaped in those humbling moments and is called to be completely dependent on God.

The beauty of a renewing church is that it knows it may not have all the strengths, but that God is helping it use what has been given. Leaders help the church to live by the hope of the resurrection. The living Christ shines through the endeavor.

Making a decision. For a congregation to become involved in such a renewal endeavor takes a thorough decision-making process. No board or committee can decide one evening that they should take up renewal. Four or even six or more months might be needed to have as many people as possible in the congregation decide to respond to the thirst and affirm there is potential to be realized. Special leadership is needed to carry this process forward in a graced-filled manner. This is not a river to be pushed in its flow. Rather, we seek to follow God's leading.

Also, the decision for renewal is more than just "doing the program" so something will happen. The decision to enter renewal is itself spiritual work: a congregation is discerning how they will respond to God's invitation to new life. Much prayer and discussion will be required. There needs to be time for waiting and for heart preparation. Once an affirmative decision for renewal is made, the church is ready to move ahead with joy and excitement. (Appendix 2 is an example of a covenanting service that could be used to celebrate the new journey awaiting the family of believers.)

Understanding the Life Cycle of a Church

For many people, both pastors in training at seminaries and lay leaders serving on renewal teams in local churches, learning and understanding the life cycle of a church has been an "aha" moment. The life cycle is a practical handle with which to take the thirst of a congregation to a new level.

The whole purpose in exploring the life cycle is to identify how to keep on the growth side rather than fall into decline. What is going on in a church and how can the church improve? To offset decline, bodies of faith learn to detect what sends churches into decline—those insidious, hidden factors that infiltrate at the very time we thought things were going well.

The point at which the life cycle is learned is critical for a church. Rather than locate where your church is on the life cycle and get discouraged, it is much better to enter the process of renewal and see that there is hope. Churches on a spiritual journey see that they have God-given strengths. Using servant leadership, the life cycle can be a tool in the spiritual journey leading to greater health and vitality.

While other models have value, the early work of Martin Saarinen on the life cycle of a congregation focuses on how energy emerges and vision develops. In *The Life Cycle of a Congregation*, he used the human life cycle to interpret what is happening in a church. Understanding these points helps churches not only in making interventions, but also in balancing factors that lead to greater maturity.

The genes of a church. Genes in the human body make up who each individual is. Saarinen uses "genes" to identify each stage of the life cycle:

> • The E factor is the *energizing* function prevalent in the origin of a congregation. In renewal we note how important energy—a sense of enthusiasm and hope—is for new life. E has an undifferentiated quality of an excited infant with arms and legs flailing.
>
> • I stands for *inclusion*, the church's ability to welcome individuals and groups in and out of the church. Inclusion has to do with how people are assimilated and how their gifts are used in ministry.[7]
>
> • The P factor stands for *programs* and services the congregation has developed in response to the needs of the members or community, such as worship, Sunday school, or a youth program. In renewal, a focused plan of ministry is important.
>
> • Finally the A factor is the conscious *administrating* of the congregation, often noted by mission statements, goals and objectives, budgets, and planning. While some feel administration is hard, in renewal it is an important function.

Applying servant leadership to the life cycle. The church renewal process in this book addresses factors of the life cycle. We look at the life cycle as described by Saarinen through the eyes of servant leadership as presented in this book. In this way, churches do not feel locked into one stage but see the path to renewal. Growth and decline characterize two phases as depicted in the diagram below.

Growth is never a straight line nor does it automatically go stage by stage. Each stage has a process of its own, with times of birth and decline. By being sensitive to factors of the life cycle that yield new energy and balance, we can build healthy churches. Let us look at the stages.

Key: E—energy; I—inclusion; P—program; A—administration;

EIPA   eIPA

EiPa   eIpA

EIpa   eipA

Eipa   eipa

1. *Birth: Eipa.* The birth of a congregation always has elements of hope and enthusiasm. Energy is high and people have a mission. The focus comes from an energetic person or group with lots of enthusiasm. Rediscovering this vision of birth is a gift.

Servant leaders help a church enter a spiritual journey. First, such leaders feel a sense of call and deepen their own spiritual life. Then through use of spiritual disciplines they help the church gain new focus and energy. A new birth is possible.

2. *Infancy: EIpa.* In infancy a congregation has a high level of enthusiasm and puts out the welcome mat. The message of inclusion is strong and members are excited about inviting others to help. Servants reach out to others and lift them up.

For a church to be renewed, such servants see that inclusion is important. People are invited to be part of something exciting. One example of this kind of inclusion is the calling of a renewal team. This team shares the load of renewal work. In turn, this team as servants invites others to come and do their part.

3. *Adolescence: EiPa.* Adolescence follows as the fledging group decides to establish some programs. A committee structure may help things get organized. A Sunday school may be established or a youth program begun. The dilemma comes if program needs override people needs.

Servants help a church enter dialogue so people communicate better and learn how to establish ministries and work together. Servant leaders help to attend to people needs so that they are not overridden by program needs. Servants help a congregation use foresight to spiritually discern a vision statement and goals.

4. *Prime: EIPA.* Balance is needed for the prime stage of the

life cycle. People factors and program factors need to be mediated. In prime, energy is optimized as activities are coordinated and conflicts are used to create a balance of ideas, styles, and emotions. The church focuses on its mission.

Servants balance people needs and program needs, budgets and resources, and one ministry with another ministry. Servants help churches be healthy by balancing all the factors that make for new life. Using foresight, they help the church maintain its health with an urgent, Christ-centered mission.

Applying servant leadership in the decline stages. The decline side of the life cycle can show what sets off the downward spiral. Often churches seeking renewal find themselves on the decline side, but this is not cause for panic. By entering the spiritual journey of renewal and applying servant leadership, hope is alive and renewal is possible.

1. *Maturity: eIPA.* As you might imagine, energy is first to go. The familiar becomes more attractive than the innovative. By listening, servant leaders read signals, use dialogue to engage in conversation, and help a church embark on a new, energized spiritual journey. They take nothing for granted. Servant leaders keep up hope and look for the way God is at work.

2. *Aristocracy: eIpA.* With less energy, all programs diminish because there are fewer people willing to become involved. The same people do the same thing and others feel excluded. Fear and anxiety play into the acceptance of the malaise. Servant leaders help a congregation ask where God is leading. Servants help their church look at strengths and build on those.

3. *Bureaucracy: eipA.* When bureaucracy sets in, checking to make sure "everyone of us is present" shifts to maintaining power. Amid resignation and frustration, the church tries to keep things going using administration. Servants start the spiritual disciplines and see the spiritual journey as the way to reestablish health and to help the church rediscover the mission to which God is calling it. Servants enter the labor-intensive work of renewal and invite and include new people and regain inactive members.

4. *Death: eipa*. If the decline cycle continues unchecked, the unavoidable happens and death comes. In renewal we learn not only how long we can hang on, but also how destructive decline can become. Servant leaders help a church look at where God is leading. They use dialogue to begin conversation and develop trust. They proclaim resurrection hope and a reason for being.

In my renewal work, I have found that wherever a church may find itself in the life cycle, people are usually encouraged that a future is ahead. Now they see a way out of their problems. They once again believe they could become a healthy church. Often they say, "Why didn't we do this before?"

Three Critical Components of Renewal

Stories of churches involved in the renewal process tell of new life. In the Springs of Living Water process, churches enter a faith journey and move through a season of renewal with a seven-fold process. Testimonials in these pages tell personal stories that illustrate where the renewal process was applied in local congregations. Spiritual growth through spiritual disciplines is the source of new energy for the church.

In the midst of spiritual disciplines, churches have congregational gatherings, build on strengths, discern a biblical text and vision, and implement a ministry plan. They continue the process that builds in sustainability and becomes a pattern for the long haul. Spiritually vibrant, servant-led congregations engage in significant ministries that spell vitality and growth. Three critical components of renewal emerge.

1. Spiritual growth. Entering the pastoral ministry years ago, I was alerted to the spiritual needs of a church that some feared would close its doors. My passion for church renewal began at that first church.[8] Focusing on the spiritual journey of individuals was fundamental for renewal. We asked, "How can an entire church enter a faith pilgrimage?" Because of this early experience, you will find a heavy emphasis on spiritual growth in the Springs process, with a variety of ways a congregation becomes involved in a regular diet of spiritual disciplines. People grow spiritually; churches grow spiritually.

2. **Servant leadership.** As I recognized that renewal takes leadership, in that first church, which feared for its future, the concept of the servant in Scripture gave me needed guidance. Out of our spiritual journey and growth, the church went out into the community with a view to serve. We listened, saw needs, and felt the call of Christ to take the basin and towel to share the Christian life. So my passion developed for servant leadership, and that interest continued to grow as we used the same principles of service to incorporate people into the church and see them use their talents and grow in the Christian life.

3. **Christ-centered mission.** This led to the third focus of having a healthy church with Christ-centered mission. If we spoke of establishing goals, how could the entire congregation be involved in that process? If led of God, how could a Scripture passage guide a church to build on its strengths rather than focus on its weaknesses? How could all this be put together in some kind of plan so that renewal would really happen? All the answers eventually came together in a seminary program in which a pastor worked with a team in the church to shape a mission, chart units of renewal, and implement a plan of ministry.

The Ongoing Renewal Process

This vision was but the beginning. The process represented in Springs of Living Water matured as I implemented it in local churches, taught it in seminaries, and used it with clusters of churches at the regional and denominational levels. Even before decline sets in, focused work is crucial to having a church take up the mission to which God is inviting it.

All congregations need to constantly be asking the questions that this book raises and answers: "Where is God leading this church?" Renewal is never a quick fix; there are no short-cuts; new life cannot be forced. Renewal happens as a church embarks and stays on a spiritual journey. Of all the things that the renewal process suggests, this discovery is central. Renewal is a spiritual journey.

The renewal process must be done from the perspective of the strengths of a church. Rather than finding out what is wrong and fixing it, we find out what is right and build on it. Discovering our strengths, we find we have something to offer, in fact, that we have a mission. Jesus is inviting us to discover living water and to share in his mission. If our desired outcome is to grow spiritually, our input is to enter that spiritual walk and build a path of continued growth and vitality.

Springs is an ongoing renewal process that a church can utilize to engage in a lifelong spiritual journey. Renewal is multifaceted and never follows a straight line. The reader is cautioned against looking for a cookie-cutter program. Church renewal is an initiative needing constant discernment on how to proceed. Renewal means entering a spiritual journey in an easily understood process involving a broad range of people. A lot of exploration will happen in Springs—not just discerning a vision, but implementing it brings renewal. Hope comes alive as we see God at work.

Tending to the Thirst

In class after class, in church after church, new life begins when one individual responds to the invitation for renewal. Unless someone does something, nothing happens. Spiritually we are prompted by our thirst.

Once we respond, not knowing what to expect, we discover good news: God's grace becomes evident. Hope is at hand. Like the woman at the well, when one person experiences God's search for her and she responds, she wants to go and tell others to meet this man Jesus.

At the heart of renewal is tending to the thirst, that spiritual longing to grow closer to God. Such tending is attuned to the pilgrimage of discovering the church's true identity, asking, "Where is God leading?" By tending to the thirst, this question shifts us into an entirely different perspective: Where is God leading us by grace into the future? For that we use a process of prayer and spiritual discernment that will be discussed in the next two chapters. In renewal we begin to engage in a faith journey and become proactive. We take step-by-step action in obedience. Tending to the thirst is a continuous process and leads us to hear the call of God.

Getting to the well and meeting Jesus is such a blessing. When we realize that God is taking the initiative to offer us living water, we can be almost overwhelmed. So long we have worked, so long we have strived, and now God is reaching out to us. The dynamic of thirst can turn into an invitation to renewal. And if this can be true for an individual, what a blessing it also is for a congregation to experience the dynamic of thirst and respond. Rather than feel caught in decline, a congregation can experience hope and a path, a spiritual journey of renewal. So we embrace the spiritual thirst and see within it the opportunity to trust totally in God and anticipate the new life to come.

For Reflection and Discussion

1. The title of this chapter is "Getting to the Well." Can you identify this thirst; have you or your church ever felt such thirst? Share with someone what you do when you have such a thirst.

2. Can you name some immediate advantages to your church entering a renewal process? What would this entail? What would be your hopes?

3. As you look at the life cycle, is there an "aha" moment for you? Can you see how servant leadership could help guide you to renewed life?

4. What are the strengths of your church? When you begin to identify them, what sense develops in you? Can you monitor your energy level as you go through this exercise?

5. If you were to begin to ask the question, "Where is God leading your church?" what thoughts arise?

2

Engaging in the Seven Steps of Renewal

Harrisburg First Church of the Brethren is an ethnically diverse church. On Sunday morning a traditional worship service is followed by a Sunday school hour and then a contemporary bilingual service. The spirit is very warm and positive. The church has active ministries in the city with strong volunteer service workers. While the church is located in the inner city, a significant number of members live in suburban communities. From the story that follows we can see how one church thoroughly went through the enlistment process so that a decision could be made whether to enter an intentional journey of spiritual renewal.

Desiring to enter a spiritually oriented renewal process, Pastor Belita Mitchell asked me and my wife, Joan, to come and meet with the core of the leadership team. In a context immersed in prayer, we listened. The leaders felt that, whether wanted or not, the church was in transition. The congregation was aging, and there was concern about the future of the church's many ministries and ongoing mission. Rather than succumb to the forces before them, they began to ask, "What is God's will? Where is God leading us?" From that point, Joan and I were invited to lead the annual leadership team retreat. We listened for what the pastor sensed would be the best way to do the retreat in order to meet their goals. We talked about enrichment, helping the group set goals, and gaining a focus set in the context of an inspirational event. We talked about having interactive time interspersed with presentations. We focused on how God was calling the church to be spiritually alive and spiritually renewed as a spiritual organism. The words *multicultural* and *Christ-centered* stood out. If a program were to die in the process, let it die. Recognizing the anxiety over finances, the hope was to identify the strengths of the church and go to the next level in its journey of faith.

Some months later, thirty-two people from the church gathered for a leadership retreat at Camp Swatara, in the foothills of the Blue Mountains. The pastor personally invited congregants who may have wondered whether they were included.

Worship on Friday evening began with singing. Then, using a genuine wooden well bucket, Joan and I did a dialogue reading of the woman at the well. I followed with a message on living water. We invited people to ponder these questions: Is Jesus asking First Church for a drink? What does First Church have to offer?

With empty cups and bottles of spring water near the well bucket on the worship table, Marisel Olivencia, the associate pastor for Hispanic Ministries, sang a beautiful and moving song about living water. People were invited to come forward and take a cup and a bottle of spring water. They were encouraged to take quiet time during the retreat to meditate on God's desire to fill their cup with living water so they could share living water with others.

On Saturday morning we had a time of worship followed by a presentation on the Springs renewal process. The group reflected on its desire to provide spiritual nurture to people of all ages and to cultivate leadership skills among both lay and ordained people. The group affirmed its call to urban ministry. They desired to be empowered to stay the course and affirmed a ministry of compassion. They wanted to be "prayed up and powered up." We also had them look at their strengths, which First Church found aplenty.

After this retreat, Joan and I were invited to bring the message to the entire church. We participated in the traditional service, the Sunday school hour to follow, and the bilingual praise service. Joan was invited to present a "moment in mission," telling about the Springs process. The pastor asked that I preach the message on the woman at the well. During Sunday school we attempted to review each of the dynamics of renewal: thirst, encounter, transformation, and mission.

Participants wrestled with what led those in the Samaritan woman's hometown to receive the previously outcast woman. What had changed in her that caused them to actually go and see this man, Jesus? A question was raised: "How can we do that if we know our lives are not yet whole?" During the second service, people received the message again, now translated into Spanish. Some were present to listen to the message a fourth time.

As they anticipated a congregational vote concerning the commitment to renewal, the leaders of the church called each congregant on the phone. The church made a leap of faith and voted to adopt the Springs model of renewal and attend to their collective thirst. (After a thorough decision-making process like the one at First Church, a covenanting service can be celebrated; see appendix 2.)

This chapter is a thumbnail sketch of the process used by many churches for renewal. Throughout the book we will explain each part of the renewal process in greater depth under the appropriate sections of encounter, transformation, and mission. An important part of this endeavor will be to have the congregation learn and adopt the process as its own, which takes time.

The Renewal Process

Springs uses the seven-fold process shown in the chart on the next page. At no time is this chart to be seen as cookie-cutter steps that, if completed, will yield renewal. Rather than go on our own schedule, we must discern God's leading. Sometimes churches have already completed parts before entering the renewal process, and they can build on those experiences. The renewal process is built to spiritually align a church and to gain the energy needed to become healthy. This chapter gives an overview of the process. Each topic will be reviewed in greater detail in subsequent chapters under the dynamics of renewal as they unfold in parts 2, 3, and 4 of the book.

The spiritual process deepens as renewal unfolds. Rather than be overwhelmed, we enter the process step by step and make needed adjustments. At each step we discern the movements of God in order to make decisions about where God is leading the body. Sometimes in the process we may loop back to go deeper spiritually or decide more training is needed for the renewal team. Spiritual development is not linear but multifaceted. Renewal is an art rather than a science. Prayer will lead to the creativity needed in the process.

Spiritual Movements and the Path of Renewal

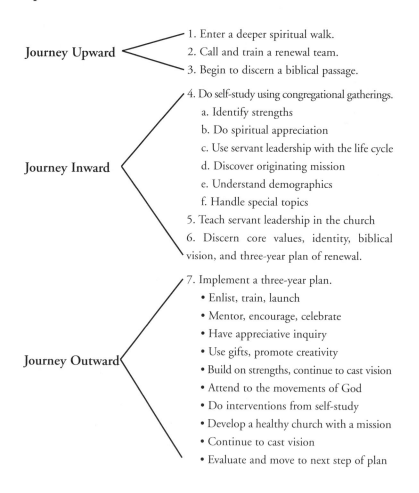

Journey Upward

1. Enter a deeper spiritual walk.
2. Call and train a renewal team.
3. Begin to discern a biblical passage.

Journey Inward

4. Do self-study using congregational gatherings.
   a. Identify strengths
   b. Do spiritual appreciation
   c. Use servant leadership with the life cycle
   d. Discover originating mission
   e. Understand demographics
   f. Handle special topics
5. Teach servant leadership in the church
6. Discern core values, identity, biblical vision, and three-year plan of renewal.

Journey Outward

7. Implement a three-year plan.
   • Enlist, train, launch
   • Mentor, encourage, celebrate
   • Have appreciative inquiry
   • Use gifts, promote creativity
   • Build on strengths, continue to cast vision
   • Attend to the movements of God
   • Do interventions from self-study
   • Develop a healthy church with a mission
   • Continue to cast vision
   • Evaluate and move to next step of plan

In the chart, the steps in the renewal process run down the right column. In Springs, it usually takes a church twelve to eighteen months to go through the first six steps, and three years to implement step 7, implementing the renewal plan.

On the left of the chart are the movements of God. As we feel the upward movement toward God as God calls us and we respond by reaching out to God, we do the first three steps of the renewal process. Then as we sense the inward movement of God, calling for inner reflection, we explore the interior movements in ourselves and the church. We go through the next three steps (steps 4-6) of the renewal process from a position of strengths. Then as we sense the outward movement, we are led into mission with the steps of implementation (step 7). The three movements of upward, inward, and outward and the stages in the steps of renewal provide benchmarks for celebration and Sabbath rest. Although each part makes its own impact, for renewal to take its full effect Springs is designed to complete the process in its entirety.

The renewal team takes time to discern the flow of congregational gatherings. It helps the church cover specific topics, but not too much in each gathering. One step should build on another. Once you get started, you will want to move with the process so as not to lose momentum. Spiritual discernment will help you keep in tune with God's invitation to renewal. (A linear step-by-step listing of the plan is included in appendix 1.)

Step 1: Enter a Deeper Spiritual Walk

The first step is entering a deeper spiritual walk through the use of spiritual disciplines. Spiritual revitalization of a church does not just occur one Sunday, but entails extended seasons of renewal. Appendix 3 contains a summary of the twelve disciplines from the book *Celebration of Discipline*. These disciplines can be taught in various settings, including Sunday school classes, small groups, in dialogues in worship, and by preaching on the disciplines. In renewal, each person discerns the next incremental step that God is inviting him to take.

One tool used in the Springs process is a spiritual disciplines folders, which the entire congregation uses to commit to disciplines for a period of spiritual growth. (The folders will be explained in chapter 5.) When a church decides to use spiritual disciplines folders or in other ways grow spiritually together, there is a sense of united growth as everyone enters the same path of spiritual growth. The spiritual walk is both a personal and a corporate journey.

Step 2: Call a Renewal Team

The second step is to train a renewal team. Rather than the pastor(s) or lay leader(s) working solo, a team of people is called to this task. Right now we will look at the selection of this team and its role, while specific aspects of a team's purpose and function are explained in chapter 5.

The team should be made up of the pastor(s), individuals who serve in an official capacity, and others who have a real commitment to the church and its renewal. Experience shows that discerning spiritually alert people is very important. Some of the team may be new in the congregation. Some may be long-term members with many experiences in the church. The most important thing is for all to have a real thirst and heart for renewal.

Throughout the process the team tries to model the renewal it wants for the church and the outcomes it hopes will be accomplished. Rather than simply telling the church what to do, the team gets as many people as possible involved in the process and works in a servant-like fashion. They do their work cooperatively in a good spirit and with joy.

Step 3: Begin to Discern a Biblical Passage

A third step of the spiritual journey is for the congregation to begin to discern a biblical passage. At such an early point in the process, this will be just to introduce the idea of discerning a text as the spiritual journey gets underway. You will see in the list of congregational gatherings below that discerning a biblical passage will be taken up again in the third congregational gathering and the outcomes shared at the fourth. The story of the woman at the well from John 4 used throughout this book is an example of a biblical passage that can define a renewal process.

The renewal team helps the entire church discern a passage. Rather than depending on organizational principles of change, a church needs to seek the spiritual journey that leads to wholeness. The church, as a collective group, studies the text to find the Good News for transformation and the dynamics of renewal leading to new life. What are the major shifts represented in the passage? How does the passage help us understand the transformational power of the gospel for us and others?

Congregations have used all kinds of passages as their guiding Scripture. It may take a good part of a year to decide which text to adopt. Some examples are "Blessed to be a Blessing" (Genesis 12:1-3), "Faithful Community" (2 Timothy 1:6-7), and "Serving Together with Jesus to Spread the Good News" (Romans 15:5-7). In renewal, a church might first discover one text, but as things progress, move to another. At strategic moments, the church will refer back to the dynamics of renewal in its text that enrich, inform, guide, and inspire them along the way.

Step 4: Do Self-Study Using Congregational Gatherings

The fourth step in the renewal process is to look inward. A self-study explores topics from which a church can gain further energy and find the balance that will lead to new life. While this step can seem like going to the doctor for a physical, when approached in prayer, the effort is gratifying. *All self-study is done to discover the strengths of the church and build on them.* The way you design these gatherings is important. A similar format seems to help people become familiar with these events and get the most from them. Follow-up is always necessary.

We will review the gatherings to show how they can be conducted, and you can see information on outcomes in chapter 9. While these are put in a specific order with letters from the chart on page 46, the renewal team can discern the number and flow of the gatherings. You may take extra time for one specific gathering or add an event if your team discerns this is the best way to get the most benefit from this part of the process. Below you will see how to design the first congregational event on strengths, which can become a pattern for gatherings to follow.

Often, wonderful surprises during these gatherings reveal deep appreciation for the church. The process helps to uncover strengths, the way of spiritual formation, servant leadership and the life cycle, originating mission, demographics, and core values of the church.[1] By doing the study as a congregation, each person in the church develops the ownership that helps the church gain impetus and energy to build for the future. The events themselves can be very meaningful and life changing.

4a. Identify strengths (first congregational gathering). This approach differs from a diagnostic model of church renewal—find out what's wrong and fix it—and uses an affirmative model—find out what's right and build on it. Our spiritual eye is on discerning strengths, sensing God-given talents, and looking for God-given potential.

Joan and I have a challenged son, and this approach is effective with him. We do not focus on what Andrew cannot do well. Rather, we look at what is possible for him—what his strengths are. I developed this approach of identifying and building on strengths while teaching pastors in seminary in 1985, and today it is known as appreciative inquiry. Strengths give us clues about God-given gifts both in individuals and in the corporate body of the church.

A good way to identify the strengths of a church is to have a congregational gathering planned by the renewal team. This may follow a fellowship meal where people first enjoy conversation. After a significant time of prayer to create a spiritual center and after reviewing the dialogue process covered in chapter 3, the larger group breaks into small groups, in which people identify the church's strengths. The rule is "If it is a strength, share it." The strengths should be recorded for sharing to follow. As the small groups conclude, a composite list of strengths, including how often each strength was named, can be put on poster board. As strengths are identified, the needs of the congregation will become apparent as well.

The list of strengths should be saved, perhaps on the original poster, for later use (especially as the congregation rediscovers the identity of the church). Strengths help define what is unique about the church. Strengths can be posted around the church and celebrated appropriately by the church. The list of strengths will also be used as the church discerns a vision and implements a plan. Saving the poster with all the strengths provides input for the fifth congregational gathering.

4b. Do spiritual appreciation (second congregational gathering). Another step in the self-study of a congregation is a congregational gathering in which everyone is given the opportunity and encouraged to share spiritual experiences that inspire and empower the congregation. These could be stories of how members of the congregation have touched people's spiritual lives—how a card or phone call, Sunday school class or retreat was a significant part of an individual's faith journey. These stories tap into the spiritual vitality of the congregation and help a church understand what it has to offer and how spiritual formation is accomplished. This knowledge is invaluable in discerning identity, vision, and a plan.

The second congregational gathering on spiritual appreciation has a design similar to the first. As the renewal team meets to plan this gathering, it can consider how to create an atmosphere conducive to such sharing. After the meal, a presentation is given about discovering how people touch each other's lives in the congregation and the significance of that for understanding how the church can touch the lives of others. Sharing can be done in small groups with points placed on poster board. After the sharing, people are given an opportunity to walk about the gathering and tell others how they have touched their life spiritually. Then the large group gathers and shares the outcomes. The posters can be placed around the church for further conversation.

Significant transformation can happen just by such sharing. These are touching moments. In the Alban Institute resource *The Inviting Church*, written after visits to sixteen growing churches, Roy Oswald and Speed Leas say people return only if they have gone deeper spiritually after one or two visits to a church.[2] As a church aligns spiritually, congregants search for ministries that nurture the soul and provide spiritually oriented ministries. As we will soon see, the Springs process works continually to nurture the spiritual life of people. Rather than just looking at putting this as the front end of a process, the church discovers how it nurtures people and sees this as integral to its mission.

4c. Use servant leadership with the life cycle (third congregational gathering; thirty minutes). The renewal team decides how to use servant leadership and the life cycle from chapter 1. The team will discern that this is just for them or for the entire congregation. If brought to the congregation, a good time to introduce it is during the third gathering, after significant new energy and momentum have been gained from the first two. This gathering could be divided into time with the life cycle and then with originating mission and demographics. The event can begin with worship, then an introduction of how servant leadership helps a church become healthier, then a follow-up time with discussion.

A presentation depicting the life cycle and how servant leadership intervenes to keep the church on the growth side can be done with PowerPoint or a chart. The church can then reflect on how an infusion of energy is needed for renewal and how entering a more intentional spiritual journey is essential. If presented in this way, people can see how the renewal process fits together and how servant leadership can approach the ups and downs of the life cycle. Churches often can have that "aha" moment of discovering what is happening and what to do about it. The congregation can see how all are invited to be renewed spiritually and to build on the strengths of the church.

4d. Discover originating mission (third congregational gathering; twenty-five minutes). Another way to regain new energy is to discover a church's originating mission.[3] This could also be done in the third gathering. Rather than just go through all the facts and details of the past, the purpose is to discover markers that signal direction for mission today. The church goes back to its roots to discover why a congregation was gathered. What was the heart and driving vision of the founders? What was the passion of faith that led to a congregation being born and continuing to this day? Discerning the originating mission includes discovering the mission new members bring as well. In this way the gathered energy from visions, histories, and commitment to the church creates new energy.

To discover its originating mission, a church usually begins by the renewal team assigning a few people to do research and report back to the team. They decide what to present to the congregation. Often there are people in the church who can be interviewed or perhaps a church historian who can tell the story of the past. There may be old records. Rather than just looking for key individuals, though important, those doing the study try to find underlying themes and dreams that rise to the surface. These outcomes can be brought to the congregational gathering for discussion.

Discovering the originating mission may reveal why the congregation is stymied spiritually. Often a church began with an urgent mission, but some factors took over, and the mission stalled along the way. In renewal, a church can feel God's grace gently inviting it to move forward. In the process of review, a church sees how past experiences can be handled creatively so that it can move forward.

4e. Understand demographics (third congregational gathering; twenty-five minutes). A task group can be called to explore the demographics of the community surrounding the church. Local school districts and chambers of commerce often are eager to share such information and happy to learn that the church is conscious of its setting and interested in the needs of the community. One church learned from the community that a larger-than-usual population of youth was entering high school, so one part of the renewal plan was to start a youth ministry. Martin Saarinen, an expert on the life cycle, says demographics can be viewed as God's way of reaching out to the church, inviting ministry.[4]

Besides doing their own research, churches can use an organization called Percept. From its studies you can learn population trends as well as what attracts people to churches in your community. Percept helps assess community issues, faith preferences, and the kind of people who live in an area. Congregations can learn the level of faith reception and preferences in church program and style that people have.[5] In looking at demographics, a church can look at its location as a unique place of mission— God's mission.

At the close of this congregational gathering, the renewal team can ask which biblical passage could take what has been covered thus far in the renewal process and express God's leading for this church. What text would build on its strengths, tie to its spiritual journey, and take into account its mission and context? Sunday school classes or small groups could study the question. (See appendix 11.)

As congregants discern a biblical passage that guides their church, they feel they are a part of the biblical story. As they discover the dynamics of renewal in the text, they see how transformation occurs in faith. Right within the biblical story is the element of hope as well as themes of repentance, guidance, and invitation to new life. The power of the text invites them to new life. The text gives biblical grounding to the entire renewal endeavor and spiritual direction for the church. Congregants can take outcomes to the fifth congregational gathering. Such efforts are transformation in the making.

4f. Handle special topics. Sometimes there is something that, if resolved, could move a church forward. An important part of revitalization is the healing of hurts. Sometimes unpleasant stories that have been sapping energy from the congregation surface during renewal. So-called secrets are not often secret. Some stories, called living-room secrets, are fairly well known. Some are kitchen secrets that people don't know about, but they nonetheless feel the effects of those secrets. They all hurt. Sometimes just naming the hurts releases their sting. Using spiritual discernment and servant leadership, people can determine how to approach such situations. (Handling special topics will be discussed in chapter 11.)

Step 5: Teach Servant Leadership in the Church

The fifth step in the renewal process is to teach a leadership style consistent with the faith journey. Servants listen to the counsel of Jesus that the greatest among us is the one who serves. Servants carry the needs of others in their hearts and know where to point people to living water. In so serving, they are lifted to leadership, what we call servant leadership. This leadership model is consistent with the kind of church we envision. Perhaps the biblical passages in this book can be studied in smaller groups and classes in order to arrive at the church's own list of traits of a servant.

The Springs renewal process utilizes servant leadership, in which the deepest desire is to serve as Christ served. Servant leadership not only impacts the work of the renewal team but also creates trust as the church goes about the renewal process and develops a healthy corporate life. From servant leadership, people discover dialogue for better communication. Servant leaders spiritually center, listen, speak in love, and discern together. With everyone learning about being a servant, the church can develop a consistent pattern of leadership faithful to Scripture. Such a study could be conducted as part of several meetings of each leadership team in the church.

Step 6: Discern Core Values, Identity, Biblical Vision, and Three-Year Plan of Renewal

In the sixth step, the church gathers information accumulated thus far, discerns its core values and identity, and begins to shape a biblical vision and three-year plan. As the steps unfold, the church takes periods of prayer.

6a. Discern core values and identity (fourth congregational gathering). One effective method for discerning core values is to use a survey that helps the church identify what is really important (see appendix 4 for a core values audit). Core values are heartfelt beliefs that are central for a church. They are those convictions that a church desires to pass on to others around it, to its children and grandchildren.

This process reveals bedrock convictions. It helps the church look at how it can come together around its passions. There needs to be a ring of authenticity; what is on the outside should match what is on the inside and vice versa. Some things that may have seemed important may now have a minor role.

The renewal team hosts a congregational gathering to discern core values and identity and what is unique about the church. The gathering begins with the group centering spiritually through worship and prayer and reviewing the dialogue process. In small groups, they look at the core values survey and the resulting tabulations. Each small group decides which three core values come to the top.

Then the large group gathers and makes a poster of the most important core values. They look at the strengths of the church from the list made at the first gathering and compare them with their top core values. They can see their identity, what makes them unique, and what they have to offer. Knowing the church's identity is a significant step toward discerning a biblical passage, biblical vision, and mission plan.

Finalizing a biblical text can provide closure to this part of the process. It prepares the church to discern its biblical vision and plan. What text pulls together the sense of where God is leading the church? What passage would build on the strengths, tie to the spiritual journey, and take into account the mission of the church? Through group spiritual discernment, the team finds a text that invites the church to new life. Then the team can facilitate a study of the dynamics of renewal and of the text as the church goes on to make this biblical passage its own.

6b. Discern a biblical vision and three-year plan of renewal

(fifth congregational gathering). The renewal team thei
follow-up congregational gathering. Again the meeting
with prayer and renewed commitment to dialogue. At thi.
ering the congregation claims its identity and discerns a biblical
text, which helps it understand itself and what God has in store.
Then it can discern a biblical vision. With this vision the church
also discerns an incremental plan. A vision is not a vision until it
has a plan, and a plan is not a plan unless it is implemented.

Small-group discussion and total-group interaction help the
congregation dialogue to arrive at a vision and plan. The list of
the church's strengths from the first gathering and the core values
and identity from the second gathering help in this process.
Information from the work done on spiritual appreciation, originating mission, and demographic trends is shared and used.

The image below can help a congregation visualize what is
happening at this fifth gathering.

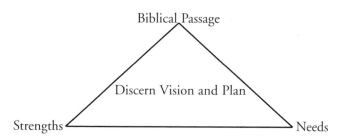

The church needs to ask, "Where is God's leading? What words
express God's calling for us?" (See, for example, the list in step 3
above). Rather than coming up with a long statement in which you
attempt to incorporate all aspects of your calling, a short vision says
a lot and is focused. It should be a statement that could be painted
boldly on the side of a bus.

As one author puts it, "Nothing becomes dynamic until it
becomes specific."[6] Perhaps a congregation immediately sees a
number of logical steps to fulfilling its vision. Dialogue will help
a church discern what needs to happen first and then next, and

what needs to wait. Any plan of ministry that emerges at this stage is open to alteration and surprises. Expressing the core values of the congregation can become instrumental in seeing this vision and plan unfold. (Chapter 10 focuses on using servant leadership to discern vision and plan.)

At this point, it is a time for the church to pause for celebration. Churches use various formats for celebration, including testimonies, a celebration of communion or foot washing, or a potluck. This is also a good time to rest. Rest can be seen as Sabbath, when we lie fallow and restore. The press of schedule is laid aside for a time of spiritual rest and nurture. The church pauses for people to recreate and know the stillness of God. Living water restores. What a joy!

Step 7: Implement a Three-Year Plan

The steps of implementation discussed briefly here are covered in greater detail later in the book. The church renewal process described thus far has laid the groundwork for establishing or reestablishing ministries that express the newly found vision. Implementation means having a clear focus, setting priorities, enlisting leaders according to gifts, and finding needed resources. Ministry means service. Implementing a renewal plan can be seen as the outward discipline of service. Ministries are at the heart of renewal. In renewal we use our gifts and implement our call to ministry. While this looks like just one step, in renewal, it can be the longest part. (We will look at implementing ministries in part 4.)

Have appreciative inquiry. While having congregational gatherings on shaping and implementing ministries, a church may decide to look at factors that make things go well. The field called appreciative inquiry, which we looked at in assessing strengths, can be effectively used in a church that has low self-image and operates from a position of weakness. In appreciative inquiry, we look for what works in an organization. Using the workshop approach, participants "stir up memories of energizing moments of success creating a new energy that is positive and synergistic," notes Ann

Hammond, who has written on appreciative inquiry.[7] In appreciative inquiry people share examples of what it feels like and looks like to have things work well. They also look at the assumptions behind the way the group operates and factors at work that made things go well.

Unlike the problem-solving approach that explores needs, analyzes causes, proposes solutions, and develops a treatment plan, in appreciative inquiry congregations value the best, envision what "might be," dialogue on what "should be," and innovate what "will be."[8] Using appreciative inquiry, churches attempt to do more of what they do well. Or, as Hammond puts it, "Doing more of what works crowds out the insoluble problems."[9] This has many applications in renewal of the church. Centering on what the church feels called to do and does well gives focus on what to do in the future. The increased energy and momentum enable the church to move forward.

New leadership emerging. By this point in the renewal process, as ministries are starting to be implemented, new leaders often begins to emerge. Sharing the load in a congregation is one visible outcome of the renewal process. To be healthy, the renewal team helps the church remedy difficulties that arise out of the self-study or perceived roadblocks in the plan. The team gives attention to the corporate culture of the church, to decision making, and to the ability to realize potential in terms of witness and service. Keeping a journal of renewal is helpful because this practice keeps us observant of the movements in renewal, helps us note progress and challenges, prompts us to reflect on renewal, and helps us express our gratitude to God.

≪

This chapter has covered the basics of the seven-fold renewal process that leads to a plan uniquely discerned for a church and built on its strengths and guiding mission. New energy comes through the spiritual journey, through congregational gatherings and identifying strengths, spiritual appreciation, and core values.

Identifying originating mission and demographics gives energy. Discerning a biblical passage, a vision, and a plan gives energy and focus.

All this is renewal, which is even more evident as implementation occurs. It will take time to establish new patterns of growth; in time, such patterns will become healthy habits. In upcoming chapters we will go over each of these seven steps in greater depth. The next step is to look at the concept of dialogue used throughout the process.

For Reflection and Discussion

1. Do the seven steps of renewal energize you? What can you do to help your church tend to its thirst? What can you do to tend to your own thirst?

2. Discuss the three larger movements of the seven steps: the journeys upward, inward, and outward. Does this progression make sense to you? Is there one that seems especially exciting?

3. Do you see the value of putting strengths before weaknesses and finding what factors are at work when a church operates at its best? What strengths come to mind when you think of your church?

4. What questions do you have about the renewal process? Can you see how each step helps a church embark on a spiritual journey? Can you see how one step builds on another?

5. Do you agree that a vision is not a vision without a plan and that a plan is not a plan without being implemented? What further ramifications do you see in this statement?

3

Discovering the Gift of Dialogue

The outcome of the gift of dialogue went far beyond expectations at Emmanuel Mennonite Church. When I introduced it at the beginning of the renewal process, I used dialogue to engage people and have them add their ideas about how the process should work. At Emmanuel people differed on styles of worship; some liked traditional and some contemporary music. The chairperson of the worship committee, Bill Parson, decided to utilize the dialogue process to approach the topic of worship.

He reported, "After hearing from several members of the congregation regarding worship issues, I decided to take some time to sit down with people on both sides of the issue and hear what they had to say. I spent most of my time listening. Occasionally, I asked questions to clarify what they were saying or to help them elaborate on a point so that we could get to the heart of the issue."

Bill was heartened to hear in the interviews that the dialogue process was catching on. "In one case, the first couple I met with actually invited the other person over for coffee, and they had a chance to listen to each other's concerns. I also found that some of the issues themselves were not as important as was the opportunity for these individuals to feel someone was listening to them and valued their opinion."

Through dialogue, Bill found that he was affected as well. "I became open to new ideas and was able to change my thinking on some issues once I heard what others had to say. It was much easier to do when I made the effort to listen and avoided trying to make my own points first before they had the opportunity to finish. I was completely tuned into what they were saying rather than trying to form my statements or arguments in my head while they were talking."

In church renewal, dialogue is important both as an intervention in decline and as a way to draw forth communication. One of the first things a church does in the Springs process is to learn to use the process of dialogue in all aspects of renewal. This four-point dialogue process has been developed with a spiritual focus.[1] Growing spiritually and growing dialogically go hand in hand. As people listen to God and speak with God, they become more attuned to the sacredness of other people. Listening ties directly into relationships. In the second half of the chapter we will discuss how dialogue is used for renewal within a cluster of churches.

The Invitation to Dialogue

When we take the John 4 passage with Jesus and the Samaritan woman and turn it into a drama, we see how Jesus initiated dialogue. Rather than telling the woman what to do, he invited conversation by asking her for a drink. That conversation ultimately led to him speaking of life-giving water and to the woman asking for some of that water. From there, Jesus gave the great "I am" proclamation: "I am he, the one who is speaking to you" (4:26 NRSV). The conversation went from a simple request for water to the woman finding the full expression of God standing before her, offering God's very life to her.

Dialogue is truly a blessing. In a monologue, one person speaks while the other listens. In dialogue, two or more people participate in a dynamic interchange that creates understanding among people who together can discern solutions to complex problems. In dialogue, each person becomes an equally important partner. Dialogue transforms individuals and churches. Once it is discovered, all relationships take on new life. When dialogue occurs, people realize it takes them beyond what they are able to create on their own. The outcomes often go far beyond our every expectation.

Ironically, I found a premier book on dialogue, *The Miracle of*

Dialogue, by Reuel Howe in the discard box at a library. Using a spiritual focus along with Howe's wisdom, I developed a four-fold dialogue process for use in the local church. Dialogue is not necessarily easy, because individuals will find that certain disciplines are needed to ensure it happens. But as they interact, this process becomes second nature. What a joy, what a gift when dialogue happens!

The Dialogue Process

The process of dialogue should be introduced at the beginning of any endeavor in church renewal and be part of the training in servant leadership. If the renewal team is not yet in place, the leadership team of the church can facilitate this training. By introducing it early in the renewal process, dialogue is not tied to any issue and creates the safe haven for discussion necessary for a church not only to survive but also to flourish. A dialogue card like the one below can be distributed so each member has a copy of the process.

Dialogue

1. Becoming Grounded Spiritually
   - Get in touch with the living Christ.
   - Release anxiety and be open to what is possible.

2. Listening
   - Set aside my agenda and listen to the other person(s).
   - Suspend judgment and be open to be influenced.

3. Speaking
   - Speak the truth in love, using my understanding.
   - Be able to reflect on the assumptions of others.

4. Spiritually Discerning
   - Seek God's will and truth together.
   - Get head, heart, and faith journey together.

The pastor or other member of the church who teaches the dialogue process should attempt to teach it dialogically. This occurs through discussions in which all are invited to give input and to invest in the process. How will dialogue work in this specific church, with these members? Perhaps the card needs to be adjusted to make it applicable to specific needs or characteristics of a church. In this way people gain ownership in a process that is workable for the group. In teaching dialogue we have found how handy it is to put the four-fold process on two sides of card stock and fold it over, creating a tent that can be set up on a discussion table.

Becoming grounded spiritually. Silence helps us enter dialogue and is perhaps the best way to become grounded spiritually. As we release anxiety we become open to what is possible. Speaking about silence, Robert Greenleaf, a Quaker, said, "One must not be afraid of a little silence. Some find silence awkward or oppressive, but a relaxed approach to dialogue will include welcoming of some silence. It is often a devastating question to ask oneself—but it is sometimes important to ask—'In saying what I have in mind will I really improve on the silence?'"[2] In silence we tend to our spiritual thirst and know the presence of Jesus' living water. Centering spiritually allows us to gain sensitivity to others and realize the gift of relationships. We become aware of the living Christ in our midst.

When we pour out the clutter of our hearts, we become present with God and others. Drawing on the work of Martin Buber, Howe connects the spiritual dimension with relationships. "Dialogue offers the only possibility for a relation between the *thou* of the other person and the *I* of myself. I can only speak to him and leave him free to respond, and out of that exchange we may both be called forth as people in a relationship of mutual trust."[3] Participants carry the attitude of prayer into dialogue and return to this oasis frequently during the conversation.

Listening. Spiritually centering ourselves leads naturally to step 2 in dialogue: listening. Communication is generally associated with speaking, but listening provides the basis for deeper communication, creating the climate for dialogue. In listening we hear elements of truth shared from the perspective of another individual. Various nuances of meaning are present, and by listening we learn from others and can understand their convictions.

In dialogue, it takes discipline not to think you know what others are going to say even before they speak. Howe calls such thoughts "calculated monologue."[4] Dialogue calls us to wait and listen, refraining from thinking how we will respond before the other person is even done speaking.

To see that we understand someone properly, we might choose to repeat what we think that person has said. This signals that we really are interested and are taking seriously what others are saying. Listening empathically does not mean compromising our own position. We listen to understand. We are open to being influenced. By listening we take initiative to create the climate that leads to greater understanding. We set the stage to form a deeper bond, to resolve differences, and to find solutions to problems.

Speaking. Speaking, the third step in dialogue, is needed for communication. But in dialogue our understanding of what speaking entails runs deeper than we might expect. For dialogue to occur, the way we speak is critically important. If we speak as if we hold the only truth in a matter, we signal that the other's opinion is not welcomed. In dialogue we speak in a way that invites people to share their truth.

Building on the work of physicist David Bohm, William Isaacs uses the analogy of people with different viewpoints being in a giant washing machine together. In this place, assumptions can be suspended and looked at from different points of view. In this cool environment, people can begin to inquire together and find insights for the good of the whole.[5] Speaking so we can discover the truth among us results in greater understanding.

Spiritually discerning. In discernment we seek God's will in a situation. We ask where God is leading. This is the thirst we desire to quench in the fourth part of dialogue: spiritually discerning the truth. Whenever I talk about spiritual discernment, I am reminded of St. Ignatius, founder of the Jesuits, who spoke about becoming attuned to the movements of God, which he described as consolation and desolation. In discerning, we see that one way leads to greater peace, hope, and love (consolation) and the other to anxiety, unsettledness, and despair (desolation).

Some modern Jesuits speak of discernment as getting the head, the heart, and the faith journey together. In addition to the feeling side (our heart), God's will uses the best thinking (our head) and calls for following the path of discipleship (our faith journey). In dialogue we explore each aspect of discernment. Dialogue helps us tend the spiritual thirst. Dialogue helps us grow in discipleship. Dialogue sets the pace for renewal. Discipline is needed so we don't push the process. We "wait for the Lord," as the psalmist says. In dialogue we discover the greater truth God gives.

The Gift of Dialogue

Dialogue is a gift because it cannot be forced or manufactured. Howe calls this the miracle of dialogue. "Dialogue therefore produces muscles of discovery opening to us the mysteries of life," Howe writes.[6] Dialogue leads to collaboration; the talents, insights, and energies of everyone are appreciated. In dialogue we face resistance, anxieties, and alienation and find a path that leads to understanding, strength, and unity. In dialogue we see God at work.

Building energy. Decline in the life cycle of a church often entails breakdown in communication. Programs may still function to some degree, but lack of communication takes the spirit out of everything. With unresolved issues, the aging process sets in and energy is the first to go. As Jesus showed in John 4, intervening with dialogue helps people find a renewed faith, understand one another, and build on common core values. Beginning to regain energy and momentum, churches benefit from having dialogue about even basic matters.

In the upswing of the life cycle, critical points emerge in which people need to communicate to reach maturity and health. Every church needs to negotiate between people needs and program needs, budgets and resources, one program and another. With dialogue, a church gains strength, captures energy for its vision, utilizes resources, and balances critical areas. When cultivated, dialogue is immeasurably useful for building healthy relationships and healthy churches. What a God-given gift!

Conflict. When conflict occurs, rather than act or react under pressure, churches can initiate the four-fold process of dialogue. The outcomes often amaze us, going beyond what we imagined possible. In *Crucial Conversations: Tools for Talking When the Stakes Are High*, the authors describe conversations that matter the most, even day-to-day exchanges that affect one's life and make all the difference in the world.[7] When under duress, the authors tell us, return to dialogue. The outcomes of dialogue reflect the values we cherish.

Through dialogue, servant leaders are in the position to act when crucial decisions need to be made. Appendix 5 has been prepared so many people in the church can review the contents of this chapter and look at how to hold a group dialogue session. Rather than be separate from an organization, servant leaders use dialogue to lead from the center of the organization and do so with humility and poise. Their grace and authenticity is evident because they are actively in dialogue with others. They use their gifts and legitimate power for the good of all and for the mission they serve.

Mission. At one church where I served we had used dialogue in the earlier stages of renewal, but now the church was ready to establish a new ministry. The church had discerned a vision statement: "Serving Together with Jesus to Spread the Good News!" and, using Romans 15:5-7 as its passage, was about to launch the first step of the plan—to have a family night. But there were various ways to go about this endeavor. There were different curriculums to use, different schedule ideas, and some wanted the family night to be weekly rather than biweekly.

After prayer, the group began to talk again about dialogue. They all acknowledged that the way was not yet determined and that they wanted to listen to each and every person. Amazingly,

after each person spoke and reviewed not only their input but also
the input of others, they came out of that meeting of one accord.
They decided to have family night every week, which could have
been seen by some to involve too much work. However, because
everyone felt heard and appreciated, the family night was a united
endeavor.

Dialogue in a Cluster of Churches

Even as Springs can be used in one church, experience has
shown that working with a cluster of churches in renewal has
advantages. (But churches working alone can pick up additional
ideas as they read about clusters.) Just as dialogue greatly enhances
conversation, think of the infusion of faith and gifts as a group of
churches gathers and helps each other along the way. Like having
a jogging partner to encourage one another and keep up the discipline, churches can walk alongside of and help one another in
the renewal process.[8]

Renewal has a wave-like effect. When a cluster is formed,
churches begin to work in league with other churches, and the effort
of renewal begins to be felt in an entire region. The dialogue widens
and the conversation brings new life and support to churches.
Imagine the new life when people work toward a common goal,
helping one another. The synergy is heartening. A region is able to
assist churches to do together what a local church finds challenging
to do alone.

What is a cluster? A cluster is a group of two to six churches
that covenant to work together to help one another discover God's
vision unique to each church and support one another in implementing a renewal plan. By working together, churches can draw
on one another for the journey and multiply the strength for
renewal. Each church has a renewal team that ranges from four to
eight to as many as sixteen people.

The teams meet for intensive training, to discuss discoveries,
and to integrate information for their geographic setting. Often
churches help each other identify their strengths and unique iden-

tity. In a cluster, these teams meet a number of times a year to listen deeply and to help one another in spiritual discernment of where God is uniquely leading a church.

Along with extensive training, cluster time allows the churches to give and receive counsel and walk with each other on the journey of renewal. Churches help one another become aware of the resources available to meet needs and may in fact have a resource, an experienced individual or published resource that another church can use. Churches can help each other as they develop a vision and a three-year plan of renewal.

In clusters, churches encourage one another through the ups and downs of renewal, help one another overcome challenges, and become a living expression of God's kingdom. Cluster churches can help each other see things not otherwise seen and give needed perspective on the overall growth in renewal.

Role of the prayer network. Any endeavor in church renewal flourishes only when built on the foundation of prayer. Providing prayer support for a cluster, churches pray not only for their own renewal but also for the renewal of the other churches. In a cluster, one of the first things to do is to enlist a prayer team. Those with a heart for prayer are called for this ministry assignment. A prayer coordinator can establish a group email list or telephone prayer chain. The team prays for response to God's invitation. It may ask regional or denominational bodies to include prayer for renewal as part of their annual meetings.

The prayer team is in prayer when an event on renewal is in progress. This can be done in its own locale or on site. On the Sunday prior to each cluster meeting, churches and the prayer team pray for the renewal of their church and each church in their cluster and for the upcoming gathering. Prayer is the foundation for all aspects of Springs. The outcomes of this prayer emphasis are astounding.

The role of a district executive or conference minister. Whatever the title (bishop, conference minister, overseer, executive minister, etc.), the person who provides leadership over several churches in a specific geographic area plays an integral role in the renewal of those churches. Executives provide the point of contact with a Springs initiative, help envision renewal in their region, work with appropriate regional boards, and lay the groundwork for renewal. They need to become familiar with the resources of the renewal process of Springs, be able to access all materials, receive information on such an initiative, and assist in renewal of the churches.[9]

As clusters are shaped, the executive helps a district discern which churches are interested and ready to be part of a renewal cluster, is an integral part of the enlistment process, assists churches as they make their covenants, and celebrates with the congregations. A district executive can serve as the coordinator of a cluster or help enlist a cluster coordinator. He encourages pastors and congregations as they go through the renewal process and points churches to appropriate resources for new ministries, lifts up the regional effort of Springs, and shares the enthusiasm of renewal.

Criteria for churches in renewal. Often we wonder what kind of churches are candidates for renewal. Just like Marriage Enrichment or Marriage Encounter, Springs is for making good churches better. A church needs to have a heart and desire for renewal and feel a thirst for new life. A pastor needs to be eager to grow spiritually and have a passion for renewal of the church. A church needs four to eight people willing to commit themselves to be on a renewal team. Such a team does not do the renewal, but is trained to facilitate renewal with the entire congregation.

Other criteria are also essential. Churches seeking renewal should have a manageable level of conflict. If this is in question, they should be willing to consult with their district on their readiness for renewal. At the same time they need to see that renewal is a long-term process, taking three to four years to mature. They also have to have a willingness to stay with the process during any possible slowdown. A church in renewal should be willing to continue to follow God, who is leading, and see challenging periods as part of renewal. Then they move on to next steps.

In terms of selection of churches, the district executive can meet with an appropriate commission and prayerfully discern which churches seem ready for renewal. Often when churches are approached their spirits are buoyed because someone sees potential in them. So discernment of churches is a vital part of renewal. Sometimes churches are in transition, such as having an interim pastor, and the process can help them to discern a vision and see the kind of leadership needed for their church.[10]

The role of the advisory council. Behind renewal is the basic assumption that we seek wise counsel. The wise counsel of Scripture is at the heart of renewal. We also seek wise counsel of the wider church and local church. Wise counsel from many perspectives helps ensure the success of the renewal effort. An advisory council called by a district broadens the perspective and ownership of a renewal effort. The council may learn of resources and people that can be utilized to meet the needs of the local churches. The council multiplies the number of contacts that can be made and the number of voices that unite in a common initiative.

In Springs, an advisory council of six to ten people is called using spiritual discernment. Such people should represent a variety of roles and functions in the various churches participating in the cluster. The advisory council can meet in person, by telephone, or through email. With eyes and ears closer to the situation, they are instrumental in shaping the initiative to meet the needs of churches.

Enlisting churches for renewal. Enlisting churches is very important in church renewal. It is, in fact, renewal and is of critical importance to the outcome of the entire endeavor. Enlistment is done from a deep spiritual orientation. Using the process of spiritual discernment (described in chapter 7), those who enlist should be in prayer around the entire experience, even before the first call is made. The churches approach should show signs and eagerness to be renewed (see appendix 6).

Since the renewal process involves a significant commitment, it is best that the enlistment process be done with a group of people. It also should not be done in one meeting. Enlistment is done by servant leaders, who first listen to the churches and their heart, see their strengths, and help them as they discern what God is calling them to do.

In the first meeting there can be significant listening and sharing. The church will need to understand the renewal process, as well as the background and methods of the Springs approach.[11] While help is assured each step of the way, the commitment required of the church should not be played down.

On the other hand, the rewards and accomplishments of renewal are emphasized and celebrated. Enlisters may find that there have been past attempts at renewal and may need to help the church process those experiences. The entire enlistment should be done with a sense of deep appreciation of and respect for the church. The process of enlistment and discernment should have positive effects. Churches asked to join in renewal feel affirmed and take the first step in renewal.

Role of a cluster coordinator. A cluster coordinator is instrumental in the success of a Springs initiative in a region. Coordinators are organizers, teaching assistants, encouragers, and helpers of churches in the renewal process. They must have a spiritual heart for renewal and be able to maintain a positive outlook. Cluster coordinators are invited to serve through a call process. They should have a real heart for the renewal of churches.

A group selecting a cluster coordinator should begin in prayer and then review the kind of person needed for this calling. Praying over the requirements for a week or so, they then return to discuss names. They discern together who would fit the call. At that point, a time to visit with the called person is set. Members of the selection group should be ready to listen as they explain a call under the vision for renewal. Give the called person time to think, pray, look at priorities, and if willing, make adjustments. Be sure to set a follow-up visit.

Cluster coordinators enter a time of prayer and take the next step in their own spiritual disciplines. They study Bible texts around the Springs theme and attend a training event where they learn the renewal process. They read resources before cluster meetings and study the topics for each session. Coordinators prepare for each cluster meeting, see that churches have materials, and welcome participants.

They help people get acquainted, assist with presentations, lead discussions, and draw conclusions from each session. Between sessions they make at least monthly contact with each church to encourage them. They contact the servant leader of Springs with updates and channel any questions to move the process forward.

Training for a cluster. From two to four times a year the renewal teams and other designated members of the churches in a cluster should gather for intensive leadership training sessions. To ensure effectiveness, all expectations of who takes initiative and time frames for sessions should be worked out well in advance so everyone knows what is happening and can effectively plan. To start the training of a cluster, a spiritual retreat may be held to establish the spiritual focus. Also, the pastors of the cluster churches may have their own session at the beginning and at other points of the process.[12]

Part of the servant-led aspect of training is teaching by learning objectives. In this servant-led style of learning, we think not of what information we want to get into people, but of where the learners are now, and then we come up with a plan that can lead them where they want and need to be.[13]

Before a training event, a letter should be sent to the renewal teams that gives the overall plan and specific learning objectives for the session. The schedule should include time for discussion and reflection, along with breaks. The agenda should have focused reading resources, which should be completed ahead of time.

Chapters in this book can be covered at team or cluster meetings. With prior preparation, people can spend the session building on the readings with discussion and discernment. Participants should leave a session with concrete steps to take upon returning to their local congregation. Training can be in an expectant spirit and done with joy.

Training for pastors of renewal. Training for pastors can be another vital aspect of a cluster. Training events can be held in the setting of a retreat that assists pastors in developing their spiritual disciplines, becoming trained in the renewal process, and taking up topics specifically related to that pastor. Introductory training topics include (1) being spiritually grounded—being spiritually renewed, (2) leading as a servant—linking to spiritual formation, (3) being servant leaders—helping facilitate the renewal process, (4) operating collaboratively—using dialogue, and (5) keeping focused—delegating appropriately. (Topics specifically related to pastors will be covered in chapter 10.)

Advanced training includes teaching pastors how to be spiritual guides of congregations and helping them enter a spiritual path and attend to the movements of God. Pastors can help churches grow spiritually through corporate spiritual disciplines, corporate spiritual direction using a biblical text, and group spiritual discernment. This training includes (1) being spiritual guides—spiritual formation of congregations, (2) being visionary—seeing things whole, (3) being messengers of good news—becoming master preachers, (4) discipling others—establishing training in discipling and becoming apostles, and (5) encouraging—the role of standing behind others.

Corporate gatherings of renewal. A final component to encourage renewal is to have a yearly, large corporate gathering of all the churches in the cluster. This could include a celebration, testimonials, inspirational messages, and training that keeps the renewal process before the churches and addresses special topics. This helps keep the enthusiasm and camaraderie alive and growing. Each such gathering can be an important part of the renewal initiative. A spirit of Christ is alive.

✦

Dialogue plays a very important role in revitalization. Dialogue exemplifies one's faith in God and demonstrates the respect people can show one another. Dialogue also exemplifies the servant leadership style, calling on people to listen and interact in a positive manner. Dialogue yields a positive outcome in relationships in which the strengths of each party are multiplied in the interaction. No wonder churches working in clusters often have a better chance in renewal than if they work alone. Praying, listening, speaking in love, and discerning together joins a body of believers working for a similar goal.

For Reflection and Discussion

1. Put the tent card on dialogue on your refrigerator or in your wallet or purse. Is there a person in your daily life (a spouse, co-worker, or friend) who would like to covenant to use dialogue in your daily conversations? What outcomes do you notice?

2. Can you reflect together on each of the parts of dialogue? How do you see silence impacting communication? Listening? Speaking in love? Discerning? Have you ever found yourself thinking of what you were going to say before someone else even spoke? How can you plan to counteract that?

3. How do spiritual disciplines and disciplines in communication fit together? Can you testify that growing spiritually helps you to grow relationally?

4. How could dialogue be of use in the life of your church? Think of specific areas, committees, issues, and so on. Can you see why dialogue is such a gift and have you ever been blessed with this gift in a way that went beyond your comprehension?

5. What are the advantages of doing renewal in a cluster of churches? If your church has no other partner, do you see how some of the same elements could be built into your renewal process? In what setting could training of pastors occur?

4

Leading with a Basin and Towel

The profound connection of the spiritual life with servant leadership and renewal of the church became evident early in my first pastorate. The challenges of leadership were before me as I began pastoral ministry in a declining church. While the voices of discouragement were strong, leadership potential was evident. The community around the church building was growing, but the unused doors of the old section of the church faced the road and signaled to the passersby, "We're closed." The church lived under the voice of doom clearly spoken by a man I met at the back door—someone I did not know and never met again. He said, "Sonny, if you think you are going to do something with this church, you better think again!"

Leaders face the challenge of tending to people's spiritual thirst while also developing a vibrant church. Coming from a scientific background and having many discussions in the graduate math department about faith at Purdue University, I knew of the spiritual hunger of our society. As I entered Bush Creek Church of the Brethren, my first congregation, I asked myself, "How do I meet the spiritual needs not only of a declining church but of a growing community?" Back then, in the early 1970s, there were few resources on the life of prayer, much less on fostering a spiritual focus in congregational life or becoming a serving community of faith. Somehow I took all this negativity as a challenge. I saw a vision of a renewed church.

The water basin and towel are symbols of servant leadership that arise from Jesus' service to his disciples in the upper room.

The basin and towel speak not only of service, but also of the very heart of spiritual formation.[1] In the act of foot washing, people have their feet washed as a symbol of cleansing and renewal of their baptism and go as refreshed vessels of God to wash the feet of others. In the same spirit I decided to go out into the community each Saturday where Bush Creek was located and stop wherever someone was doing lawn work or knock on doors when someone was obviously home.

I went with the mindset to serve. Not thinking of what people could offer us or how we could get them to come to church, I sought to discover how the church could serve and enter the spiritual journey with them. One couple asked outright, "Are you conducting a membership drive?"

"No," I replied. "I am here to be with you and visit."

I purposely took little literature so people would not feel I had something to push. Just letting people know the church was there and interested in their lives attracted newcomers. As new people came to church, the church looked not at what we could do for us but how we could assist them in their faith journey. We would look at how they could develop their gifts and offer their talents. We would connect them with others with whom they could share their spiritual journey. Through this approach, the couple that asked the membership drive question became part of a stream of new attendees. The spiritual focus we nurtured in the church impacted the way we began to relate in the community and vice versa. A whole new climate began to develop around and in the church.

Writing my doctoral project, *How the Pastor Can Help Motivate and Supervise Renewal in the Local Congregation*, I studied marks of ministry from the Gospel of John. Servanthood stood out as a hallmark for ministry of renewal in the church.[2] When Robert Greenleaf wrote his booklet *The Servant as Leader*, it was like holding up a mirror to what was happening at Bush Creek.

We approached ministry as service, the Greek meaning of ministry, and followed what that called for day by day. As Greenleaf put it, "The servant leader is servant first. . . . It begins with the natural feeling that one wants to serve, to serve first. Then the conscious choice brings one to aspire to lead."[3] Indeed, through serving, the church was gaining leadership in the community.

Tending to the thirst lifts up the importance of leadership. Each of our personal spiritual journeys impacts the way we view leadership. Rather than beginning with where we want other people to be, we need to begin by tending to our own spiritual thirst and seeing how we can be vessels to serve others. Understanding ourselves as servants, we become more attentive to God and more in tune with people. Through prayer we become more compassionate and more sensitive to people's spiritual and practical needs.

Servanthood gives integrity to the power held by those in authority, because people feel the leader has their interests in mind. Servant leaders develop relationships of trust with people. Servant leadership is about taking on the manner of Christ, who chose not to be served but to serve and gave his life as a ransom (see Matthew 20:28). As people feel served by Christ, they respond to Christ and begin to be able to tend to their spiritual thirst. At Bush Creek, the adult Sunday school class, which had grown to fifty, decided to tend their thirst by doing a quarter on the topic of prayer. We had to travel the whole way to the Washington Cathedral to discover E. Herman's little classic *Creative Prayer*.[4]

At the same time, at Bush Creek we discovered people in the community who were physically in need, so the church decided to form a clothing room. The Women's Aid group, which quilted each Wednesday at the church, grew in numbers and decided to assist those who came for clothing. Soon a group was doing a Bible study and folding the regular and community newsletters. Brown-bag lunches turned into feasts of fellowship, with the menu including hog maw (pig's stomach) filled with sausage, a food of the long-standing members of the church. Soon a small-group Bible study started in the community and provided women with a special fellowship of faith.

The newfound spiritual depth and the desire to serve could

be seen in interpersonal relationships as well. When I first came to Bush Creek, there was a lot of apprehension among some life-long members about new people who might come and how that might change their church. New people soon said that they came because of what they found at the church. It was amazing to see fears overcome and vibrant relationships formed.

One new member, Duane Lippy, who was a CPA and worked in the Watergate complex in Washington, D.C., formed a bond with our longtime church treasurer John Main. John was a White House gardener, and he used paper and pencil to figure all the finances. Duane said that every penny was accounted for, and he did not want to change the system of a man who had given so many years of conscientious service to the church. As pastor, my heart was warmed to see the respect and mutual service in this and many other relationships that developed in a vibrant, serving con-gregation.

Servant Leadership: A Biblical Model

In the upper room, Jesus exemplified being a servant leader. Since beginning to work with church renewal using servant lead-ership, I have carried a replica of a water basin with a towel into every class and church. This symbol serves as a reminder that at the heart of the gospel message is the drama of Christ the servant who brings reconciliation to God and others. As we have our feet washed and cleansed by Christ, we in turn wash the feet of others in his name.

Scripture defines servant leadership for the church. We find traits of the servant in Old Testament readings in the suffering ser-vant songs in Isaiah 42:1-4; 49:1-6; 50:4-9; and 52:13–53:12. In the New Testament the attributes of a servant are described in Revelation 7:17 and John 13, among others. When studying Scripture, it is important to remember the concept of the one and the many. On the one hand, when we talk about servants we are thinking about what one individual is and can do. On the other hand, the servant can be a group of people like the nation Israel or the church today.

After looking at biblical passages on servant leadership at a Springs pre-Renovaré conference, a small group from a wide range of denominations was adroit in lifting up attributes of the servant.[5] Its list included the following: "a servant is called, humble, persistent, not about him or her, no whining, an instrument in God's hand, filled with light, obedient in sharing the light, hidden until the proper time, brings back the stray, formative from the moment of birth, has a keen sense of awareness of self and God, determined, listens to God, courageous, trusts in God, secure in his or her identity."

Scripture reveals that people were called to be servants in a framework of hardship. In the book of Isaiah, Israel, which had been in bondage, returned to its destroyed homeland. In the suffering servant songs, God called them to be a servant people—a light to the nations.

In Revelation, John was in exile on the Isle of Patmos because emperor Domitian of Rome demanded everyone call him "Lord and God." Refusing, Christians were put to death. The author gives a "church consultation." Some churches in Asia Minor sold out to the culture. In contrast, John wrote about being a faithful servant following the Lamb.

John 13 recounts Jesus in his final hours. The path to the cross was set in motion. In that context, Jesus met with his closest associates and did the unusual—he took a towel. Here is the model of redemptive love as God reaches out to humanity. In church renewal we can identify with these Scriptures as we face the challenges set before us.

Tucked away in these Scriptures are at least ten traits of servant leadership. In this chapter we look at the first eight traits—all from the suffering servant songs in Isaiah. Chapter 10 of this book discusses the ninth trait, which is that the servant leads in spiritual transformation, as found in Revelation 7:17. In chapter 14, the tenth trait of servant leadership is that the servant enters the drama of reconciliation as found in John 13:1-17. (All ten traits are listed in appendix 7.)

1. Called and Strengthened

Servant leaders feel a call to serve God, assured that God will provide the strength for the task and that they will be blessed (see Isaiah 42:1). As servants they are to be a light to the nations, taking God's saving power to everyone (see Isaiah 49:6).

When we read the five servant songs in Isaiah, we find ourselves at the center of church renewal. Due to their unfaithfulness, Israel was in captivity and certainly an unlikely candidate for leadership for spiritual formation. Calling their state "exilic despair," Walter Brueggemann says that God calls a grieving nation from being preoccupied and self-absorbed with its own destiny, even comfortable in it, to become a servant people.[6]

What powerful words for a church seeking renewal! How often is a church, region, or denomination caught in dynamics of exilic despair, comfortable in decline, unsure of the future, and focused on maintaining what is left? Broken, God's people are called to be servants, called to a mission—to be a light to the nations. What an unlikely light!

The servant's call, strength, and blessing are wrapped up in the opening verse of the first servant song of Isaiah: "Here is my servant, whom I uphold, my chosen, in whom my soul delights" (42:1 NRSV). As Claus Westermann observes, "Out of many who might have performed the task, this is the one whom God chooses for it, and the designation makes the choice public."[7] Most likely Israel was as surprised as everyone else.

As Brueggemann notes, "In exile, Israel tended to be more self-preoccupied and self-absorbed with its own destiny. In this utterance, however, Yahweh changes the subject and summons grieving Israel out beyond its own self-preoccupation to other work."[8] Their role was identified. The servant was called to mission to bring God's order to society and ensure the dignity of the dispossessed.

Call is a significant feature in every renewal ministry, whether it be for individuals or for the corporate body. People feel a call within themselves to initiate renewal in a local church, to become part of a renewal team, to attend a congregational gathering, or to take up a ministry that has meaning. God speaks.

In terms of calling people, our experience has been that members have been enthusiastic to be part of something that is going to be done for their church. You can't seem to hold that kind of person back. The call needs to be confirmed by other people. Can others also sense how this call has come to this person and see how this person can be instrumental in leading the church to renewal? Other people who feel this sense of call can serve and assist in renewal of the church.

Servants take up spiritual disciplines to help place themselves before God. Potential members of a renewal team should pray about a call to serve. It will be a commitment of time, resources, and talents. Sometimes other things need to be given up. Whatever the call in the renewal process, it takes time to consider and pray, asking God to lead. Saying yes, individuals surrender to God and open themselves to the call, a crucial posture for renewal to occur.

Just as Isaiah affirmed that call, so he lifted up the strength God provided. The servant soon realizes that to fulfill that call takes power. And that for which God calls, God gives the strength to fulfill. Here, calling and tending thirst connect. The call to fulfill ministry invites us back to prayer and spiritual disciplines to keep up the supply of energy, to align with God's purpose, to grow in Christ. Looking at the ministry of Jesus, we see that often he did not just go to prayer after some major event in his life, but before he set out in ministry. Jesus knew his need to rest, to replenish, and to be strengthened.

2. Spiritually Centered

Servant leaders lead from a heart of peace. They lead from within (the center), are attuned to healing, and sacrifice unselfishly to bring wholeness (see Isaiah 53:4-5).

Servants lead not by anxiety or in reaction to circumstances, but from a heart of peace. Anxiety drives a system down. By tending to their thirst, servants release the anxieties in their

[handwritten margin note: Anxiety drives a system down!]

"wait until clearness comes."

Amen !!!

hearts and help churches do the same. It is then that a sense of peace enters. Out of that peace, servants can operate.

Rather than think leadership is in externals, servants lead from within. In their personal manner, servants carry truth gently. In spiritual discernment, people do not act when anxiety is present but wait until clearness comes. In leadership this rule is essential. Peace within translates to peace around. Waiting until clarity comes sets the purpose, direction, and pace of leadership.

Applying servant leadership to the task of being a lay leader who makes sure the physical needs of the church building are maintained (sometimes called a trustee) is illustrative of leading from a heart of peace. The furnace breaks, the roof leaks, someone is hot, someone cold. Trustees often find it challenging to worship in the same congregation where they are responsible for everything being in working order. How can the needs of everyone be met? In terms of all the human variables, a servant trustee can focus on how to serve and to relate to people as ministry. He can imagine being in the position of someone who is hard of hearing, cold, or just out of sorts over everything today. Servants lead by peacefulness in such circumstances.

In his original essay *The Servant as Leader*, Robert Greenleaf wrote, "And if there is a flaw in the world to be remedied, to the servant the process of change starts in here, in the servant, not *out there.*"[9] In a unique way, as they tend to their thirst, servants become centers of healing. Servants exemplify self-sacrifice and work in a spirit of reconciliation. Because service means coming alongside other people and walking with them, servants send out waves of goodwill. Service speaks to the anxieties people face. The renewal process in the church begins inwardly, building on its strengths, and then moves outward.

3. Listening

Servant leaders listen first to God, who opens the servant's ears each morning. In like manner, servants listen to people. This is an outgrowth of their spiritual life and a hallmark of their efforts (see Isaiah 50:4-5).

Listening is central to the servant; it is a key trait in renewal. In Isaiah, God actually opens the ear of the servant each morning: "Morning by morning he wakens—wakens my ear to listen as those who are taught" (50:4 NRSV). As church leaders, tending to the thirst means being in tune with what God is saying and paying attention to the promptings that come in times of prayer. Renewal puts one in a receptive mode, with God as initiator. Throughout this book we will see examples of people who listened for God to speak and then proceeded. Servants become aware of the movements of God. So attuned, servants develop a steadiness in their leadership.

Servants listen, making sure people feel heard. Careful listening helps people understand more of what they are saying. When someone listens, the level of the conversation goes deeper. In servant leadership, Greenleaf says,

> I have a bias about this which suggests that only a true natural servant automatically responds to any problem by listening *first*. When he is a leader, this disposition causes him to be *seen* as servant first. This suggests a nonservant who wants to be a servant might become a natural servant through a long arduous discipline of learning to listen, a discipline sufficiently sustained that the automatic response to any problem is to listen first. I have seen enough remarkable transformations in people who have been trained to listen to have some confidence in this approach. It is because true listening builds strength in other people.[10]

Seeking to listen before speaking, servants see the effect of their spiritual life in conversations with others in the church. In the dialogue process, the first step is spiritual centering, entering a quiet, receptive mode to listen. Then the servant listens and only then speaks in love. Tending the thirst has a direct impact on communication and renewal because it sets us in that listening mode. Servants develop a listening heart.

Listening is the needed intervention at any point in the downward spiral of a church's decline. We listen in times of

(handwritten margin note: a leader's automatic response to a problem = listening)

growth, because God will provide the direction to keep us moving in a positive direction. Seeing renewal as an ongoing process, we don't have to have all the answers. We learn by listening to God and to others. Then through dialogue and discernment we come to a truth that is larger than any of us. (See chapter 3 for more on the process of dialogue and listening.)

4. Manner of Love

Servant leaders lead in a kind and humble manner. Rather than overpower people, they respect people and treat them with love (see Isaiah 42:3).

"And now faith, hope, and love abide, these three; and the greatest of these is love" (1 Corinthians 13:13 NRSV). Servant leaders know how important the way people are treated is for renewal. According to Isaiah 42:3, "a bruised reed he will not break, and a dimly burning wick he will not quench" (NRSV). The servant will have love prevail. Renewal is an effort of goodwill and self-sacrifice. Servants make sure justice is done, and churches in renewal discover a new level of love among their people.

Like the reed in Isaiah, churches in decline can be easily bruised by experiences or by people. In decline, their light can be very dim. A dim wick can easily be snuffed out. Churches in decline often feel bad about themselves. In this situation, how leaders act and communicate is critical. A "quick fix" that forces a situation can snuff out the remaining life. Leaders can vent frustration in an inappropriate manner. Little blurbs in newsletters or blistering announcements get few results. Memos that express dissatisfaction fail to open lines of communication. Often such notices do more harm than good. Love seeks a way to build.

In the work of renewal, love becomes so evident. In church after church you begin to see people reaching out. In entering spiritual disciplines, people become more attuned to others and to the call of Scriptures. Intentionality emerges in people's hearts to be the church; a new unity develops. We start to see the positive traits of people. In spiritual appreciation we begin to see what people have done to touch our lives. In renewal, the inner work of reorientation occurs.

What has been taken for granted is no longer taken for granted. We saw how being presumptuous sends the church into decline. In renewal teams we see how someone tries to make spiritual disciplines "user friendly." They begin thinking how someone can be led to make a commitment without being forced or embarrassed. People begin to think more about putting themselves in the shoes of others when it comes around to spiritual growth. And they think about including others who might feel left out.

The love expands as the renewal team makes sure that no one is left out in congregational gatherings. The youth of the congregation may be called on to create a special seating arrangement at the carry-in meal. Maybe they put a tag under certain chairs and have a gift for each person who sits at one. As older adults learn what is happening in youth ministry at such an event, they can support the youth. Another example of love expanding is when someone reaches out to a handicapped person or an individual who has had to make a special effort to come. Servants operate in the manner of love, and renewal flourishes.

5. Mission

Servant leaders have a clear vision and use foresight to see things whole—to bring justice near and far. Using the wisdom of discernment, servants act as God's appointed with an urgent mission (see Isaiah 42:1; 49:5).

In tending to the thirst, servants see the big picture. So often in decline, churches are just struggling with day-to-day existence. In that state they easily become reactionary. Here is a principle I have discovered: if you are focused on one thing coming in the front door, beware of some bigger problem coming in the back door. One way to get out of the cycle that spells decline is to see the bigger picture.

As God did with the Israelites in defeat, God can call the church to a clear vision and an urgent mission. Foresight—seeing things whole and discerning a vision path—is a God-given gift. Servants work out of the big picture and take the first steps to reach what is possible.

The entire renewal process is missional. At each point servant leadership can be used to help a church identify its strengths, claim its unique identity, and discern a vision that becomes a working reality. Each step, even in the self-study stage, is part of this big picture. In fact, this helps a church because the process can be clearly understood.

Isaiah expresses this vision so well, not in giant dreams of grandeur, but by what he says: "my God has become my strength" (Isaiah 49:5 NRSV). By its very creation, mission has the ring of servanthood at its heart. <u>Mission is service; service is mission</u>.

6. Paradoxical Expectation

Servant leaders at first sight may seem to be the least likely people to make an impact, but they are used by God in a role beyond which their appearance would seem to warrant (see Isaiah 53:2).

In any congregation are those people who, like the woman at the well, seem to be the least likely to have any contribution to make. Perhaps they are just quiet by nature or awkward socially. We then remember that it was the woman at the well who brought others to a discovery of faith.

Israel, who had been unfaithful and seemingly the least likely, is the one God uses to be a "light to the nations." It has "no form nor comeliness" (53:2 KJV). Perhaps such people have known what it is like to be down and have developed a total dependency on God and can lead others who are hurting to Jesus. Whatever the dynamics, when servants discover that God wants to use them, even they are surprised at the outcomes.

Churches in renewal discover often that the least likely one comes up with the solution to problem or identifies a fresh biblical vision. In my renewal work, I can specifically remember two congregational gatherings in which the least likely person to speak came up with a statement that put a crisp vision together.

The role of the servant is to lift up what this least one is offering or to offer encouragement by saying, "Now make sure you say what you are sensing on your heart." Often this least likely one needs extra encouragement. In the same way, a church in decline may feel it is the least likely place that God will do something significant. The servant lifts up discouraged people and churches, alerting them to God's call for their life.

7. Paradoxical Outcome

Servant leaders trust that God brings dramatic reversals through their efforts. In suffering and sacrifice they act redemptively and believe God's will is accomplished (see Isaiah 53:10-11).

Renewal often reveals a unique paradox. By tending to the thirst, new life comes. The transformation comes not in some fancy program or by convincing others to follow this or that strategy. Rather, as people grow in faith through focusing on their spiritual journey, taking their next step in the spiritual disciplines, and entering a spiritually focused process, God brings reversals.

Servant leaders stand back and acknowledge that the growth was not even the design of what they were doing. This new life is of God. Servants are not about to take credit. They are simply happy for what has happened.

Illustrations of renewal in unlikely places are found throughout this book. The story of Bush Creek at the beginning of this chapter, the congregation where my interest in renewal began, is one such example. The message of doom from that man at the back door was not the last word. No one could have imagined that things would come together as they did. There was nothing that unique at Bush Creek—except faithfulness to Christ and a commitment to new life.

The passage from Isaiah 53 answers other questions: What if you don't see results? What about the sacrifice and suffering that might come with leadership, including the feeling of not being appreciated?

While servant leaders should by all means be appreciated

God brings about reversals!

and valued, sacrifice is entailed in servanthood. Servant leaders act redemptively. But the flip side is that servant leaders believe such efforts will lead to God's will being accomplished. In other words, servants so believe in what they are doing that they know it will be worth the effort even when sacrifice is called for. Such devotion is accompanied by joy.

8. Joyful

Servant leaders carry joy in their hearts. There is a sense of surprise, victory, and peace. They go out in joy (see Isaiah 55:12).

In all my research on the servant, I have never found why the suffering servant songs are called songs. The best reason I see comes from examples in church renewal. You see it in the faces of people who try to make the renewal process something exciting. It grows out of their genuine growth in their faith journey. As they begin growing closer to God in their life of prayer, and as they connect that faith journey with their daily lives, you can see the change. People speak the joy as their church takes on new life.

You may think servants would be very somber types, but just the opposite is the case. Servants carry joy in their hearts. To be gleeful or falsely optimistic that everything will work out all right can be rejected outright and is ill advised. Tending the thirst, servants carry gratitude in their hearts that results in a unique sense of joy. Joy does not have to depend on everything being okay; neither does it have to carry a sense of defeat, which will not help the situation. The approach of this book is for servants to find out what is right with the church and build on it. Servants keep the balance of reality and hope. In renewal, churches find that they can have joy again.

❧

In this chapter we have explored the role of the servant. In the basin and towel are the very dynamics of being served by Christ, having our lives transformed, and in turn taking on the role of Christ so others can experience the reconciliation of the gospel in

Joy does not depend on everything being okay...

their lives. A powerful image of leadership emerges from this drama of the upper room, where we experience the transforming power of the cross for the church. By exploring the biblical traits of the servant, we have seen their special role as they are called to be leaders. We have seen the kind of vessel, the spirit, and the manner of those called to be God's instrument. Even the least likely can bring results we never anticipated. What a joy we see as servants become agents of reconciliation.

For Reflection and Discussion

1. Servants in Scripture were born in hardship. Why do you think that was the case? Is that the case today? How do servants gain strength to fulfill their calling?

2. Reflect on the traits of the servant from Scripture. Which one or ones really speak to you? Is there anything about a servant that enlarged your perspective?

3. Explore the concepts of service and reconciliation. By figuratively having our feet washed and cleansed, we feel the dynamics of reconciliation as we kneel and wash the feet of others. Where have you experienced new life in that process?

4. What would you add to the profile of the servant started by the small group at the pre-Renovaré conference (see page 81)? As a group, try a study of Scriptures on the servant and list the traits you discover.

5. How is it that servants become leaders? Do you see any immediate help for a leadership challenge you face? How can you use the biblical traits of a servant leader to be more effective in the variety of roles you fill each day (as a parent, co-worker, sibling, etc.)?

6. You have probably seen the joy in the face of servants who have their heart in what they are doing and are doing it in faith. Can you share an example of when you met a real servant and what that meant to you? What call do you feel to be a servant today?

Part 2

Encounter

Jesus answered her, "If you knew the gift of God and who it is that asks you for a drink, you would have asked him and he would have given you living water."

"Sir," the woman said, "you have nothing to draw with and the well is deep. Where can you get this living water? Are you greater than our father Jacob, who gave us the well and drank from it himself, as did also his sons and his flocks and herds?"

Jesus answered, "Everyone who drinks this water will be thirsty again, but whoever drinks the water I give him will never thirst. Indeed, the water I give him will become in him a spring of water welling up to eternal life."

The woman said to him, Sir, give me this water so that I won't get thirsty and have to keep coming here to draw water."

—John 4:10-15

5

Embarking on a Church's Spiritual Journey

Peering from the prayer room in the steeple of Leffler Chapel at Elizabethtown College, I was deeply moved by the sight of people eagerly streaming into the chapel to learn about spiritual disciplines. This was the year 2000, and the spiritual renewal team of the Atlantic Northeast District of the Church of the Brethren, which I lead, had planned a regional Renovaré conference. Richard J. Foster and Emilie Griffin came to teach us how to grow in faith through spiritual disciplines.

The coordinating committee invited people to the conference using the Springs enlistment approach described in this book. We did a skit at the district conference likening the necessity of regular spiritual renewal to getting the oil changed regularly in your car. With our attempt to get young adults to the conference, we kept the registration fee below the cost of an oil change. We also provided childcare for young families.

But as the date approached for the conference, we were faced with a problem we had not anticipated. Leffler Chapel holds 850 people, and we were going to have to turn people away. As the number of registrants grew, we considered having an overflow location to accommodate five hundred more. The logistics seemed insurmountable. The potential to compromise the entire event led to a hard decision to hold the registration at 850 people. What a spiritual thirst this crisis represented!

The attendees were not let down. Foster and Griffin presented the disciplines, such as meditation, fasting, study, service, and worship, in a lively and engaging manner. These were not represented as somber practices that needed to be done, but rather as disciplines undertaken with joy. Foster said that practicing the disciplines is placing ourselves before God so our lives can be transformed. Griffin talked about having our souls in full sail. The anointing service at the close of the conference prepared each of us for the next step of faith.

But all that was just the beginning. The conference made a lasting impact on pastors, individuals, and churches. As a follow-up to the conference, I taught a class for licensed ministers to help them discern the next step in their own spiritual disciplines. In terms of impact in churches, various small groups sprang up, some using the Renovaré workbook.[1] Six years later, a pastor of a church with a Renovaré prayer group that grew out of the conference said the group was now leading in the renewal of the entire church.

The Dynamic of Encounter

Encounter is the second dynamic of renewal in John 4. The woman came to know Jesus as living water. Imagine that moment when she discovered him. In a similar manner churches can sense that God is inviting them to embark on a spiritual journey to meet Jesus. Like the woman at the well, they can discover that life has a purpose and their congregation a mission.

In Springs, churches enter a spiritual journey and put form and shape to it. If spiritual vitality is our desired outcome, we need to create a path to discover where God is leading and have that as input. In chapter 2 we covered the overall design of the renewal process. In this chapter we will cover in detail the first three steps presented in chapter 2 (see the chart "Spiritual Movements and the Path of Renewal").

This entire section helps us to encounter Jesus. The first three steps of the seven-step process are part of the journey upward. A church begins to sense the call of God to enter a spiritual journey.

It calls a renewal team, starts corporate spiritual disciplines, and begins to discern a biblical text.

The Renewal Team

Throughout Scripture, teams are used to accomplish mission. Jesus had a team of disciples who went with him. Paul took helpers on his missionary tours. Teams maximize leadership potential for renewal. Teams model the way Christ drew together his disciples. Teams become a ready expression of servant leadership.

The first way for a church to enter a spiritual journey is to call a team to facilitate the renewal. This team is critically important for the renewal process. It functions as a facilitating committee and sets the tone for the renewal work. Rather than make decisions about congregational direction, the team facilitates the entire church's renewal process.

Selection of the team. There are various ways to choose the members of the renewal team. At one church the leaders (paid staff and lay leaders) took two sessions to discern their team. At the first meeting, after prayer, dialogue, and discernment, they developed a long list of names. They then went home and prayed, returning with the names that stood out. At the second meeting, a final list of names was established and confirmed.

Often four to eight people are called, although large teams of sixteen have been used. Some people may be new in the church. Experience shows that spiritual growth, a positive attitude, and maturity are essential characteristics for a team member. Also, other people in the church, though not on the renewal team, can be used and may attend the team meetings from time to time or be a representative at a cluster meeting.

Leadership of the renewal team. A pastor or member with leadership qualities can serve as chairperson of a renewal team. A nice arrangement is to have the pastor work with some person or people in shared leadership. The leaders of the renewal team need to be servant leaders who serve and "get down on the floor" with people. They need to be able to help the team develop, figure things out with others, and move the process forward. Leaders of the team see that all aspects of the process are covered and that the entire endeavor is coordinated.

Leaders of the team will need to coordinate activities with other leaders in the church, problem solve with the team, and see that everything is communicated between the team and the rest of the church. Rather than needing to be knowledgeable in everything, the leaders assist the team by providing a structure, drawing forth the talents of the team, and conducting sessions.

Role of the renewal team. As a facilitating committee, the team sets the tone for all the renewal work. Members of the team work to have the entire church become involved in discovering their faith journey. The team does not form policies per se, but rather helps the church through the renewal process; it helps the church discover its identity, vision, plan, and the implementation of the plan. Team members spend time being trained in renewal work, spiritual disciplines, dialogue, and servant leadership. The team then trains others in the church.

The team builds enthusiasm, rallies people, and conducts congregational gatherings that draw on each person's input. Teams do practical things like organize meals, help people get seated with potential new friends at congregational gatherings, or lead small groups in that setting. Members of the team need to be ready to do a lot of hands-on planning and work—like setting up the chairs for proper seating at congregational events.

Once the congregation establishes the vision, the team continues by helping revitalize old ministries and shape new ones. In both cases, the renewal team works with committees in the church to call leaders, see to their training, establish an appropriate launch, and provide support (like mentors or prayer or whatever is needed so the ministry is fulfilling and fruitful). The team works with the official decision-making bodies of the church throughout the process.

The renewal team should also be attuned to the timing of renewal. At times the team may slow the process to build spiritual depth. It also may engage the church in an experience of growing in awareness of God. It might even host a retreat or a program of spiritual growth for a period of weeks. Or the team may see how the church can take a step with confidence. The time may come when a specific topic will be handled so that there is greater clarity and sense of direction. Or the team may see that the church needs a period of rest.

A significant role of the renewal team is simply to be an example. Pastors and church leaders repeatedly say that if they want their church to grow, they themselves need to grow. Their spiritual growth not only benefits them but also sets the climate for the team and for the church. The importance of a renewal team cannot be underestimated. A team can model renewal and, invite others into the process and into new life.

Leading congregational gatherings. One of the renewal team's important roles is to organize, conduct, and process congregational gatherings. These gatherings are important in the renewal process; they are opportunities for everyone in the church to become involved and excited about renewal. The first goal is to get everyone to attend. There are many different ways to encourage attendance: skits during the worship service, phone calls to each member, email reminders, and ways that have proven successful in that particular congregation in the past. One, of course, is to have a congregational meal.

The team may plan a creative way to have people sit with those they do not know at the gatherings. The team discerns how best to design the gathering with worship, presentations, and small-group and large-group discussions. Sessions should be of reasonable length, about one and three-quarter hours, so they can be a positive and productive experience. There should be a clear objective and agenda for each gathering so people can leave knowing exactly what was accomplished and what needs to be done next in the process.

With a standard format for gatherings, everyone becomes familiar with what to expect. Starting in a timely way after the meal, the session can begin with singing and prayer. Then there can be a

[handwritten margin note: Be an example!]

short presentation of the topic of the day and a reminder of the dialogue process for conversations. It helps to have small-group discussion on the topic of the day so that people can get involved. Finally, there is time in the full group for the smaller groups to report findings and to have leaders pull together a summary. At the close of the gathering some spontaneous time can be used for people to express affirmations and offer gratitude to God. In such moments you can literally feel the Spirit at work and experience renewal of the church. (In chapter 9, as we look at the transformative power of each gathering, we'll see some adaptations of this outline.)

Leading small groups. One important area of training for a renewal team is in leadership of small groups. Small groups will be used at congregational gatherings, often with people around tables after the meal, taking up a topic. In small groups, people need structure; without it, they flounder. Discussion needs to stay on a positive course in which strengths are lifted up. Leaders need to keep things on track. Guidelines can be helpful to see that group discussions move toward a constructive outcome. (See appendix 8, "How to Lead a Discussion.")[2]

The group leader needs to stay neutral and encourage everyone to participate. The leader helps people express their opinions by listening to make sure the group has received all of what each person has to offer. The leader may say, "If I understand it, you are saying this: _____. Do I have it all?" The leader can keep interaction moving by saying, "Well, I am hearing two people who feel this way: _____. What are your thoughts?" The leader can help the group summarize by saying, "I am hearing _____. Is that everything you wish to offer?" Seeing that there may be silent members, the leader will respect their quiet manner. One person can serve as a scribe and report the conclusions of the group.

Regular communication with the church. Another renewal team role is regular communication with the church. A variety of methods are needed, such as a special page in the church newsletter, weekly emails, and fliers placed in mailboxes. One creative and visually unifying idea is to assign a "renewal color" to all communications from the renewal team. Green Tree Church had the "Green Team." It also had a regular "Green Page" in the newsletter. Whatever specific method and name is used, for clarity in this book we will call this a renewal page.

A renewal page can call for prayer, tell of renewal team meetings, invite people to upcoming events, and carry educational articles on renewal. (See appendix 9 for a sample.) A distinctive graphic used for upcoming congregational gatherings is effective. Creativity helps convey a message that something exciting and important is happening in the church. Newsletters also can be used to invite new people to renewal events.

Another way to communicate can come in the form of encouragement. Cedar Hills (American) Baptist Church in Portland, Oregon, wrote its strengths on building blocks (the cardboard kind for children) and placed them on the platform in front of the sanctuary. The renewal team illustrated how God was building something from the raw materials of people's lives. Communication builds understanding and momentum, so renewal teams use whatever manner they can to tell the church about what is happening and how God is working.

Working with the ebb and flow of congregational life. One thing for renewal teams to be aware of is the ebb and flow of congregational life and how to work within those parameters. A church can work with spiritual disciplines at various times of the year. Often the fall is a time to have a spiritual disciplines folder (see below) to begin the year. Special seasons like Advent, Epiphany, and Easter are natural times for the church to work on a spiritual disciplines folder together. Often fall, late winter and early spring are the best times for congregational gatherings.

Renewal team meetings. The renewal team meets regularly. Each meeting includes training in renewal, as well as planning on how the congregation will go through the renewal process. Meetings should be immersed in prayer, properly communicated and prepared for, and lead to specific action that builds up the church and the renewal process.

A great way to begin meeting as a renewal team is to hold a spiritual retreat. In such a setting, team members can discern the next step in spiritual disciplines to which God is inviting them personally. The renewal team can review the classic twelve spiritual disciplines.[3] After they discern the next step in their spiritual disciplines, they begin the practice and then share the outcomes with others on the team and in the church. In turn they help church members and friends take their own next step in spiritual disciplines.

Setting the agenda. Renewal teams meet regularly, either monthly or every other month. A letter that includes minutes from the previous meeting and an agenda for the upcoming meeting should go out to all the members of the team several weeks in advance, if possible. Each meeting's agenda should include preparatory readings, such as study of Scripture, a section from this book, or research on the originating mission of their church. Team members also can spend time praying for the renewal of the church.

The training portion of the meeting could follow this book. Time can be spent studying the renewal process, discussing servant leadership and its approach to the life cycle, and learning spiritual discernment. The team can see that the spiritual disciplines folders are readied and discern how to present them for the congregation's use. Also the team can prepare for upcoming congregational gatherings. There can be specific training on how to conduct aspects of the gathering, such as how to lead small-group discussions (see appendix 8).

Developing a format for meetings. Church leaders need to determine who will do the training component for the renewal team and for congregational gatherings. (See chapter 2 and the section on the path of renewal for the topics that need to be covered in training for each step in the process.) Leaders should discern how best to do training, whether it be through presentations with question-and-answer periods or an interactive style with breakout groups. One church I worked with wanted interactive training during which they could experience the concepts, such as dialogue or discernment, before they led small groups themselves.

The sky is the limit in terms of how sessions are done. The appendices, such as the ones on dialogue (appendix 5) and spiritual discernment (appendix 12), can serve as teaching aids. PowerPoint presentations, guest speakers, and church leaders may be used as well. Sessions should always be steeped in prayer by the team leaders, the team members, and the entire congregation. It is good to begin each meeting with worship.

Dialogue should, of course, be encouraged. Questions at the end of each chapter of this book can help get conversation going. There are additional resources in footnotes of this book, as well as at resource centers locally or from church denominational offices. (The Springs website, www.churchrenewalservant.org, points to further training opportunities and resources for renewal teams.) Then an agenda can be created for items in upcoming events in the renewal process. A letter can be included (as illustrated in chapter 10).

Conducting a renewal team meeting. In his book *Preparing Instructional Objectives*, Robert Mager proposes a style of teaching consistent with the concept of servant leadership.[4] In this style, leaders are sensitive to people and determine what participants want to accomplish and how they are going to get to the desired outcome. Being servant leaders, those doing the training keep the needs of the team in mind, encourage them, and create a learning environment in which everyone feels a part.

Perhaps the greatest learning comes while training others. Since leadership is done as teamwork, the leaders of the renewal team should encourage all members to contribute in the training process by using their gifts. Often individuals right on the team have expertise on a topic specific to that church's needs. At Green Tree Church of the Brethren, a licensed minister, Rod O'Donnell, who works in sales in a steel corporation, is very active on the renewal team. When the team decided to contact all the inactive members of the church, Rod did a wonderful job training them in making "marketing" phone calls. Despite the statistics often quoted, those calls had success.

Follow-up. The real work of renewal is done as people are encouraged and enlisted in this endeavor, so follow-up is needed after each meeting. People soon catch the spirit of what is happening. In follow-up the team ensures that communication is happening on all levels and that people understand what to do.

A basic tool in follow-up is listening. Just by calling people on the phone, you can listen to how they are doing with the renewal efforts. They may have many other things going on in their life and may even need some assistance. At that point, other help can be enlisted that will lighten the load and get others involved.

On the other hand, things may be coming along quite well. Touching base with one another can be an occasion to offer thanks and to see possibilities that have arisen in the work. All this is building up the body of Christ. People begin to relate at deeper levels, share about their faith and daily discipleship, and even have some laughter.

Follow-up is a positive experience because people see an increase in both personal and corporate energy. They feel they are serving in a meaningful endeavor and see hope come alive as they grow in this spiritual journey. Step by step their work is part of the church's corporate mission.

Embracing Corporate Spiritual Disciplines

Conscious of God's invitation to renewal, the renewal team assists the congregation to enter spiritual disciplines. A seasonal spiritual disciplines folder helps to support the spiritual journey of a congregation.

The renewal team needs to inquire of all the existing leadership groups whether they wish to take up such an endeavor. In this way everyone is fully apprised of what is happening, and the church has an investment in seeing a positive outcome. A disciplines folder requires interpretation and can be explained on the renewal page or during a worship service.

The spiritual disciplines folder. Developing a folder takes several weeks and several steps to accomplish.

Selecting a theme. The pastor, if not a member of the renewal team already, should work in conjunction with the renewal team to decide on the theme. Because it is connected to preaching, pastors will want to be involved in the process. (For example, appendix 10 is an example of a folder in English and Spanish used in a season of renewal with a study of the twelve spiritual disciplines.)

Usually an overall theme emerges that goes with the spiritual journey of the renewal process, particularly once the church has discerned a Bible passage for renewal. If a congregation is accustomed to observing church seasons, the theme can go with those. When the church has discerned its mission, the theme of the folder can dovetail with implementing the vision. Such themes can be a crisp presentation of the Good News.

After extended study of Scriptures for the season, a theme can be discerned. The Easter season comes after Easter Sunday, lasts until Pentecost, and is a great season of celebration. The lectionary texts move through sightings of the risen Lord.

After Green Tree Church claimed its mission to be a faith center in the community, they chose "Go Forth, Proclaim the Power of the Resurrection" as their Easter season theme. Emmanuel Mennonite Church's folder for the season of Epiphany was "Carrying Emmanuel's Light." This theme highlighted the topic of light and was an obvious tie to the name of the church. Hatfield Church of the Brethren, whose renewal vision was "Faithful Community," chose the theme "Renewal of the Faithful" for the season of Pentecost. Such themes are very helpful in developing a season of spiritual growth.

Developing a format. Whatever format is ultimately chosen, keeping it consistent throughout the renewal process is important to the overall success of the spiritual disciplines folders. As each folder is presented to the congregation, people appreciate and more readily use a folder they recognize and feel comfortable with.

If a bulletin-style folder is used, the theme can be put on the cover and a brief explanation of the topic and purpose of the folder can be placed on the inside of the bulletin. Clip art on the cover can highlight the theme and give a visual representation of the spiritual work in process. Sunday services should be listed inside, with Scripture and sermon topics. Special services like communion should be noted. Events in the renewal process such as congregational gatherings should be listed.

Each week should have Scripture readings for the day. The international Daily Bible Reading Guide from the American Bible Society is one option.[5] The International Sunday School series also has daily readings for adult education classes. Another option is readings that go along with the theme of the folder. Everyone reading the same Bible passage each day brings continuity. Over the years people have spoken of a feeling of unity as everyone works through a folder together.

An insert for commitments to spiritual disciplines. This bulletin insert carries options of the various disciplines, and people are invited to put a mark on which discipline they feel God leading them to for their next season of growth. A blank space can be placed on the insert for other disciplines as well. Each time a disciplines folder is made, the pastor and renewal team, along with other spiritual leaders in the church, can decide on options for spiritual growth on the insert.

After people have had a chance to fill out their inserts, a service of commitment should be held for the entire congregation under the guidance of the renewal team. If this is done, a second copy of the insert should be placed in the folder so one copy can be used for the commitment service and the other for people to retain in their folder. Commitment services can include a public expression like walking forward to the foot of the cross and dedicating the commitment insert, or placing it in the offering plate or a special box in the lobby.

Follow-up to disciplines. The renewal team in one congregation decided to each take names of people who committed to disciplines. They prayed for these individuals, asking that God would help them in their disciplines. The team also made contact with people doing disciplines that led to interaction and formed spiritual friendships in the church.

When the time comes for another folder, leadership bodies can discern how to proceed. Subsequent folders will be easier to design and implement as people know what to expect. The renewal team can help select disciplines that its senses will lead to spiritual growth for people in the church and plan on the kind of commitment service to have and the follow-up that will be needed. It also can plan the frequency of use of folders and sometimes will sense the need for a break from having a folder.

Other collective spiritual disciplines options. Although spiritual disciplines folders are a very effective way to collectively engage in spiritual disciplines, there is certainly value in incorporating other methods for spiritual growth. The renewal team should search how best to assist people and various groups to go deeper spiritually. There are a variety of resources on the spiritual disciplines for classes and small groups in the church.

Renovaré provides *A Spiritual Formation Workbook*, which gives a format for small groups and seven sessions built around various classic traditions.[6] Upper Room provides the Pathway series resources, which are quite helpful (go to www.upperroom.org.) Knowing that individuals are intentionally engaged in spiritual disciplines will have an impact on the church. The congregation will feel it is on a spiritual journey.

Finding Themselves in the Biblical Story

A third way for a church to discover it is on a faith journey is to find itself in the biblical story. The concept of using Scripture for congregational transformation emerged quite naturally as I taught classes in church renewal. Students often found themselves in a text that helped them get unstuck, become focused, and move forward spiritually. In the same way, each church discerns a text that defines its own felt sense of calling and also defines its mission for others.

Guided by Scripture. As churches enter more deeply into spiritual disciplines, they often gravitate toward a Scripture text. Whether it is Abraham leaving Ur with his people, the Israelites going to the Promised Land, or the early church developing a vibrant faith community, a congregation can recognize itself somewhere in the biblical story and discover God's call to faithfulness.

The text provides instruction. What did God have to say in this situation? When the load became too heavy, what was God's advice to Moses? When the church became lethargic, what words did John speak from the Isle of Patmos, as recorded in Revelation? Because we are people of the Word, the very authority of the Scriptures aids us in understanding the call, the pain, and the process of transformation. As the church we center on the Word and are guided by the hope of the gospel; the church becomes a "people of the book."

In the renewal process, various biblical texts may emerge. Sharing those texts in a spirit of dialogue, people might be drawn to several texts. Each text provides some understanding of where they are at present and where they feel God is leading. The church should study these texts in-depth and look for spiritual dynamics of renewal. A Bible study guide that looks at the background of the text can be composed. Things to highlight would be the setting in life, translations, and key words and concepts in the passage. (See appendix 11 for a sample Bible study guide.)

This guide could be part of the renewal page. All small groups or Sunday school classes in the church could use the guide and search for the message for them as individuals and as a church. All could report their findings at a congregational gathering and share the reality and hope of the resurrection that is central to renewal.

Looking deeper, the gathered people may find themes. In Springs, as we studied John 4 we discovered dynamics of thirst, encounter, spiritual transformation, and mission. In conversations, congregational gatherings, renewal team meetings, and sermons, people find direction for their church. With self-study, they don't just do analytical work but also prayerfully consider what their discerned text has to say in their journey of faith and find spiritual companions in the Bible. God reached out and called out a people and led them. Similarly, God is calling us today.

Shaped by the text. Being shaped by a text is a profound part of the spiritual renewal of a church. In *Shaped by the Word: The Power of Scripture in Spiritual Formation,* Robert Mulholland differentiates between operating on a functional or a relational mode with Scripture. He asks, "Are we operating on a functional basis, somehow trying to get ourselves closer to God or to what we think God wants us to be; or are we operating on a relational basis, where, in responsiveness to God, we are allowing God to draw us into genuine spiritual formation?"[7] Being drawn to a relationship with Christ is central in the renewal process.

As Scriptures for spiritual formation become more present in our hearts, we begin to live out of their meaning, call, and direction. Mulholland goes on: "Do we come to Scripture open, to yield, to submit, to humble ourselves, to bow ourselves in God's presence and allow God to speak to us and then to be obedient?"[8] Renewal is a gradual process. Sometimes we take a leap forward, sometimes backward. Continually the text calls us. Continually the Word shapes and transforms us.

As a church discerns a biblical vision, it lets the text speak to it and call it to new life. As they discern their identity as a church, the text helps them understand themselves in new ways. As they find a focus, the text moves them to a biblical vision. The church's vision statement comes out as a few inspirational words. Sometimes one word suffices. The church can return to that Scripture often and draw from its meaning. The church literally lives out of the Bible. A church's plan for ministry is much more focused and has much more strength when guided by the Word.

❧

In renewal, churches take strong steps by entering a spiritual journey and renewing their lives of faith. A renewal team is put in place so the pastor is not working solo and the team embarks on a spiritual journey that follows God's leading. Nothing restores

The Word shapes and transforms us.

energy to a pastor, lay leader, or entire church like beginning afresh in regular practice of spiritual disciplines and finding itself in a Bible verse or passage. This is so important for getting on the growth curve of the life cycle. The church begins to feel new vitality; it is on the way to a positive future.

For Reflection and Discussion

1. Can you share ways you have experienced a church entering a deeper spiritual journey? Can you share an encounter in which you felt you met Jesus, who was searching for you at the well?

2. Discuss the role of the renewal team as a facilitating committee that helps the entire congregation be part of the renewal process. Have you ever been part of this kind of team, and if so, can you share experiences you found helpful?

3. After studying Scriptures for a season of the year, what themes for spiritual disciplines folders would you suggest? Roughly sketch out a folder with a small group or by yourself. Include a daily Scripture reading and disciplines insert.

4. Can you see that growth and faith sharing can arise out of the use of the disciplines folder? What about dialogues used in worship, classes, and small groups as everyone studies the disciplines?

5. What Scripture passages come to mind as you anticipate renewal in your own life? In the life of your church? What dynamics of renewal right in those texts could guide you?

6

Encountering Christ Through Prayer

Over the years, as my spiritual life as a renewal servant developed, I kept prayer quiet because it is so precious and seems best done in the secret closet. However, with prayer being at the heart of the church renewal process and people wanting to know how to develop a life of prayer, I began teaching out of my own practice. In my experience, a life of prayer unfolds step by step. Hopefully sharing my pilgrimage will encourage readers in their own journey. Oh what strength and blessing come from a life of prayer!

Three Seminal Spiritual Disciplines

The discipline of prayer unfolded in my own life over a number of years and continues to grow at significant junctures. As a senior in seminary in the 1960s, I formed a prayer partnership with a fellow student to go to the prayer chapel at 7 a.m. every day. We sought to listen to God's calling and seek whether to enter pastoral ministry. The Bible and the *Book of Common Prayer* were in the pew racks. After reading Scripture, I meditated on the words. The *Book of Common Prayer*, new to me, provided devotional thoughts. The woodcut above the communion table with a dove and God's Spirit descending symbolized God reaching to humanity. My prayer partner and I shared discoveries. Through this daily discipline I sensed God's leading to enter pastoral ministry—a decision I have never regretted.

When I began ministry in a local church, I organized and

attended a pastors' conference on preaching led by Merrill Abbey.[1] He told of his daily meditative reading of a few verses of the Bible and writing in a prayer journal. I was inspired to try this. This daily devotional practice went beyond usual sermon preparation. As I practiced this pattern of Bible reading, praying, and keeping a prayer journal, I found that Scripture guided my ministry in a new way. Very often, later that day I met the very issue the Scripture was addressing. I discovered devotional readings of the saints and eventually obtained a shelf of spiritual classics telling the faith journey of other pilgrims. Over the years I have discovered that out of seemingly unrelated duties and events comes God's invitation to walk deeper in my own devotional life.

Some ten years later I entered spiritual care ministry with hospice. At the same time, I was invited to teach church renewal at the American Baptist school Eastern Baptist Seminary, now Palmer Theological Seminary, near Philadelphia. With so many draws on my spiritual energy, I knew I needed a time of rejuvenation. I felt led to add a weekly, extended time to be with God. At that point I did not know what shape this time would take, but I went expectantly. I went far enough away from home to be removed from my daily surroundings, but close enough to be easily accessible. The same location week in and week out helped me get into the stream of prayer.

I continue this practice of removing myself from familiar surroundings to this day. I go early Saturday morning and find a place that is open, where I will be uninterrupted. I like to go to the same place, in this case a retreat center. Having the chair in the same position helps me reenter the Presence. I spend two or more hours weekly in this discipline and discover rest, renewal, and a sense of God's direction. Continuing this practice for over twenty years, I find stages in my prayer development, but the pattern of my prayer time stays basically the same.

Prayer pattern. My prayer pattern includes four things, all of which will be treated in more depth later in the chapter. First, I release all things to God—all feelings, situations, and concerns—and attempt to sense God's love for me personally. For this part I may get up and walk outside and throw my arms up in a gesture of releasing all to God. While a sense of God's care might feel faint, I attempt to sense God's love for me.

Second, I read a short portion of Scripture in a devotional manner and meditate on some of the words. When choosing Scripture I find the international lectionary text helpful. There is one for each day. The advantage of the international lectionary is that it provides a balanced reading of Scripture that takes into account the seasons of the year. Often a phrase or a few words catch my attention.

Meditating on Scripture means to listen to its message, ponder it deeply, and let it soak into my being.[2] I encounter great themes in the Bible, discover how they touch my life, and see how I can live them. I may write in a prayer journal. I have prayers of intention, asking God to help me live guided by themes in the Scripture of the day.

Third, I read from a devotional classic and meditate on it. This is a secondary source to the Bible. Here I meet fellow pilgrims in the faith who have lived across the span of centuries in many locations and circumstances. What is so helpful is the way they have discovered the faith. Great themes of the Christian life and the sharing of the Divine Center emerge from these devotions. These classics have led many to the heart of God.[3] Needs of people may come into my mind, and I offer prayers of intercession for them. At this point I often take a break for early-morning tea.

Finally, I spend time in contemplation, feeling God's great love and presence. I am struck by the tremendous sense of gratitude that emerges in this fourth period. Deep rest comes; refreshment occurs. I discover creative thoughts, new perspectives, solutions for unsolved problems, and sensitivity to people in my life. In this fourth time, discernment often arises. Considering one direction leads to a sense of peace and rest, another, a sense of anxiety and fear.

Classically this is known as discerning the spirits, and it will be explained in greater detail in the next chapter. Discernment provides clearness in making decisions. After anguishing over a complex situation, with the extra time that contemplation affords, a breakthrough comes. I become attentive to where God is calling. New energy courses through my being, and I feel a sense of being in the loving Presence. Often creative thoughts begin to flow.

Through the years, other aspects of my spiritual disciplines have been built on this foundation—fasting, making sketches of Scripture, observing the hours of prayer,[4] and personal worship playing the harp. After twenty years, I still draw away to Saturday-morning prayer. As much as this might sound rigorous, as a pilgrim I agree with those who say we always reside in the foothills of prayer. The journey is ever new, something I look forward to each week.

Encountering Jesus Through Prayer

The second dynamic of renewal found in John 4 is to encounter Jesus. The woman at the well came face to face with the Son of God. This is what happens in prayer and all spiritual practices. We come to Jesus, who is seeking us.

Because prayer is the base for all other disciplines, we explore this discipline in detail in this chapter. My purpose is to assist people in developing their life of prayer.

The role of prayer in the renewal of the church cannot be overstated. Aligned with prayer, a church has new energy. Aligned with prayer, servant leadership is strengthened. Aligned with prayer, leaders discern the movements of God. Aligned with prayer, people are strengthened to invite new people to church. Aligned with prayer, people needs are balanced with program needs. As a church becomes aligned with a life of prayer, prayer turns into action. In other words, a congregation infused with prayer brings people and churches to fresh encounters with Jesus.

Developing a Life of Prayer

While the encounter of Jesus with the women at the well was

not prayer as such, the elements show the style and outcome of an encounter with God. In prayer, Jesus meets us and invites us into conversation. Prayer is time to be with God and have dialogue with God. In prayer we thank God, listen to God, speak to God, repent of our sins, seek God's direction, and reconnect with God's purpose for our lives. In that context, we can bring our petitions, intervene for others, and pray through concerns. The outcome is greater strength, gratitude, and readiness for whatever situation is before us.

Connecting with God. First there is time to be with God. Life-giving encounters "at the well" happen in different ways, at different times, and in different contexts. Sometimes they come because we are tired and thirsty and we pause to cry out to God for help. Sometimes we come to God with great thankfulness on our heart, wanting to express our deepest appreciation. So prayer might well begin simply with an affirmation of our relationship with God. Just as spending time with someone strengthens our bond, in prayer we reconnect with God.

Observing Jesus, who had an active prayer life, we see that he didn't pray just when exhausted. Rather, he often prayed before he went into ministry. He spent time with God and took counsel with God. As our prayer life grows, promptings from God remind us that there is an eternal connection going on continuously in which God is reaching out. The more we develop that conversation, the more we know God is present. The more we get into renewal, the more we realize how valued such a relationship becomes. Often we will seek God's counsel. Often we will rely on God's grace.

Locating a place for prayer. People in the Bible had places of prayer that became regular. In one passage Paul was locating a prayer place and in a later passage was returning to it. On the Sabbath, Paul went outside the gate by the river, where he thought there was a place of prayer, and there he met Lydia. "The Lord opened her heart to listen eagerly to what was said by Paul" (Acts 16:14 NRSV). Prayer was certainly a vital part of the life of the early church.

Part of developing any relationship is arranging for it to happen. What kind of place do you find for solitude on a regular basis? Special places of retreat are wonderful, but are not practical for most people as a regular option. The challenge is to make arrangements— obtain access to a church, clean up the attic, locate a quiet corner in the house—anything to have a space free of distractions. Solitude invites the stillness prayer requires. Just making the arrangements becomes part of the process of prayer.

In his book *Living Simply Through the Day*, Tilden Edwards gives wise council about developing a prayer space at home. Noting it as an old Christian practice, Edwards tells of having just basic elements like a chair to sit on or a cushion to kneel on. In his own prayer center, he has an icon of Christ with a colored candle beneath. He has a Bible and books of Christian poetry. Needing less time to secure and prepare a prayer space facilitates deeper openness.[5] Something about regularity and sameness assists prayer. Regular times provide a schedule that frees us from having to consider whether we have time to pray. The disciplines become a blessing to have us encounter Jesus.

Keep it simple. An initial temptation might be to make an elaborate plan for spiritual growth and a renewed prayer life. A month after a Renovaré conference, I met with a group of ministers getting credentialed. Many who experienced the conference weekend tried to implement a comprehensive plan of spiritual growth, but felt overwhelmed. So we stepped back and looked at the next incremental step to which God was inviting them in the disciplines. Each person spiritually discerned the next step and built from there.

In the church renewal process, people need to take the next incremental step that they feel God is inviting them to in order to come closer to Christ. For each individual this will take a different shape. Trying various patterns for spiritual disciplines calls for perseverance. In the introduction to the spiritual retreat center guide *A Place for God*, Tim Jones tells of author and editor Philip Zaleski, who turned back five or six times until he steeled himself to knock at the retreat house door and enter a time a prayer.[6] Spiritual disciplines take discipline, so I suggest building support systems like partners, regular blocks of time, patterns, and a practical goal that will not overwhelm or discourage you.

Finding a Pattern for Prayer

My memory of this forty-year plus journey includes searching for how to pray. At each step I considered what pattern I would use. Along the way I have found benefit in exploring other prayer styles like centering prayer and Examen of Consciousness.[7] But often I return to the basic path that I discovered when I entered hospice ministry and began teaching church renewal, described at the beginning of this chapter. My prayer pattern has release and centering in God's love, reading and meditating over Scripture and devotional writings, and contemplation and spiritual discernment. This pattern can get you started on your journey, but you will, no doubt, find the right pattern for you.

Releasing all to God. In prayer we release all to God. We probably come with concerns and things on our mind. Being one who loves us, God is ready to receive us and is, in fact, seeking us out. This opening time with God is an occasion to experience God's love and develop a God consciousness. If we look at prayer as dialogue, we have someone to talk with, someone ready to listen to us, someone who is for us. I find if I release all to God and feel God's love for me, I am better able to be present with God. Thoughts that invade the quiet time can be given to God. If these need to be remembered, I jot them down for later reference and then return to prayer, releasing all anxieties and concerns to God.

Use of Scriptures. A second part of a pattern of prayer entails the Scriptures. At first, people may wonder why the Bible would be used as part of prayer. But in the Bible you meet almost any situation of life. In Genesis you find the magnificence of creation. In the Psalms the authors pour out their hearts to God. In psalms of lament, the psalmist asks, "Why O Lord?" and then often reaffirms his trust in God: "But in thee O Lord is my strength." In the Gospels, we have the Good News of Jesus. All prayer needs the Good News of Jesus, in which God's love is made real in this dialogue called prayer. Very slowly reading the Gospel of Luke or John is uplifting.

We read in a meditative fashion, pausing at a word, a verse. We let the passage speak to us on a personal basis. We read and reread perhaps one word or phrase. We let it soak in. We write reflections in a prayer journal. Or we pick up a pencil and pad and sketch a picture. Or we pick up a musical instrument and play what we feel in the moment. The psalmist had his harp raise him up before dawn. By placing the Scriptures as an integral part of one's prayer life, we place the gospel at the center of our faith development and discover living water.

As we meditate on a single word or verse, we enter deeper into prayer. We may pray prayers of intention, asking God's help to follow the message of this verse. We may express our sorrow for times when we have been unfaithful in regard to this verse. In prayer we seek alternatives. We look at things from all angles. People who need prayer come into our minds. We pray for them. We can also visualize how they would look whole again. Longer times of prayer afford us time to intercede for people and situations. What is amazing in longer times of prayer is the sensitivity that develops in us for people and their needs. We lift them up in prayer.

Thinking of Jesus, we remember the words of the ultimate pattern prayer, the Lord's Prayer, and may use that pattern to express thanksgiving and worship, to lift up simple needs, to ask forgiveness and grant pardon, to seek to not be led into temptation, and to determine to live for the kingdom with one's life. In the prayer of the Master, the Bible shapes our lives. The Good News becomes reality, hope emerges, deliverance is our promise. We realize that everywhere we go, God is there.

Reading from devotional classics. Another aspect of prayer is reading a short portion from a devotional classic. In this portion of prayer time, we read faith journeys of other pilgrims. With the variety of books available today, you may consult with your pastor or a spiritual friend for suggestions. With the great pilgrims we find comrades in the faith across the centuries.

The Testament of Devotion, my first resource in this journey, arose after author Thomas Kelly found peace in his own life. Kelly's quieting words speak with a poetic ring: "The basic response of the soul to the Light is internal adoration and joy, thanksgiving and worship, self-surrender and listening. The secret places of the heart cease to be our noisy workshop. They become a holy sanctuary of adoration and of self-oblation, where we are kept in perfect peace if our minds be stayed on Him who has found us in the inward springs of our life."[8]

In a totally different vein I was referred to the book *Showings* at a time in my pilgrimage when I was discovering so many evidences of God. Even though quite ill, its author, Julian of Norwich, saw God's goodness and pondered over a hazelnut and considered the great love of God, who creates us and loves us.[9]

We can also read current authors. With my own life impacted by the world of the handicapped, I enjoy the writing of Jan Vanier, founder of the L'Arche movement, in which disabled people and their assistants live together in Christian community. Vanier conveys how the weak portray the power of the gospel and are ones through whom we can see Jesus.

Devotional classics attune us to the way of humility. Many of them were written as a way to convey people's discoveries of God. *Spiritual Classics* and *Devotional Classics* provide introductions to spiritual companions from throughout the centuries.[10]

Perhaps you will choose to write your own prayer in your journal after you have read from a devotional. You may express your adoration, your confession, and your acknowledgment of God's love. Yes, you may also pray for practical things, such as God's help in terms of some challenge or for some person or situation. Such prayers draw together one's expressions of faith.

Contemplation. Finally there is contemplation. During this time, you sit with God and experience God's tremendous love for you. You have read the Good News in a portion of Scripture. You have read from the life of faith of a fellow pilgrim. You might want to reflect specifically on how God has called you by name for a purpose that will bring glory to God. By now your own concerns come into mind and you seek some resolution.

Perhaps you reflect on Gethsemane and see Jesus in prayer. One can only imagine the love conveyed by Christ and the identification you can feel with him when he said, "Not my will, but thine, be done" (Luke 22:42 KJV). In contemplation we experience the reality of God in all situations of our lives. We enter a time when the equation of God's love can change our perspective, give us hope, and reveal a direction.

In these quiet moments, the dilemmas of life will be before us. Often feelings of consolation (peace) and desolation (anxiety) arise. Looking in one direction we sense comfort, in another, anxiety. As we attend to these feelings we can test the spirits and see whether the road of comfort, while hard, will lead us to trust more in God and challenge us to grow in faith. Sometimes decisive action is needed so we do not continue down a road of desolation. Like the woman at the well, we may see destructive patterns in our lives and need to ask God's forgiveness and help to carve out new patterns. In prayer we can make some significant decisions in our lives.

We can also grow by expressing thanksgiving for what God is providing, like the love of a family member or the provisions of the basics of life, things otherwise taken for granted. In time of contemplation we become alert to the blessings we have but would otherwise not cherish. We might come to understand people in our lives and develop sensitivity to them in this period of prayer. We may discover that the signals we were getting from someone represent the tensions in their life or in our own. Prayer just gives us a whole new perspective. Moments of grace appear. Creative thoughts flow.

Regularly I take the major decisions of my life or areas in renewal of the church needing clarity to my Saturday extended prayer. People begin to respect this pattern and seem to appreciate that situations are handled in prayer, even though it takes extra time. Solutions to complicated situations arise. As a church we ask ourselves, "Why hadn't we thought of that before?" Prayer gives us opportunity to step back and see with the eyes of God and experience the love of God. Prayer does change things; prayer does change us. The time after such prayer sessions is filled with renewed energy and hope.

The *lectio* process. Fifteen years into the practice of this prayer pattern, I learned a format similar to *lectio divina*, a fourfold method of prayer.[11] This classic prayer process has four parts:

• *lectio*: Reading, being attentive to God and reading Scripture,

• *meditatio*: Reflecting, reading the passage slowly and lingering over the words and seeing how it speaks to you,

• *oratio*: Praying and turning your heart over to God, praying in petition and gratitude, and committing oneself to following,

• *contemplatio*: Receiving, listening, resting in God's love, and feeling the power of his presence.[12]

Rather than going to prayer just with requests, we go to be with God, to open ourselves to God awareness, to give ourselves more to God, to seek God's direction, and to renew in God. The pattern leads to peace, refreshment, direction, and gratitude.

Prayer card. The prayer card below, properly explained, could be a great asset to people. The very style of longer prayer can be placed on a prayer card to help individuals both in shorter period of prayer and in potentially longer periods, offering a pattern for prayer. Often people welcome having a resource on how to pray. In this case the experience includes reading Scripture and a devotional, and time to bring one's life before God. (This card can be copied for people to use.)

A Simple Prayer Form
Being Alone with God

• Release all to God—feelings, situations, stresses, concerns. Pour all out to God. Receive God's love.

• Read a Bible portion in a meditative manner and ponder the meaning for your life. Pray for God's help to follow the Scripture and pray for others who come to mind.

• Read a short passage in a devotional classic. Read the words of others who attempted to be faithful, and find the inspiration of their lives of faith.

• Take time to feel the in-filling of God's love. Sit quietly with God, and sense that going in one direction leads to peace but another to anxiety. Listen to God speak to you.

Resources that will aid you. *Celebration of Discipline* by Richard J. Foster has grown into an organization known as Renovaré, which holds conferences around the world. *Spiritual Classics* is a companion volume and gives additional resources on each of the twelve disciplines, including Scripture readings, readings from devotional classics in each area, discussion questions, and suggested exercises. *A Guide to Prayer* contains invocations, daily readings from Scripture, devotional readings, reflections, prayers, and hymns, along with a helpful and practical format for daily prayer.[13]

The Rewards of Prayer

The rewards of prayer are many; they are summarized here in terms of leadership and renewal of the church. If our desired outcome for the church is a more vibrant faith and more vibrant witness, then the investment in prayer directly correlates with this outcome. Prayer is like cultivating the soil for the transformation we yearn for in our lives and in the life of the church.

Pastors are renewed. Pastors who commit to taking the next step to which they feel God is inviting them set the tone for the congregation. They move into the servant leadership style. In addition, they set themselves to be alert to strengths and talents in their church. Prayer prepares the soil—prepares us—for what God has in store. Prayer builds hope, anticipation, and direction. Over the years, pastors frequently note how God's invitation to prayer has come at a timely moment for them and their congregation.

Individuals are renewed. Through spiritual disciplines folders people often become more regular in daily Bible reading and prayer. The folders can be used at the beginning of the day or be carried to school or work. A helpful practice can be to read the Scripture of the new day the night before, thereby sleeping on the theme and allowing it to become part of you, making you ready to rise in prayer.[14] When the Team Mennonite crew built our house, they laid out the tools the night before and were ready to work the next day. This practice for prayer may help some to enter into the Scriptures more fully.

The church becomes renewed. Another reward is that churches in renewal start learning more about prayer. There can be classes on prayer, such as in the adult Sunday school class at that first church in which I did renewal. There can be preaching on prayer, with a series of sermons and maybe a study guide. One of the suggestions in this book is the disciplines folder on the twelve disciplines; sermons can be delivered on each of the disciplines (see appendix 3).

You can creatively share with the church ideas on prayer from this book. The renewal team could have a teaching session during worship on such topics. Such suggestions as finding a standard location and pattern for prayer can be most helpful to people. Laying out materials the evening before for prayer in the morning can be a great help to be ready for a new day. These ideas can be put into the church newsletter. As we encounter

Jesus, who seeks us daily, we find prayer at the heart of a renewing church.

Prayer becomes integrated into daily living. Integrating prayer into daily living can and should become quite natural. I look forward to rising in prayer, and I find I need that reading of Scripture before anything else to help guide my day. Prayer becomes part of the day. Through the disciplines we can live with a God consciousness, seeing God in all of life. We see that we are partners with Christ in what we do in the most ordinary events of our days. Our relationships change because we see people as God's children and relate to them in a manner of love.

Times of offering confession don't have to wait until a formal prayer time but come as we become conscious of violating relationships or find ourselves living totally for self. In the same breath we can experience God's forgiveness and God's guidance for a different way of living. The prayer-filled life is one of hope, even in times of greatest difficulties. In times of greatest stress, we reassert the disciplines even more intentionally, and the rewards come.

Spiritual discernment. Prayer is integral to the decision making of both the individual and the church. I make no major decisions without first going to an extended time of prayer. As a pastor, I've found that members appreciate that the pastor goes to prayer, even when it slows down the decision making of the church body. For a church in crisis, healthy and Spirit-led decision making is crucial. The next chapter is devoted to this fruit of prayer.

Renewed energy. A church in renewal becomes a praying church. The character of the church changes, with greater unity and purpose. The reward comes in greater love, commitment, and enthusiasm. With energy, the key component in renewal, a church begins to experience greater strength and power in its ministries. A praying church has depth and is attractive to others.

Transformed. Just as people are transformed from the inside out, so congregations are transformed from the inside out. This is why instigating a program in the church never quite does it. Only an encounter with Jesus transforms. The encounter of the woman at the well points to transformation. The old had to go; the new arrived. Caught in old patterns and always thirsty, the woman encountered Jesus, who called for a lifestyle change and gave purpose to her life.

In *Celebration of Discipline*, Richard J. Foster says transformation is an inside job with a central paradox. On the one hand, God gives us the gift of grace, which can never be forced by sheer determination. On the other hand, there is something we can do. Spiritual disciplines are the door of liberation. They "allow us to place ourselves before God so that he can transform us."[15]

∽

Each person develops her own life of prayer. This might happen through experiences in which a person feels God's call to a closer walk. Out of that call a person may find a pattern and place for prayer. The pattern for prayer can serve to bring us to encounters with Jesus. The Scriptures are a vital part of prayer and can lead us into themes that draw us closer to God and invite us to a new way of life. Developing the life of prayer is central to the renewal of the church. Out of prayer arises spiritual discernment, which we will cover in the next chapter.

For Reflection and Discussion

1. What reflections do you have on prayer as being a way to encounter Jesus?

2. What disciplines of prayer have affected your life and how? After reading this chapter, what next step do you feel God is inviting you to take in your life of prayer?

3. What strikes you about the idea of an entire congregation joining in a discipline of Bible reading and prayer together?

4. Reflect on the rewards of a prayer-filled life presented in this chapter. Are there any others that come to mind?

5. We talk a lot about prayer in this resource. What openings and invitations to prayer do you have that will help you to the next step?

7

Discovering the Gift of Spiritual Discernment

Spiritual discernment was a gift I was not necessarily seeking or knew anything about when I first experienced it. In fact, I always say spiritual discernment discovered me in my weekly, extended prayer time. I have also discovered how spiritual discernment is integral to renewal. The discernment process gives guidance in how the Good News, in all its dimensions, has application in personal situations and in the spiritual journey of new life for the church. In decision making, in seeking the mind of Christ, in discovering where God is leading the church, spiritual discernment is central.

As I developed an extended time of prayer, I realized that in the second hour of prayer a deep rest and inner peace came, along with insights into unsolved problems and a heightened sensitivity to others. During this time, I discovered that looking at a problem one way brought a distinct sense of peace, while looking at it another way brought unrest. At first I did not understand what this was about but found the time rich because I found answers to questions I faced. Now I know that what happens in that extended time of prayer is spiritual discernment—an integral part of the renewal process.

As I began thinking about a resource for church renewal, I wondered what theme would capture how renewal occurs in a local congregation. From my experience I knew the title and direction would naturally arise out of focused prayer. For the theme to have depth, it needed to come from a biblical text. And for application, the theme should be incorporated throughout the book. So I went to my prayer place for retreat. I sat in my favorite chair, where I pray on Saturday mornings. The question on my heart was, "What theme, what text would serve to capture how renewal occurs?"

The more I sat, the more I realized that the way renewal occurs is like water bubbling up, sometimes quietly, sometimes vigorously, but with a refreshing peace. In my experience, renewal is not as much a fire that quickly ignites as a spring that bubbles up quietly and energetically. At that point I was drawn to the woman at the well and looked at John 4 in more depth. The theme of water and springs came more and more to the fore and seemed so real. In the midst of the need for renewal, the theme of a spring expressed the life-giving, transforming power given by God and needed in our churches.

Various considerations came to mind. Would this theme be exciting enough to invite renewal? Would it be expansive enough for interpreting renewal to individuals and churches? Would it be inspirational enough to provide challenge and encouragement? The more I meditated, the more the theme of water and springs seemed right. Springs of life-giving water are given by God and always keep flowing, thus bringing new life.

This was just the beginning of the discernment process. The theme of water and renewal developed over more than just one day. This discernment hasn't just happened in solitary prayer either. It has been a continuous journey of discovery and application with individuals and churches.

In time, I visited various springs. I thought I would see water gushing up like a water fountain you turn on to get a drink. That was not the case. What I first noticed was how the vegetation around the area was green. I saw how the spring water just oozed out of the ground. At another location the water was directed through a pipe that spilled out into a pool. The flow was constant. In all locations the visit was refreshing. Was it positive ions? Was it the serenity? Was it the refreshment? Probably all of those. But above all else, it reminded me that the source of new life is God and that life all around it becomes renewed.

As a further part of discernment I studied the theme of water in Scripture and was drawn to John 4. The source of new life bubbles up and is never-ending. There is strength to it, and renewal.

Spiritual discernment often happens over time and is itself instrumental in renewal. Building on chapter 6 on prayer, this chapter explores how spiritual discernment is used throughout the renewal process.

The Nature of the Gift

Rather than a technique, spiritual discernment is a gift. Not forced or done in one's own wisdom, and never self-serving, discernment is part of the journey of faith in which, as partners with Christ, we attempt to do God's will. We can speak of this as finding the "mind of Christ," finding the will and way of Christ who seeks to lead us (1 Corinthians 2:16). "Christ is present at the center of each person and alive in a group—speaking, forming, and touching—waiting to be heard and recognized."[1] (Appendix 12 is a summary of this chapter that can be used to teach this invaluable way of decision making.)

Rooted in a life of prayer. Discernment is rooted in our prayer life, as we pause to take time to get in tune with God. Thomas Green, a noted author in the field of discernment says, "Discernment is . . . a function of one's personal relationship to God. It is where prayer meets action; the more deeply one knows the Lord, the easier is will be to 'read his face' and to sense what he desires us to do." Thomas Green summarizes: "I felt that the real problem in discernment is not at the communal but at the personal level. That is, to have a discerning community you must have discerning people, discerning members of the community. And to be a discerning person you need to be a praying person."[2]

Spiritual discernment is a fruit of prayer rather than something to pick up at will. We have to think through what we mean when we say we are going to a meeting to discern something. Will we begin by having the prayer time needed for the time of discernment to take place? Often discernment will occur through a whole season of prayer with Bible reading and soul preparation in stages of spiritual discovery that incorporate reflection and action.

Having the right motivation. The motivation behind discernment is important. Speaking of solitude, Thomas Merton says, "Nor does he seek solitude as a favorable means for obtaining something he wants—contemplation. He seeks solitude as an expression of his total gift of himself to God. His solitude is not a means of getting, but a gift of himself."[3] Discernment will not come if all you want to do is "fix" this or that problem in the church. Rather, discernment arises out of a discipline of prayer in which the desire is to be in communication with God and to do God's will. Obedience is a hallmark of right motivation.

The goal of discerning love. In his book on discernment, *Weeds Among the Wheat*, Green describes the process of finding resolution to spiritual needs as one that follows a line. This line starts out with *experience*, such as the experience the woman at the well had with Jesus, or a church when it encounters Jesus and begins to be transformed. After the initial encounter comes an *afterglow*. This is when the church is awash with astonishment, thankfulness, and joy for what is happening.

Finally the church comes to discover the *habit of discerning love*. This is when the church has a sense of spiritual discernment as integrated into its very way of operating. The members feel at one with God and are able to know what pleases God and to do what such love requires. "The habit of discerning love means integration, and integration means simplification."[4] What a beautiful picture of a church growing into greater health and mission!

Where is God leading? The question in all discernment is, Where is God leading? From Scripture we learn that the will of God is for people to prosper. In Jeremiah 29:11 we read, "'For I know the plans I have for you,' declares the Lord, 'plans to prosper you and not to harm you, plans to give you hope and a future.'" What greater words of promise for a church! A spiritual director once said, "God doesn't want us just to cope but to flourish." God leads us into health and wholeness. As we discern God's will and live God's vision for us, our horizons do expand. In the church, God is leading us to discover living water in all its dimensions.

An alternative to hide and seek. Discerning God's will has sometimes reminded me of the game of Hide and Seek. As children, we fabricated a more interesting, albeit challenging, version called Tin Can Turkey Lurkey. I have since heard that others play something similar called Kick the Can. Whatever the name, the rules are the same. Home base is an old tin can. The person who is "It" places a foot on the can, holds closed his eyes, and counts to fifty as everyone hides. While still trying to guard the can, the It player ventures out to find the hiders. When It sees someone, he runs back to home base, puts his foot on the can, and calls out the name and hiding place. This hider then has to come out and stand by home base. However, at any time, other hiders can sneak back to home base and kick the can. This frees everyone already found and makes so that It has to not only retrieve the kicked can, but also count to fifty all over again while people hide. Being It can go on for a long time.

When going through life, we may sometimes feel that God hides and we seek. Searching is an awkward position to be in, especially when what we are looking for is allowed to change locations. In this disadvantaged position, we may feel we are trying on our own to be faithful to a God who is so much greater than we are. In this position God's will seems enigmatic. Thinking of Hide and Seek helps us look at our theology and assumptions. In spiritual discernment we affirm that we do not have to live in fear. Rather, we live in God's love.

God as initiator. In the familiar John 3:16, we affirm that God so loves the world that he sent his only Son, and that believing in him we have the very life of life. God takes the initiative to find us. This is the Good News of the gospel. In *Testament of Devotion*, Thomas Kelly says,

In this humanistic age we suppose man is the initiator and God is the responder. But the Living Christ within us is the initiator and we are the responders. God, the lover, the accuser, the revealer of light and darkness presses within us. "Behold I stand at the door and knock." All our apparent initiative is already a response, a testimonial to His secret presence and working within us.[5]

Partners with God. Spiritual discernment is not playing Hide and Seek. When we seek to know God's will, even our seeking is God at work, leading us to fullness of life. Rather than being It, we are God's partners. God wants and needs us to be partners in order to do God's work. "I do not call you servants any longer, because the servant does not know what the master is doing; but I have called you friends" (John 15:15 NRSV). Partners do not kick each other's can, send the other forever running, or cause endless fatigue. Spiritual discernment is about restoration, confidence, and peace.

Our approach to discernment is to become aware of God, listen to God, and decide not on the easiest course but on the faithful journey. In church renewal, this perspective is grace-filled. Challenged, we may feel we are always running to get back to base, pursuing some program in the church that might work, or getting our can set back up and counting to fifty before we venture forth. Renewal is not anxiously seeking God before someone runs and kicks our can again. Since anxiety is what drives a system down, prayer and spiritual discernment help us gain inner stillness and strength.

Getting the Head, Heart, and Faith Journey Together

The sixteenth-century Catholic priest Ignatius of Loyola, a principal founder of the Jesuits, has played a key role in the understanding of discernment. He covered the topic of spiritual discernment in his classic *Spiritual Exercises*, which was designed for a four-week retreat process.[6] Ignatius writes of consolation (peace) and desolation (anxiety), and now many resources written on spiritual discernment refer to these concepts. A new approach to discernment in a modern Ignatian tradition is to get the head, the heart, and the faith journey together. This understanding of discernment is extraordinarily helpful in church renewal as it is integrated as part of corporate spiritual discernment.[7]

The head. While discernment has to do with feelings, it also uses the mind and rational thought to make decisions that are realistic and concrete. Discernment will call us to sharpen our mind and have the external components in place. Part of decision making is determining the cost entailed and using the mind to evaluate the nuts and bolts of an endeavor. Doing one's homework is part of making a good decision. My wife constantly reminds me of this in our renewal work with churches: "Keep it practical," she says.

In church renewal, we need to use the best of our minds to analyze and make sense of any situation. As we explore the depths of a Scripture passage and look for dynamics of renewal in the text, we need the best of biblical scholarship. As we look at being a healthy church, we study key concepts and principles that help us understand decline and growth. Then we seek to understand our vision and plan for ministry. We ask, "How much will this new ministry cost? How will we pay for it? Are there written resources on this type of ministry? Do we have the practical things to sustain this initiative?"

The heart. Classically, the heart is the center of discernment. With a decidedly feeling or affective tone, spiritual discernment means sensing the movements of God—desolation and consolation. Being attentive to God, we consider alternatives. Some may be impulses, others suggestions, others may be thoughts based on anxiety. Consolation may not be the first thought that comes into our mind. We need to turn to the way that provides peace in our heart through a sense of God's love. Ignatius defines consolation this way:

> I call it consolation when there is excited in the soul some interior movement by which it begins to be inflamed with love of its Creator and Lord, and when consequentially, it cannot love any created thing on the face of the earth in itself,

but only in the Creator of all. Likewise when it pours forth tears, moving it to the love of its Lord, whether it be from sorrow for its sins, or for the Passion of Christ our Lord, or for other things expressed directed to His service and praise. In short, I call by the name consolation every increase of hope, faith, and charity, and all interior joy which calls and attracts the soul to heavenly things and to its own salvation, rendering it quiet and at peace in its Creator and Lord.[8]

There is a sense of one direction being right. Some call it clearness. Consolation gives focus and increases energy. Rather than pointing us in a direction that leads to our personal gain, consolation calls us to be a servant.

On the other hand, we can sense desolation in the heart. Ignatius defines desolation:

I call by the name desolation all that is contrary to what is described in the third rule [consolation, cited above], such as darkness and confusion of soul, attraction towards base and earthly objects, disquietude caused by various agitations and temptations, which make the soul distrustful, without hope and love, so that earthly, restlessness arising from many disturbances so that it finds itself altogether slothful, tepid, sad, and as it were, separated from its Creator and Lord. For as consolation is contrary to desolation, so the thoughts that spring from consolation are contrary to those that spring from desolation.[9]

Desolation is like a dark rain cloud. When it cover us, no sunshine is present. We may continue to try to hold onto one direction, but the heart will tell us that clearly it is not the way. Additional time in prayer helps us to discover the way of consolation.

The faith journey. Besides the head and heart, the faith journey plays an important role in discernment. While the mind leads to rational thinking and the heart is attuned to inner feeling, our faith journey calls us to costly discipleship and is essential in spiritual discernment. Ignatius warns of false consolations—feelings that seem right and comfortable but are not God's will and trick even the most prayerful person. The faith journey is the way of the cross. Decisions that call us to grow in faith are in tune with God's will and way. The way of Christ is the journey of discipleship in which we live out the life and teachings of Jesus.

In the *Imitation of Christ*, Thomas à Kempis speaks about the way of the cross.

> It is not our strength but Christ's grace which can and does accomplish such great things in us. Christ's grace enables us to embrace warmly those things from which we naturally recoil. It is not in our nature to bear the cross, to love the cross, to discipline ourselves, to avoid seeking praise, to suffer insults willingly, to think humbly of ourselves, to appear humble to others, to endure adversity and loss, and not to seek prosperity as our first goal. If you take a look at yourself, you will see that you can do none of this alone, but if you confide in the Lord, he will give you heavenly strength and all you have chosen to do will become easier.[10]

Spiritual discernment moves us in this direction.

The faith journey is the way of abiding hope. All church renewal is built on a resurrection theology. Just as we believe in the abiding faith for individuals, so we believe God is the one restoring the church. Things that happen in renewal are clearly beyond our own doing. We cannot make things happen. The faith journey means we grow in trust in God, who will raise up the church. Having that belief is fundamental in spiritual discernment.

Discernment Card

Discernment plays such an important role for individuals growing in faith and for churches that enter the renewal process. We have created a card for use by individuals and churches that summarizes the discernment process.

Spiritual Discernment

Seeking God's will and truth by getting head, heart, and faith journey together.

• Getting Spiritually Grounded: Spending extended time in prayer

• The Head: Using your rational tools, what are the practical aspects and results of this situation?

• The Heart: Being present with God in prayer, where is there peace, where anxiety?

• The Faith Journey: Asking which direction will lead to growth in faith and in the journey of costly discipleship.

Going About Spiritual Discernment

Given all this background, how do we practically go about discernment? Sometimes we face a particular situation and attempt to find direction. We try to get clarity or try to make a decision. We may purposefully delay making a decision because the way is not clear. In such moments we need to decide whether individual discernment or group discernment is needed. In church renewal, both types are helpful, depending on those involved in making the decision. Discernment is never a step-by-step process and is slightly different for each person and church, but here are some suggestions to help your discernment journey.

St. Ignatius's rules of discernment. St. Ignatius did Christians a wonderful service by giving two sets of guidelines for the discernment of spirits. These "rules" help when trying to discern direction. We've already looked at two of these rules: consolation and desolation. Now let's look at other guidelines.

Giving ourselves even more to prayer.

While the bad spirit tries to add one evil desire upon another, the good spirit makes us uneasy about false direction. Another rule is never to make a change in time of desolation. Stay firm to one's resolution and give oneself even more to prayer. God has not left us and consolation will return. Patience is needed in the face of desolation. When consolation comes again, the person of prayer will take strength from it, grow in humility, and be grateful. This provides the memory that God's grace will be sufficient if desolation arises again.[11]

Beware of self-sufficient thinking. The second set of rules from Ignatius are given as progress is made in the spiritual life. These rules address even more subtle but errant movements when all seems to be pointing to God. The evil spirit raises anxieties and doubts. How much that applies to church renewal! A confidence can develop in us that we are on the right path. But we might begin to wonder if things are as good as we think they are and yield to false worries. Equally troubling is a time when consolation is overtaken by self-sufficient thinking: "I can do this on my own!" Consolation does not come by great commotion and noise; Ignatius compares consolation to the way a drop of water enters a sponge.

Spontaneous or sought out? One good way to discern is to enter into your own style of prayer. (A personal example of a style of prayer was given in chapter 6.) In prayer we release all to God and enter a space where we know God's presence and get in touch with God's will and heart.

At other times, discernment arises unexpectedly. You may be mowing the lawn or waiting for the bus or helping a child. In a peculiar way, direction comes for decisions that may not have even been on your mind. The more your life gets in sync with God's love, the more you attend to the movement of God, and the more such spontaneous moments arise. We have the divine visitation that Thomas Kelly speaks about.

Entertaining the unexpected. To enter discernment, be ready for the unexpected. A new perspective may arise for some situation. You may feel the tug for immediate action. Discernment opens the doors to new thinking and to solutions to problems you did not know you had. Love and sensitivity emerge. New energy comes. Discernment is never a program; it is never forced into what you want.

Difficulty might come when we don't want to give up something that feels right on some levels. One example comes from my work with the American Baptist Churches. Looking at the originating mission of the Baptists on the frontier, I learned about chapel cars hooked on the back of trains. Evangelists would take the gospel to railroad towns and address social problems.

Since we were going to be using virtual technology to broadcast training sessions for renewal teams, I had an image of a virtual chapel car. But then I learned that many workers who laid the tracks west by the sweat of their brow were African-Americans. With discrimination part of the image, we dropped the chapel car idea immediately.

However, something better took its place. Reflecting on what various American Baptists wanted—some revival, some transformation, some renewal—I wondered, "Why not find a biblical word that incorporates all of them?" I spent time in prayer, and the passage of 2 Timothy 1:6-7 emerged. This is where Paul tells his younger companion, Timothy, to rekindle the gift within him. *Rekindle* is an active verb that gave direction for the American Baptist initiative. Further study in the Amplified Bible led to this expression: "rekindle the gift, fan the flame, and keep it burning." Any person, any church can find itself in that continuum. Here was an expansive theme with power.

Temptations in discernment. Not surprisingly Jesus faced temptations while in the wilderness. We also face temptations. When alone and faced with uncertainties, stray thoughts may come into your mind. These are simply white noise. What do you do with them? The best way is to pay them no heed and quickly dismiss them.

Sometimes, counterproductive options mask themselves as having potential. We can learn from Jesus here. Tempted to break his fast, he said, "One does not live by bread alone" (Matthew 4:4 NRSV). Faced with the cost of inheriting all the kingdoms, he said, "Worship the Lord your God, and serve him only" (v. 10). Faced with the temptation of a dramatic display of power and protection, he said, "Do not put the Lord your God to the test" (v. 7). In each case, discernment meant decisive response and action. This pattern of handling temptations by focusing on God's will is critical for discernment. Discernment leads you into the truth of the gospel. Discernment aligns you to the will of God.

Taking the time for discernment. As the illustration from my life at the opening of this chapter showed, discernment takes more than one session. The clarity that comes during prayer might be that more facts are needed, and you need to do more research or seek counsel before making a decision. We need to sit with a decision over an extended period and weigh it in our heart. We need to know more of what the faith journey will entail in order to discern between false and true consolations.

Rightful discernment leads to being stretched in faith to put beliefs in practice in new ways, to live Christ's way. Spiritual discernment occurs as you see these three streams of head, heart, and faith journey come together. Waiting on God is an active part of such discernment. What we have said about renewal elsewhere in this book applies here as well: spiritual discernment takes longer than you would like, but not as long as you might fear, and is more right than you ever will know. Spiritual discernment is not the easiest route, but the one in which you find peace.

A different pace. Spiritual discernment has a different pace than dialogue. While dialogue helps open conversation, discernment is often slower; it cannot be rushed. At those points when you feel clearness, a breakthrough comes. I always told our young-adult son that the darkest part of the night is right before the dawn. But the wait is worth it. We can see how we could never have come up with the outcomes of spiritual discernment on our own.

This different pace speaks to several concerns in church renewal. When we feel nothing is happening, we must remind ourselves that the outcomes of spiritual disciplines are not necessarily immediate. Simply deciding to do disciplines is renewal. This pace also speaks when we want to enthusiastically move forward. We might wonder why others don't get it, and we may grow impatient when we feel enthusiasm but don't see that in other people. When the need for renewal is so great, how do we wait for God's time? Spiritual discernment speaks to such concerns. Through servant leadership we learn how important it is to go with the group to the springs. Sometimes we will be ahead and sometimes behind others, but in renewal we attempt to go *with* God and *with* people.

Doing Group Spiritual Discernment

In group discernment, one person may comment about how his thinking was stirred. Someone may yield to another. Some may be able to see the common thread of God's leading emerge. It is a priceless treasure as the variety of people and their different faith experiences bring greater clarity for the church. You will actually be able to feel how God is molding people as you discern identity, vision, and a plan together.

Building on dialogue. Group spiritual direction naturally flows out of the dialogue process but calls us to an even slower tempo than dialogue. We have gathered not just to communicate, though that does happen, but also to become aware of the movement of God and to align ourselves with God's direction. The focus goes beyond dialogue, in which people gather to have conversation and grow to mutual understanding. In spiritual discernment the focus of our conversation is God and others as God's partners in doing God's will.

Preparing the setting. Arranging an appropriate environment for corporate discernment is very important. Meeting with a group, you might light a candle or oil lamp to remind everyone of the presence of Christ and the activity of God. Nature also provides an appropriate setting. The sights and sounds calm the spirit and signal God's creative activity. There may be a symbol that the group finds meaningful, such as a banner or a poster. The convener should clear out clutter ahead of time—broken pencils, a lost coat, or a broken chair. The setting is important for discernment.

Preparing the group. The convener recognizes that deeper preparation is needed for discernment than for a dialogue or social gathering. How do we get a group prepared to meet, ready to give their hearts to seeking God's will? How do we develop the humility and the openness and the peace to be totally present? In an article on Ignatian discernment, Philip Boroughs lists predispositions for discernment as "interior freedom, sufficient knowledge of self and the world, imagination, patience, and the courage to act responsibly." He defines interior freedom as indifference to inordinate attachments (such as temptations to riches, honor, and pride).[12]

By having first engaged in spiritual disciplines, a church will be more able to display those traits that Boroughs suggests. Also, courage and humility and quietness are essential attributes for discernment. The outcomes will attest to the preparation.

Laying out the format. A group gathered for discernment begins with everyone becoming comfortable. Small talk of the day can be important. Praises of thanksgivings as well as the sharing of concerns can be part of the process as people give their joys and burdens to God. Sometimes people want to sing, sometimes be quiet. The convener needs to be sensitive to what is most helpful. Group members can also take initiative to express what is needed.

In discernment, a group gathers to seek the will of God and ask where God is now leading. If a particular item is before them, someone may explain the decision that needs to be made and give updates on the situation. Then the convener lays out a format, beginning with prayer and reminding the body of the various aspects of discernment—how the head, heart, and faith journey need to come together.

The collective wisdom of the head. Sometime during discernment, the group can specifically look at the head, the rational and practical part of this decision. What are the various aspects of the matter before us? What will the schedule be? What will the cost be? What will the cost be if we do nothing? What are the alternatives? Often thoughts just come forth with the wealth of knowledge and experience a group holds.

Now is the time when the group looks at practical matters such as facilities, accessibility, and the schedule of church activities. Are there resources to keep the initiative alive for the long term? Having the number of people needed for a ministry to function well is an important part of any decision about renewing old ministries or initiating new ones. Perhaps an endeavor needs to wait until the right time comes when more of the practical matters are in place. All initiatives need to be sustainable.

The collective feeling of the heart. When we prayerfully consider going in one direction, what does the community of faith sense in terms of the movement of God? Additional prayer time may be needed. Where is consolation? Where is desolation? Is there a signal to wait? As a group, waiting together becomes very important. If we made a decision at this point, would we just be operating out of anxiety? Is there clearness? As we listen with the heart, someone else's voice can help move discernment forward. Here is where we need to listen intently to the least likely voice. The collective heart emerges.

The collective challenge of the faith journey. Then the group considers its corporate faith journey. If we take one direction, will we just be comfortable as a church or will we be stretched to grow in faith? The advantage of being in group discernment is that often the faith journey calls for sacrifice. If the group discerning God's call is made up of those who will sacrifice, they are more likely to consider the cost of discipleship and whether they will commit themselves to the outcome. "Count well the cost" is not just an admonition but the challenge of discipleship. When we make decisions, rarely is all the information in; rarely can we anticipate all that is entailed. So we ask which direction will be in accordance with the gospel.

Closing. The session can close with expressions of thanksgiving. Familiar praise choruses may be sung. The doxology "Praise God from Whom All Blessings Flow" is simple and, if sung slowly, can be very moving.

The role of the convener. Throughout the process of discernment, the convener keeps the process moving. At points the convener may slow the course down, at other points determine where an opening for resolution lies. Never to be rushed, the convener might say, "It seems we are coming to a decision, but it also seems we need more time for prayerful discernment. We'll set another date, and perhaps you can all spend some quality time with this question in your individual prayer time."

Helpful information for group discernment can be found on various Quaker websites. In Australia, if a decision is controversial, a "threshing session" is held beforehand to get out various feelings about the matter. Then a period of quietness is observed in order to settle into a discerning spirit.

The convener is a servant. Servants are not trying to advance their own position but to draw forth the views of others. Group discernment engages everyone in the process.

Discernment Leads to Mission

Discernment turns into prayer-filled action that has a sense of confidence and direction. Here spiritual discernment serves us well. We move with God. We move with people. In church renewal we see how our vision moves into a workable plan and how discernment is used in each step of the plan. While the initial part of the renewal process may take great energy in order to overcome inertia, implementation will take the most time. Here the encounter with Jesus takes deeper and deeper root. A mission emerges that we can give our heart to.

The woman at the well's encounter with Jesus led her to discern that she had a mission. She saw what to give up and what to take up. In a guide for spiritual directors on the spiritual exercises of St. Ignatius, *Beyond Individuation to Discipleship*, George

Schemel presents a sequence in discernment that can also be used in corporate spiritual formation. The dynamics of the exercises move us from the Word to identity to vocation and to the name of grace to which God is calling us.[13] We are "missioned." Partaking of living water, we feel an urgent mission for spreading the Good News to others.

Spiritual discernment is a gift. Out of deep prayer and being in tune with God, we can live by the promptings of the Spirit. Often the way is already being paved, and we need to enter a listening stillness to understand God's way. Renewal takes time and faithfulness in the many small decisions that make the difference. Spiritual discernment should lead us all the way. With spiritual discernment, ministries become stronger, the unity of the congregation becomes evident, and the spirit conveys spontaneous energy. What can be used on an individual basis can also be used in a corporate setting. Together, the church can discern where God is leading, which will be a giant step in discerning a vision and plan. Getting the head, heart, and faith journey together leads us to places more right than we will ever know.

For Reflection and Discussion

1. What experiences have you had with spiritual discernment? Are there things you would like to change in the way you approach problems or decisions?

2. What do you think about the concept of discernment as getting the head, heart, and faith journey together? What do you find helpful in this combination? (Consider teaching from appendix 12 on discernment and having a discussion on the topic.)

3. How might your church use group spiritual discernment more as part of informal gatherings and official meetings? What has been your experience of corporate spiritual discernment so far?

4. What do you think about the sacrifice discernment requires, the growth of faith, and the road of costly discipleship?

5. What do you do when discernment takes longer than you would like? Have you ever waited in prayer and the right decision came to light?

6. What role does spiritual discernment play in finding the courage to do mission? How can active prayer be integrated into entering mission?

8

Discerning the Spiritual Movements of Renewal

Bush Creek Church of the Brethren is set in a rural area, with the suburban population of Washington, D.C., growing up around it. In such a context, the name Bush Creek probably does not sound very exciting nor have much meaning. But that's the name of the creek that flows nearby. In former days, this creek was used for baptisms. At the heart of this church's name is the symbol of encountering Jesus with life-changing outcomes.

The spiritual needs of members and newcomers led to a call for renewal. After I came to Bush Creek, we worked out a ministry plan that responded to the congregation's discerned need to make faith development its top priority. The desired outcome was for people to speak of a relationship with Christ in the first person and discover their own ministry as a unique person.

As a church we had conducted a successful retreat-like experience. People from other congregations came and in a very simple and honest way told of their faith and experience. In the spirit of love and with a lack of pretense, the weekend helped people to grow spiritually and brought a new love and freedom. People discovered their faith pilgrimage in daily life. Faith became a first-person reality, and people felt freer to share their faith.[1]

The ministry plan called for a second such weekend, but this one turned out different than the first. Many people were involved in the planning, but the former enthusiasm did not carry over. Events were over-planned, which led to a lag in the schedule. You could sense people's frustration about feeling pressured to come to faith and be converted. The church was disappointed.

However, through the experience, the congregation grew in faith in ways we did not anticipate. Several debriefing sessions were held. The positives and negatives were listed. Persons affirmed that faith cannot be forced by pressure or fear but is given by God in the simple experiences of life. This was the real intent of the successful weekend, but we had not come to it in the way we had planned. God was at work!

The congregation learned that renewal needs to be an ongoing part of the church's life. The Christian faith is not learned in the high experiences of a conference, but rather in a daily discovery of God, who is available to us all the time. Further, a theology of grace rather than guilt leads us to grow. Faith can never be thrust on another person. Neither can a faith experience be recreated or forced on another person.

The church learned to depend on its own strengths. Listening to one another led to an even greater openness to God. We also learned that there should be more opportunities for people in the congregation to share their witness informally or in congregational settings. The church learned to affirm its own leadership, not excluding outsiders, but recognizing that faith experiences grow as we actively explore our life with God.

The outcome of all this led to several faith renewal weekends with speakers who guided growth experiences in total Christian living. The church learned to stress how personal faith is discovered through ministering. People could teach Sunday school, hold the hand of a sick loved one, or visit someone and share a meal. As the church began to talk more about issues of faith it met daily, it discovered grace afresh. The church committed to carry renewal through the year.

Renewal is not a straightforward path for a congregation. Unplanned outcomes draw us up short and help us realize that only in and through Jesus can things be accomplished. At Bush Creek, growing spiritually together as a church—and taking the time to do that—kept the renewal process alive and, indeed, allowed it to flourish.

The entire renewal process is about entering a spiritual journey. Through inner spiritual growth and self-study, the church discerns a biblical vision and plan of ministry to be implemented. The continual question is, Where is God leading?

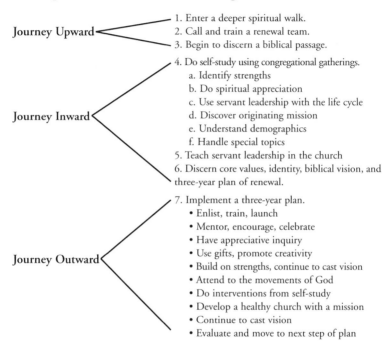

Journey Upward
1. Enter a deeper spiritual walk.
2. Call and train a renewal team.
3. Begin to discern a biblical passage.

Journey Inward
4. Do self-study using congregational gatherings.
   a. Identify strengths
   b. Do spiritual appreciation
   c. Use servant leadership with the life cycle
   d. Discover originating mission
   e. Understand demographics
   f. Handle special topics
5. Teach servant leadership in the church
6. Discern core values, identity, biblical vision, and three-year plan of renewal.

Journey Outward
7. Implement a three-year plan.
   • Enlist, train, launch
   • Mentor, encourage, celebrate
   • Have appreciative inquiry
   • Use gifts, promote creativity
   • Build on strengths, continue to cast vision
   • Attend to the movements of God
   • Do interventions from self-study
   • Develop a healthy church with a mission
   • Continue to cast vision
   • Evaluate and move to next step of plan

Congregational Spiritual Direction

In this chapter we'll explore corporate spiritual direction. People who receive individual spiritual direction discover where God is leading and where God's grace is inviting them in their lives. The spiritual director is a servant leader who listens in order to help others develop greater faithfulness and fruitfulness. In a similar way churches need congregational spiritual direction to stay on a spiritual journey. Someone can assist them in setting a direction by listening for the movements of God so that they will stay on the course and be found faithful with their gifts. Such attentiveness will help churches as they make decisions in the renewal process and implement a renewal plan.

First we'll look at discerning the three larger movements of God—the paths upward, inward, and outward—on the renewal process chart above. Then, having worked on the larger picture of how God shapes the life of the total church, we can turn to individuals and see how their growth in faith can take place. Finally, we'll look at how nurturing ministries can lead to encountering Jesus in the church. In all three ways congregations are guided in spiritual formation.

Linking the Movements of God with the Path of Renewal

The more I have worked in church renewal, the more I have found that various movements of God can be linked with the path of renewal of a church. You can actually feel the movement of consolation if you go in one direction and desolation if you choose another. This can help leaders decide where to go next. As Isaiah said, "Whether you turn to the right or to the left, your ears will hear a voice behind you saying, 'This is the way; walk in it'" (30:21). Following God's movements we encounter Jesus in the renewal process.

The challenge will be to follow the outcome of spiritual discernment and lean into the direction that discernment takes the church. Spiritual movements are indicators of where we feel God is leading and which way provides consolation. Getting beyond the temptation to program renewal or identify stages that a church must go through, we see how God invites new life. In the chart above, the spiritual movements of upward, inward, and outward are on the left of the chart, and the seven stages of renewal are on the right. Let us look at the movements and see the direction they suggest for our efforts in renewal.

The movement upward. In the movement upward, we feel we are drawn closer to God, but it is actually God reaching out to draw us to new life. This movement can be tied to the first three steps of the renewal process: entering a deeper spiritual walk, training a renewal team, and feeling led to a Scripture text. Churches that enter the Springs process find great help in learning and practicing classic spiritual disciplines. In terms of disciplines, Richard J. Foster says "We place ourselves before God so He can transform us."[2] The church embarks on a spiritual journey. During training, both the renewal team and the congregation find themselves drawn more to live their lives for God. They feel invited to be partners with God.

When we are tempted to move pell-mell through the process, the movement upward reminds us to stop and listen—to encounter God. Moses would not have encountered God if he had failed to stop and take off his shoes. By being attentive, the Israelites learned to follow the pillar of fire. People who stop and tend to the thirst when they feel the presence of God discover new life.

When preaching on church renewal, Marcia Bailey at Mayfair Conwell Baptist Church used the example of a tree in her office. Sometimes she tended it, but often she forgot it, and it showed the results. In the same way she found sometimes she tended to her faith, but at times took it for granted. She discovered that, like the tree, renewal has to be cared for and tended.[3] Being attentive to God is crucial for renewal.

In his book *Thirsty for God: A Brief History of Christian Spirituality*, Bradley Holt says, "Part of the human predicament is not always knowing what one really needs or longs for. Another part is difficulty of acting consistently on what one does know."[4] Holt says that when his body gets tired and listless, he gets upset and discouraged and heads to the refrigerator to eat. For a long time he did not realize his body craved water, not food. Thirst is different from hunger. As spiritual beings, we thirst. Holt says Christian spirituality identifies our real need, our thirst for the life-giving living water, "fresh, sparkling, and pure." Equally important is realizing that God's love actively seeks the thirsty.

Looking at the chart and the renewal process, how do we respond practically to the movement upward to God? In terms of the spiritual disciplines, we do our daily disciplines, or we may sense that we need to take a day of retreat to meditate and study Scripture. In terms of the renewal team, we see the movement upward when we lift one another up in prayer. Rather than just move forward with the business at hand, we see that acting as a team *is* the business at hand. Or we see a team uniting in approach when faced with something potentially divisive. Or in the renewal process we feel drawn to a biblical text. All of a sudden we see how God is calling us, uniting us in a biblical vision. Such a Scripture empowers us and guides us in mission. In all these things and more, we experience an encounter with Jesus in which we are drawn upward to God.

The movement inward. The movement inward is linked to the next three steps of the renewal process: self-study (including identifying the strengths and needs of a congregation with spiritual appreciation), teaching servant leadership, and discerning a biblical vision and plan of renewal. In the movement inward, we begin to claim the strengths given by God within us. Rather than just focus on weaknesses or deficiencies, we see how God has blessed us and will use people like us. This is how Jesus treated the woman at the well.

Part of the renewal process are congregational gatherings at which we look at the strengths of our church and share how other congregants have touched us spiritually. At junctures of feeling new energy in those experiences, we pause and offer genuine gratitude and can feel the movement of God. In a similar vein, as we look at servant leadership, we see how the unlikely one can make all the difference. We listen to the invitations of God and follow the promptings of God.

As we saw with the woman at the well, Jesus takes the despised, the lonely, and the rejected, offers them living water, and uses their lives for the purpose for which they were created. Even today, God takes discouraged and dispirited churches and uses them as a mission center to do Christ's work in their community. The good news is that we don't have to be perfect to get started. God's qualification is that we be but servants. Churches find this season of self-reflection upbuilding as they gain new energy. The excitement begins to show and others are often drawn in, whether they are new attendees or those who simply become more involved.

Renewal is not an end state, but is becoming aware of what God is doing now. The process itself is renewal. We can't determine how a church is going to change. Rather, we feel the movement of God and set out to discover a whole new way of living. Renewal comes more in small victories, step by step, than in monumental breakthroughs. In some ways, it is easier than we thought. In other ways, the journey of obedience calls for commitment and courage that takes more than we ever imagined. Renewal takes hard, hard work. It is not for those who give up easily.

Speaking practically, through the period of looking within we discover the strengths with which God has blessed us and how they can be turned into a vision. At those times in the process when we feel we don't have what it takes, the movement of God within reminds us that God's help is sufficient for the task to which we are called. We feel gratitude. The load lightens.

In a similar way we see how our church spiritually touches the lives of others. In a congregational gathering on spiritual appreciation, we identify how our lives of faith are formed. We can feel a movement within as we see how God used a person or a situation to draw us closer in faith. This inner movement calls us to savor such an experience and see how it can help others as well. In the movement inward, we discover what it means to have a discerned vision and to live from the inside out. Such a vision will have power.

The movement outward. The movement outward means that we feel a tug to use our gifts and strengths to engage in ministries, go through all that it takes to engage others, and appreciate the new life that comes. There may be moments when the way does not seem clear. We pause to sense where the movement of God is leading and ask what steps to take next. There may be moments when our breath is taken away. Making progress, we give a sigh of relief. We rejoice and begin to work even more diligently. We discover we can't overcome dehydration by just one sip, but we do know that God is leading us forth to greater life.

As renewal begins in a church, there is movement in our faith walk. As a pastor in renewal, I learned that what is called for in our faith response may seem paradoxical, the opposite of what we would normally think. Just when we thought that all of this was at our initiative, we learn that all of renewal is a gift. Just when we thought all would be easy, we discover what transformation entails; we discover that discipleship is costly. As renewal unfolds, we encounter new challenges and give up old patterns. Ministries stretch us and call us to become new people. The movement of God leads us even closer to Christ. As Paul says in Ephesians, "The church is Christ's body and is filled with Christ who completely fills everything" (1:23 CEV).

Paying attention to God is a wonderful blessing as we engage in mission. We can only imagine what the woman at the well faced going to her hometown. Following God's leading, she gained the courage she needed and was able to enter a dialogue, inviting others to go to discover who this person was for themselves. Following the movement outward leads us into unknown territory with situations and uncertainties we never imagined we would face. With God within, we can face the fears. William Barry notes, "Could it be then, that what we most deeply yearn for we most deeply fear? When we are united with God, we see reality whole, and we are not at the center of it." And then the paradox: "the closer we are united with God, the more ourselves we are."[5]

The movement of God draws us closer to Christ to become partners in mission. Embarking on a mission means we personally and corporately feel we are on assignment. In *Sleeping with Bread*, the authors speak of having "sealed orders," the way we are gifted to give and receive love.[6] The church understands it has a unique mission. The movements of God are not a linear progression, but an invitation to release all to Christ in order to receive new life. Lest we get disheartened, miss the proper course, or lose the creative spark, we trust God's leadings. In surrender there is a peace. Life-giving water will refresh us and fill us and invite us to go deeper in our encounter with Jesus.

Faith Development of Newcomers and Returnees

Having worked on the larger picture of congregational spiritual direction for renewal and how God shapes the life of the total church, we turn to individuals and see how their faith development can take place. As we work on the total picture, we don't want to lose sight of the individual. Specifically we have to look at the faith development of newcomers and those who return to the church in a time of renewal, as well as resident members who potentially go to a deeper level in their faith development. (We will return to this topic, especially in chapter 15.)

When Jesus approached the woman at the well and asked for a drink, he signaled that he would bridge barriers and conveyed that her life had purpose. Within the dialogue and encounter came a series of events that led to further growth. In a similar way, the church in renewal becomes a community of faith out of which each person encounters Jesus. Everyone is a vital part. Members should discover that their ministry is part of growing in the faith journey. Often it can be helpful to think about how a new person enters a church or how a long-standing member can start over again.

Thinking of the woman at the well, we can see how faith development occurred over time. She processed significant factors, including facing her current condition, meeting this man Jesus, understanding aspects of faith, coming to terms with her current life, receiving living water, and setting a new life purpose. In the inner faith development of individuals, be they newcomers, returnees, or those being renewed in their faith, we see a parallel spiritual development that moves from thirst to encounter to transformation to mission. Renewal is becoming attuned to the faith development of people.

Thirsting. Thirsting, new people walk over the threshold of the church for the first time. The importance of what happens in the first minutes cannot be underestimated.[7] Hospitality is critical for people to feel welcomed. Churches that demonstrate biblical hospitality are friendly places where people work together and feel connected even if diverse in background and circumstances. They convey a positive faith and concern for one another. Resources like *The First Thirty Seconds* help us understand how to provide hospitality to people entering the church. Like Jesus, the church can lift them up. If newcomers are welcomed, they may return.

In renewal, we find that many people who have been around a long time also thirst. Life situations press on them. Like the woman at the well, they are thirsty at high noon. Members and friends may wonder what this renewal is about. Like the woman at the well, they may wonder if they are included. Is this really for them? Some may wonder if they should take a wait-and-see attitude. The woman at the well had questions that she openly expressed, and some people in reentry will do the same. John 4 gives us clues as we see Jesus set a climate of dialogue in which the woman felt respected and could explore what a deeper faith would mean.

When a church enters renewal, people begin to welcome each other in a new way. Greetings are more heartfelt. Exchanges between people are filled with more energy. As the church enters more intentional spiritual disciplines, a new orientation occurs. In one church, on the very Sunday of implementing the discipline folders, complaints stopped. Members began to anticipate what spiritual growth could mean. As a renewal team is formed, the emphasis on cooperation sends a positive signal. Starting dialogue creates a place of understanding so people can explore their questions. The renewal process helps people check out the new life. Thirsting, people can encounter Jesus in a new way.

Encountering. Those who find their thirst addressed will most likely return. They no longer visit various churches but become more regular in attendance. They may wonder if they can grow spiritually in this faith community. Can nurturing relationships be established? It is important for a church to make contact with those who have visited one or two times. Contact also can help if a person has missed services on consecutive Sundays. Pastoral and lay visits play a significant role. In an Alban study on sixteen growing churches, the consultants identified what they call commitment anxiety, which results when too many things are offered that only extract energy.[8]

Like the woman at the well, those who thirst enter more and more into conversation with Jesus. In this stage, people begin to want to be a part, and they begin to associate more with others. People take an interest in each other; you see them lingering longer with one another. Like the woman at the well, people might have questions about various topics. People may still be testing whether there is trust in this place.

In a similar way, long-time members may affiliate in a new way. They become more intentional in their relationship with the church. Members who visited other churches may decide to return. They begin to rekindle old relationships and make new friends. With the efforts of the renewal team, a church can track those who are present or not present and provide follow-up. Checking in on how things are going is important in this stage. Listening is vital. Contacts should be made in the style of the servant leader, sensitively communicating the positive spiritual journey the church has entered. Someone on the periphery may come to a congregational gathering and become involved. People begin to feel that they can encounter Jesus in this church again, perhaps in ways they never did before.

Transforming. After thirsting and encountering, the woman at the well asked for living water. Often this kind of life change is confirmed in baptism. Some formal service and new member recognition is offered. Authors Speed Leas and Roy Oswald found that people were looking for a spiritual journey that would help them find answers to life's dilemmas and give them hope.[9] In this stage, further discipling is important. (We address this topic in chapter 15.) Growth in faith is a continuous development. In the Alban study, researchers found that people may not come to get involved, but unless they do get involved, they do not stay. Ongoing development may lead to gifts discernment through which people discover how they can become more involved.

Churches need to be careful to invite others to get involved and do their part without overloading them. One congregation in renewal identified that they were making a mistake by putting new members into major leadership positions almost immediately. This compromised the new members' faith development. People need time to grow in faith. All must find an involvement that will nurture their faith, not strain it.

Members may consider entering into the renewal activities and ministries of the church. Making a commitment to spiritual disciplines is certainly one big step, as is joining a class on the disciplines. Someone may join or rejoin the choir. A long-time member may help in a membership class. A pastor or deacon may invite noninvolved members to assist in some manner, and they wind up rejoining the church. Some denominations have people make a recommitment to membership on a yearly basis. This can be a very moving experience in the renewal process. In renewal, some members may decide they want to be rebaptized or to recommit themselves to their vows to Christ and the church.

Entering mission. Finally comes the stage of going deeper in faith and feeling sent in mission. As the woman at the well went deeper in her faith, she went back to her hometown to invite others to meet and know Jesus. Being sent means people really become a part of the church. It is no longer them and us. Here is where they take on leadership. When someone asks them about the church, they feel they can speak for it. Entering mission may include going on a mission trip as giving of selfless service to others, as well as help with their own enrichment.

Like the woman at the well, they share their faith with others. They are helped to discover their unique ministry and feel they are growing in it. In a study on lay leader burnout, Oswald and Leas discovered that lay leaders are less likely to burn out if they are doing ministries related to their spiritual growth.[10] Assimilation is still important so that people do not get lost in the process. Here is why ministry to active members is crucial in a church. As people go deeper, they take initiative. They feel a sense of assurance and in gratitude often see their vocation as a ministry.

Going deeper is extremely important in renewal. Often in this stage people readjust what they do in the church. In Springs we advise that people do at most two assignments in the church. Often as a result of renewal, leadership shifts because more people are involved in roles more suited to their talents. They no longer do what they do because no one else can be found. People feel unity of purpose and have a mentor or a support group to help them fulfill their ministry. The church finds resources and experiences to help members grow in their faith while serving. Also, the church develops nurturing ministries.

Developing Nurturing Ministries

Nurture ministries are vital to the church's corporate spiritual formation. Corporate direction can happen by guiding these ministries, making sure they are helping both individuals and the church to become a living body of Christian growth. For the church in renewal, these ministries are critical. Both long-term members, including those who reenter, and new people in the church can grow in their encounter with Jesus. The challenge is to develop nurturing ministries that lead to spiritual growth and also help people as they get involved in their ministries in daily life. Let us look at some options for ministries that can do both.

Sunday school. Yes, it is traditional, and yes it is institutionalized, yet Bush Creek discovered that the Sunday school program provided fifty-two sessions each year to strengthen people in faith. Surprisingly that growth did not start in the children's department, as important as it is, but with adults. The adult class of about eight people, of which I was a part, began to ask what they wanted to learn. Each member contributed to establishing topics, locating curriculum, calling teachers, and studying for teaching.

As the class grew, it had to transition to bigger quarters in the fellowship hall, which became a friendly, welcoming space. As we reached fifty participants, the question of whether to split the class came up. An experiment discovered diminishing results; the group liked being together. So the teaching style was changed to incorporate breakout discussion groups. We learned that as the church grew, entirely new classes should be formed instead of splitting existing ones.

Equally important to the success of Bush Creek's Sunday school program was developing a teacher training series. With the growing number of children, rotating teachers, and teaching teams, we needed more personnel. How were we ever going to find enough people to teach? Just as we had spiritual growth experiences at our own church building, we planned teacher training onsite. Mingling among our own created a spirit among teachers.

Obtaining an outstanding trainer brought a blessing in disguise. Not only did he charge one hundred dollars, a high figure for a small church in the 1970s, but he required that twenty people be present. The breakdown of five dollars per person was reasonable, but what about getting twenty people? So we shook the bushes and came up with twenty. Now, that was inclusion! And people got excited about teaching Sunday school.

Training proved to be a time saver as well as a point of renewal. As ministries like vacation Bible school grew, a cadre of teachers was trained and ready to teach. Out of this initiative arose a family night, which is described later. Ultimately Bush Creek was chosen for an interdenominational, successful Sunday school project. In the study we learned that adult education stood at the top of the list for churches. Some years later, I was asked to do a similar study that revealed the same findings.[11] Not surprisingly, building on strengths was also a factor in these churches.

In its renewal endeavor, one congregation decided to hold a congregational gathering about the Sunday school program and a follow-up by having trainers come right into the classroom to assist teachers. We found a state Sunday school association with excellent resources.[12] That Sunday the president of the association, Rodney Pry, gave an excellent sermon in worship on the purpose of Sunday school: to assist people to grow spiritually in life situations.

Pry stressed the need for active participation by young adults in the program. Then, following a potluck lunch, he helped the church look at how everyone can be involved at helping the Sunday school to grow. He gave tips like visiting, hosting an open house, and people inviting people. The influence of Sunday school for reaching out to people, both in ministry and personal spiritual growth is unlimited and well worth a church's investment.

Family-night endeavors. Midweek family-night programs, covered more extensively in part 4, can be significant in encountering Jesus. The intentionality of the ministry's use of sponsors, a variety of formats, and family involvement helps ensure success. In one congregation, my role as pastor was to help teach the fifth- and sixth-grade Bible study class. I invited a very creative person, who was having a hard time fitting into the church, to be the co-teacher. This was a wonderful way for her to use her talents.

Using the curriculum "Paul, Such a Different Man," she brought a sculpture of Paul kneeling, made out of chicken wire.[13] As the children listened to a recording she made on the life of Paul, they draped stripes of paper mache over the wire mesh. Upon completion, their recall of the facts of the life of Paul was outstanding. At a subsequent session, they painted the model. Then we designed a worship service with the figure set in the center of the chancel. The whole service became an unparalleled faith experience integrating nurture and worship.

Bible studies and small groups. Bible study groups provide a time for encounter with Jesus. At a congregational gathering on spiritual appreciation at the inner-city First Church of the Brethren, a man shared how he had become a part of the church. First Church had a food distribution center. Seeing the lines of people, the church decided to hold a Bible study. This man attended the Bible study and subsequently found a Sunday school class as his place for Christian growth.

In Bible study, people study the Scriptures, grapple with life experiences, and grow in their Christian walk. One need is finding appropriate material to use with the Bible. The Covenant Bible series is a relational Bible study series emphasizing growth in covenant with Christ and the church. This includes personal preparation, study of the Bible, and questions for study and action.[14]

Small groups make an impact on people and can be a life-changing experience. Some way is needed for getting to know people on a more personal level and for encountering Jesus on a regular basis. Small-group formats vary widely, and a number of factors are important to consider. Small groups need a focus, whether a study of the Bible or of another faith resource. Materials need to be uplifting to individuals. The group needs to set guidelines for appropriate interpersonal sharing. Accountability and prayer should remain on a positive course.

Renovaré provides a format for small groups. *A Spiritual Formation Workbook* gives eight beginning sessions on becoming a spiritual formation group.[15] The sessions are built around living the spiritual traditions explored in *Streams of Living Water* by Foster. Sessions such as "Practicing the Sacramental Life" include exercises in the incarnational tradition.

Seven years after starting a spiritual formation group using Renovaré at their church, one group found it was providing the impetus for renewal. In another church, I could tell that a successful Sunday school program had something significant happening.[16] Upon investigation I learned that this congregation was broken down into shepherding groups, and the leaders (called shepherds) met weekly for their own spiritual growth. Small-group leaders need their own ongoing spiritual growth. The small groups in this church were playing a significant role in nurturing the faith of its members and giving congregational spiritual direction for renewal.

Youth ministry. We will cover youth ministry in chapter 13, so I will say just a few words here. In my work in church renewal, the development of a youth ministry topped the list of most churches. Once a church goes through the process, they often see the call and potential for this vital work. Youth-group models differ from one church to another, as do the activities and what they hope to accomplish. But asking where God is leading and experiencing increasing energy through renewal seem to result in gravitating to this important ministry. New life through youth ministry represents the claim that the church has a future that is now!

∽

Spiritual direction and formation are vital for renewal. Understanding where God is leading becomes the path. Through spiritual discernment we can respond to the movements of God that guide the church in its spiritual pilgrimage. In making decisions, a renewal team and others seek guidance. Becoming attuned to the movements of God helps in those choices. The dynamics of renewal also help us to think about the faith development of people. Just as the woman at the well went through a process of faith development by encountering Jesus, so people can discover the blessing of receiving living water. Out of that they develop a mission for their lives.

For Reflection and Discussion

1. What strikes you about the discoveries at Bush Creek? Can you see how this church worked on faith development of people?

2. What do you think of discerning movements (upward, inward, outward) of God and the parallels with the renewal process? Use the discerning movements of God to share your faith story.

3. In reflecting on the stages of faith development of the woman at the well, can you see how people can be invited into a deeper faith and become more integrated into the church? What next steps could your church take to facilitate this journey?

4. What nurturing ministries have helped you grow in faith? Can you think of new nurturing ministries that would be good for your church? Are there existing ministries that could be a part of the renewal process?

5. Reflect on Sunday school and what it has meant to you over the years. What are the strengths of your church's Sunday school?

Part 3

Transformation

"Go call your husband," said Jesus to her, "and come back here." The woman answered, "I have no husband." He said to her, "You are right to say, 'I have no husband', for although you have five, the one you have now is not your husband. You spoke the truth there." "I see you are a prophet, sir," said the woman. "Our fathers worshiped on this mountain, while you say that Jerusalem is the place where one ought to worship." Jesus said:

"Believe me, woman, the hour is coming
when you will worship the Father
neither on this mountain nor in Jerusalem.
You worship what you do not know;
we worship what we do know;
for salvation comes from the Jews.
But the hour will come—in fact it is here already—
when true worshipers will worship the Father in spirit and truth
that is the kind of worshiper
the Father wants.
God is spirit,
and those who worship
must worship in spirit and truth."
The woman said to him. "I know that Messiah—that is, Christ—is coming; and when he comes he will tell us everything." "I who am speaking to you," said Jesus,
"I am he."

—John 4:16-26 Jerusalem Bible

9

Experiencing Transformation, New Life, and Motivation

Given Sabbath rest after renewal ministry at a church, I thought, "Why not visit four growing churches of our denomination for Sunday worship?" I was interested in learning more about healthy churches and the renewal process. Andrew, our challenged adult son, is a good barometer of the spirit of a church. With his neurological makeup, Andrew lets us know by his actions what is happening. When things are together, he settles more easily in the seat. When there is conflict, he is restless and unsettled.

When *Messenger*, our denominational magazine, was doing an issue on disabilities, they asked Joan and me how Andrew was received in these churches. We agreed to reflect on our visits and wrote an article entitled "Hospitality, Andrew Style."[1] Hospitality, in relation to Andrew, takes an unusual twist and gives a refreshing perspective on the transformation of a church.

Our only challenge in these four churches was that none had greeters at the door to help newcomers find a restroom. But beyond that, our visits were sheer delights. By Andrew's actions we could tell these churches had a low level of unresolved conflict.

Each of the four pastors had high energy and called Andrew by name. None of these pastors tried to "high five" Andrew, which increases his excitability, which we then must deal with as parents for the rest of the day. These pastors treated Andrew like an adult, which settles him and shows respect.

Each of these churches tried to put us at ease with Andrew.

While we often sit in the back of a sanctuary so as not to be disruptive, people tried to alleviate our concern that he might make noise. At one church, we were invited to the church dinner directly following the service. They were comfortable even if some food fell on the floor and reassured us his presence was not an inconvenience.

At each of these churches, parking was at a premium, hallways were packed, and buildings were clean but older. For Andrew, externals mean nothing. Taking time to speak with him makes a connection—not the fact that the carpet is new and the right color. Churches where people take the time to say hello to him and then wait for him to respond make an impact. Building relationships is definitely a factor in hospitality for Andrew.

Andrew shies away from negative people, those who complain about others and those who look angry. As visitors to these four congregations, we never heard anything negative about people or other annoyances with the church, even when there was opportunity. The crowded parking was a "good problem." It wasn't something people were unconcerned about, but not a point to complain about either. This positive spirit made Andrew happy and at ease.

Another important factor for Andrew was that each of these churches had clear beliefs. In every case the pastor expressed the church's ideals. We heard about Jesus, discipleship, counting well the cost, family values, and service. Andrew frequently talks about making peace, caring for the poor, and not fighting. When pastors would preach, we could hear Andrew repeating quietly what the pastor was saying. He feels at home when he hears Christian beliefs expressed.

While these congregations showed us hospitality, they accepted Andrew's contribution as well. People were receptive to him holding the door open for them. People answered his constant questions, such as the man whose leg was in a cast. Andrew inquired about his leg, and this led to an extended conversation in the parking lot.

The strength of these healthy churches translates into a welcoming space. Their transformed life as a church allows them to be open and welcoming, put visitors and regular attendees at ease, let others give back to them, possess a positive spirit, and clearly state their beliefs and values. There was spiritual energy in these places, and it made us want to be a part of it.

The Dynamic of Transformation

Spiritual transformation, the third dynamic of renewal, concerns what actually happens to churches in the renewal process. The woman at the well experienced transformation through the grace-filled manner of Jesus, who showed her respect, asked for her help, and gave her wisdom and new life. Through this experience, Jesus offered life-giving water. Not only did she experience new life, she was also given a mission. In the renewal process, transformation happens before our very eyes as people find a deep inner faith and churches discover a vibrant mission.

In chapter 2 we explored the steps of renewal. We looked at steps 1-3 in chapter 5. Now we turn to steps 4-6 to see how transformation happens in people and the church. Andrew may not understand the whole process, but he can tell the outcome in a church striving to be healthy and life-giving.

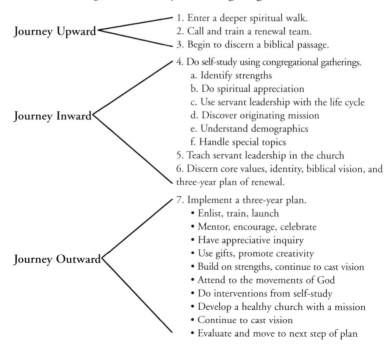

Journey Upward
1. Enter a deeper spiritual walk.
2. Call and train a renewal team.
3. Begin to discern a biblical passage.

Journey Inward
4. Do self-study using congregational gatherings.
   a. Identify strengths
   b. Do spiritual appreciation
   c. Use servant leadership with the life cycle
   d. Discover originating mission
   e. Understand demographics
   f. Handle special topics
5. Teach servant leadership in the church
6. Discern core values, identity, biblical vision, and three-year plan of renewal.

Journey Outward
7. Implement a three-year plan.
   • Enlist, train, launch
   • Mentor, encourage, celebrate
   • Have appreciative inquiry
   • Use gifts, promote creativity
   • Build on strengths, continue to cast vision
   • Attend to the movements of God
   • Do interventions from self-study
   • Develop a healthy church with a mission
   • Continue to cast vision
   • Evaluate and move to next step of plan

Step 4: Do Self-Study Using Congregational Gatherings

Congregational gatherings can be life-changing. At step 4, the church holds a series of congregational gatherings. While a gathering after a meal might last only an hour and a half, the outcome of having the entire congregation work together is significant. People will probably share in ways they never have before in the church. All of these gatherings focus on the strengths of the church.

In chapter 2 we explained how the renewal team members work to discern the flow of the congregational gatherings. They do this in order to have the time of self-study build up the church. The outcome of the gatherings will help build renewal. All the effort will pay dividends. The congregation will feel that there is a sense of direction to all of this. During this time it is not unusual for people to join in who usually are not involved in such events, so the team works to make them feel included.

Using the dialogue process for conversation in gatherings helps lead to positive outcomes where everyone is involved and everyone has a voice. The journey affirms who they are as a church. People often say they lose sight of all the good that is happening. A congregational gathering brings those things back in focus. Relationships change and energy increases as more people are included in the renewal process. Done in the right manner, such events transform and propel the church forward. There are six aspects to the self-study.

4a. Identify strengths (first congregational gathering). If we look at the woman at the well, we see that Jesus asked her to use what she had—a water pot. Jesus asked for a drink. That is what she could do. Being in her condition, she pointed out the disparities in the situation, with Jesus being a Jew and a man. Jesus was not put off but rather could see her situation and stick with her observations long enough to offer her what she most needed—life-giving water, flowing like a fountain that bubbles up, giving eternal life.

Churches that discover they have something to offer discover

Jesus coming to them. Rather than feeling the strain of exhaustion, they begin to see how God wishes to use their lives. Rather than just feeling frustrated that things are not going as well as they would like, they begin to see Jesus reaching out to them, asking for help. The only thing worse than feeling hopeless is feeling useless. Jesus has a way of coming to us personally and corporately to affirm our worth and call us to be his partners in mission. When churches discover Jesus inviting them to offer what they have, renewal takes a giant step.

A wonderful way to take the next steps in the spiritual journey is to discover and affirm strengths in the congregation. This can be done with a congregational gathering on the church's strengths. Something happens as people start sharing in small groups about what their strengths are. Rather than look for what is wrong and fix it, transformation happens as people find out what is right and build on it. Such a congregational gathering follows the regular format with a presentation on the importance of this outlook and ties strengths to God-given gifts. After reviewing the dialogue procedure, small groups identify the strengths of their church. Then a leader makes a compiled list and takes time for reflection and worship.

One transformative moment I remember involved the Harrisburg First Church of the Brethren. At a board retreat, leaders of the church identified strengths of the church. Later the entire congregation had a gathering to share strengths. All the people shared, some of them speaking Spanish. The lists of strengths grew.

Whereas at the retreat the leaders listed seventy-two identified strengths, at the congregational gathering the people named 270! When the compilation was done, the chairperson of the renewal team recorded page after page of strengths. You could feel the new energy and excitement building in the room.

An interesting strength mentioned repeatedly at this gathering was that First Church has "a deep bench." Just as a successful sports team has a deep bench from which to draw reserve players, First Church has strong backup people who readily step in when needed. What a blessing for a church to have other people who can step in to help!

Any list of strengths should be saved for when the biblical vision is discerned.

At the end of the gathering a most meaningful moment occurred spontaneously. Seeing the power of what was shared, we took time for people to say what was on their heart. Tears came to people's eyes as they said how blessed they felt. This time of sharing turned into spontaneous worship. Transformation was literally happening before our eyes.

4b. Do spiritual appreciation (second congregational gathering). The transformation in the second congregational gathering happens as people begin to talk about how their lives in the church have been touched spiritually. Founded to share the Good News and to nurture people spiritually, the church regains focus by talking about the center of life together. Here is something so central that we no longer want to take it for granted. The insight and energy created by such an event is powerful. Be available for conversation as the small group discussions break up. Look at the lists posted about the church and see the stories of faith. Listen in to conversations after the event.

This information can be helpful in knowing how people are touched spiritually, and as the renewal team assists the church in forming a vision and renewal plan. Perhaps spiritual formation happened with someone in a youth program, a teacher in a Bible study who arose from a community outreach program, or a pastor whose sermon spoke to someone even when attendance was slim. A church learns how people's involvements tie to their development of faith. Since developing the spiritual life of a church is so central and churches want to develop ministries of spiritual growth in renewal, this gathering is very important in the renewal process. The substance of this gathering will be immediately useful in all ministry groups and in establishing the renewal plan.

4c. Use servant leadership with the life cycle (third congregational gathering; thirty minutes). After looking at servant leadership and the life cycle found in chapter 1, the renewal team can decide at what point and how to introduce these concepts to help the church rally to gain new life. Even this discernment is transformational in that the renewal team assesses how best to see the renewal move forward. The focus is on gaining new energy and vitality. Often people see parallel applications in other areas of their life and welcome learning how to regain energy and vitality. By everyone working together, the exploration of the life cycle can become part of the transformation of the church.

The important thing is that churches look not just at where they are in the life cycle but do so with momentum already built and as they feel God's invitation to new life. The group can look at the points of inclusion where commitment is built in, at the dynamics of program needs overtaking people needs, and at the need for balance of all factors for maturity. The church is alerted to how to offset decline, build new life, and act if and when signs of decline appear. Leadership is given for new life.

4d. Discover originating mission (third congregational gathering; twenty-five minutes). A church can experience significant transformation by exploring its originating mission. The renewal team may look at the originating mission of the church and the invitation to ministry that comes out of the study of demographics. In the originating mission we are looking at the commitment and vision of those who founded the church. Persons become excited to learn about the faith of the founding members.

At one congregation where I was involved in renewal work, there had been a church split forty years earlier. Even though few members from that era still attended the church, the congregation was held captive by stinging comments of departed members, who had said, "We're taking God with us." Frequently these harsh words were remembered and repeated. Since the church was not growing, the members wondered whether the departed ones were right after all. Through the Springs renewal process, the congregation looked at its history before the church split. Discovering the originating mission literally transformed them. The church learned how they had lived peacefully with Native Americans on adjacent land. The close proximity to what could have been disputing parties reflected the peace tradition of the church. The church also learned that it had many preaching points and spread the gospel throughout the area. Years ago, some very dedicated members conducted services and established locations for the church. In the community the church built a path for people to walk to church and for farmers to travel to market with their livestock. That path became a heavily traveled highway.

The original church was a creative, eight-sided building that doubled as a school. The membership provided many educators for the community, and cooperation was seen in the dual use of the church. Here was a multipurpose facility way before its time. Through this discovery of its originating mission, this church began to see itself as an evangelistic, cooperative, creative group that did significant ministry and mission. By finding the originating mission, the church was transformed and began to find a new path. Never again did I hear about the comments of years gone by. New energy came as the church moved forward. Transformation was happening.

4e. Understand demographics (third congregational gathering; twenty-five minutes). Studying demographics, Hatfield Church of the Brethren became aware of the people surrounding the church and felt a new connection with them. The church learned about employment opportunities, trends in the schools, and even about green space being created. Explorations like this can help a church move to the next step of meeting people personally through visitation or outreach programs. Newcomers provide a fresh understanding of the needs and opportunities surrounding the church. Discussions at a gathering help the church understand its field of mission and how to invite people to meet Jesus.

At the close of this third congregational gathering, the renewal team can ask which biblical passage might, based on what has been covered thus far in the renewal process, express God's leading for the church. As a follow-up to this discussion, the outcome can be taken to Sunday school classes or smaller groups in the church. They can study the texts using appendix 11, have discussions, and get ready to report. As churches discern a biblical passage that guides their life, they feel they are part of the biblical story.

4f. Handling special topics. Sometimes handling a topic at the heart of a ministry is best done through a congregational gathering. This does not have to be something associated with conflict; it may be for strengthening a certain area in the life of the church. Such a gathering can happen in moving toward a vision or may come as the vision is being implemented. Just because the ministry plan is being carried out does not mean that the congregation does not need to keep growing. Transformation happens throughout the renewal process.

There may be congregational gatherings to learn about a ministry that needs revitalization, such as Sunday school. Another important topic is how to witness to your faith. A gathering on this subject might look at the materials in chapter 15, which contains resources for discipling and training apostles. Hospitality and faith sharing could be effectively explored at a congregational event, also in chapter 15. Such gatherings may come during the self-study portion of the renewal process or while the renewal plan is implemented.

Sometimes a resource person needs to be enlisted to teach a special topic. In some cases, such as exploring a Wednesday-evening family night or a soup kitchen ministry, people may visit another church to observe that ministry and report what they discovered. At Emmanuel Mennonite Church, where there were a variety of tastes in music, the renewal team decided to look at the whole area of worship in the life of the church. We studied the five elements of worship found in Isaiah 6: praise, confession, pardon, challenge, and response.

Then we planned a unit on a weekend with a guest, Art Dyck, director of music at Neffsville Mennonite Church. On Saturday evening, Art helped us look at worship as he led us in hymns and looked at the background and history of songs. On Sunday Art gave a message on the meaning of worship, helping us see how we become the sanctuary. God invites us into an intimate personal relationship and to become immersed in Christ in worship.

Finally, our guest led a service Sunday evening that incorporated many styles of music. Art helped us look at the purpose of worship from Colossians 3:16-17: "Let the word of Christ dwell in you richly with all wisdom, and as you sing psalms, hymns, and spiritual songs with gratitude in your hearts to God . . . and do all in the name of the Lord Jesus, giving thanks to God the Father through him." The newsletter said, "Renewal is happening."

Step 5: Teach Servant Leadership in the Church

This step takes place in an additional congregational gathering or some other setting. We see the effect of the servant leadership style throughout the renewal process, but we see even fuller results as we move through self-study and into the implementation of ministries. From servant leadership we glean four relevant topics: seeing things whole, using foresight and ethics, having urgency to mission, and moving with the lead of the leader.[2]

In servant leadership there are two factors to keep in mind. One is that foresight builds on spiritual discernment and occurs only within the context of regular spiritual disciplines. The outcome we desire in a vision and a plan is spiritual vitality. Foresight is built on the synergy of the inner and outer life.

The other factor is that we are attempting to discover the mission and go to the springs together. At the same time as renewal happens for others, spiritual growth and transformation happens in us as well.

Seeing things whole. Servant leaders begin with seeing the big picture. They do this from a position of kneeling and looking up. The prophet Isaiah had a vision of when justice would rule and society would reflect the moral values of the faith. With a deep abiding faith, the servant conceptualizes how things should be and begins to work in that direction. This happened to me as I walked out the back door at Bush Creek and saw how established church members and new community could grow in the church.

Spiritually discerning a vision will occur in this vein. Rather than going piecemeal and then seeing how things add up together, the servant looks for the big picture and fills in the pieces. When the pieces come into place, the big picture becomes clearer. Here is where the practice of listening first to God and then to those around us is essential. As servants, we can know only in part. But as we act in faith, the fuller picture develops. Seeing things whole is vital to discerning a biblical vision and plan.

Over the years in the renewal process, churches have used this gift of foresight in discerning a vision and a plan. In looking into that triangle (see page 181), a church can see beyond the present to how things can fit together and how the church can be life-giving. The church has to go on and see a renewal plan developed and use dialogue and discernment to see which things should come first and which things will be needed to build to the larger vision. And the servant leader keeps that vision before the group.[3]

Using foresight and ethics. The servant leader uses the gift of foresight to see where things will be in the future if they follow in a certain direction and then casts a vision with the church for where things can go according to God's leading. Biblically we think of this as prophecy, which not only foresees what will happen but also calls us back to faithfulness. Isaiah uses foresight to call the Israelites to faithfulness and casts a vision to be servants, a light to the nations.

Robert Greenleaf said, "Foresight is the 'lead' that the leader has. Once he loses this lead and events start to force his hand, he is leader in name only. He is not leading; he is reacting to immediate events and he probably will not long be a leader."[4] With foresight, the servant sees the possibilities for new life and sees the steps that it will take to arrive at that vision. Such leadership is active and dynamic and faithful.

Being faithful to a vision is a deep ethical concern. Foresight moves from just an interesting discussion of the future to a call to be proactive. With vision being a gift of God, servants act when there is opportunity to move toward vision. As James 4:17 says, "Anyone, then, who knows the right thing to do and fails to do it, commits sin" (NRSV). Servant leaders have an ethical responsibility to use foresight to engage in mission.

Having urgency to do mission. In church renewal, foresight gives urgency to act while there is time to do so. When a church has a window of opportunity, servants have the clear call to move ahead. "Prescience, or foresight, is a better than average guess about *what* is going to happen *when* in the future," writes Greenleaf. The challenge is to make that future the course of faithfulness, however costly. He also says, "The servant-leader is functionally superior because he is closer to the ground—he hears things, sees things, knows things, and his intuitive insight is an exception. Because of this he is dependable and trusted."[5] Servants of Christ carry basin and towel into the mission field.

In Springs, congregations build the energy of faith and see how critical it is to fulfill the mission in front of them. Churches replace complacency and inertia with actively engaging in meaningful ministries. Servant leadership is not about wild-eyed dreams for the church; Bonhoeffer says these need to be shattered before real community can emerge.[6] Servant leaders roll up the sleeves of vision and go to work. With this comes a sense of authenticity, humility, and authentic authority. The integrity of the servant speaks volumes both within and outside the church.

Moving with the lead of the leader. Servant leadership is not passive or retiring. Once a church body gains a vision, servant leaders move with people to fulfill the goals of the vision. In personal correspondence to me in 1986, Greenleaf wrote, "There is no magic, I believe, to leading. One simply has it in oneself to put top priority on building strength in other people, rather than trying to do it all oneself." By serving, servant leaders gain respect because they hold the interests of others in mind and are working on their behalf.

In such leadership there is also risk. Often leadership is forging new ground, and spiritual discernment is needed to find the way. Servant leadership is an intuitive approach, but in discernment it is balanced both by logical reasoning and by developing the faith journey. Often in this regard servant leaders must make decisions that are not totally clear at the time. However, in all decisions the servant leader, along with the congregation, should be able to answer three fundamental questions with a powerful yes: Is this what God is calling us to become? Does this express the gospel? Are we doing our mission in joy?

Step 6: Discern Core Values, Identity, Biblical Vision, and a Three-Year Plan of Renewal

We turn now to the sixth step and examine it in its various parts.

Discern core values (fourth congregational gathering). As part of self-study, the renewal team can host a fourth congregational gathering to help the church understand its core values. (Chapter 2 details the steps in discerning these values.) The church asks, "Who are we? What do we have to offer? What makes us unique?" As a congregational survey and gathering are conducted, there is a greater sense of unity and understanding. The value of doing this in a congregational gathering is that there can be open discussion in which people can dialogue and come to a greater understanding of their purpose. (Appendix 4 is a helpful core values audit.)

Core values help define a church not in terms of who is most known but what is of most value. Inclusion is broadened as the church centers on core values and what is important to the entire church. As a church rallies around a set of core values, it experiences the spiritual energy and transformation that comes in the process. One congregation in rough waters found it was totally united on three core values. This was a launching pad for moving to the next step, and all ministries were evaluated on whether they were fulfilling the church's core values. This helps a church understand its identity and moves it closer to a vision.

Discern identity (usually during fourth congregational

gathering). Having discerned core values, a church discerns its identity. Usually this step can be taken during the fourth congregational gathering, but the renewal team can determine whether to combine it with the gathering on core values or to wait for the gathering on discerning vision. Input can come by reviewing the strengths of the church and discerned core values. The full group can explore the very identity of the church. For a congregation, this can be a lively discussion.

There can be the presentation exploring identity. What is it that makes us uniquely who we are, and what does that mean for us as God's people at this place? In faith, our identity is a gift of God. God breathes into us, making us uniquely who we are as individuals and as the church. We are called by name. In the Bible, a person's name is changed to represent his role in the faith.

Developmental psychologist Erik Erikson says, "An optimal sense of identity . . . is experienced . . . as a sense of psychosocial well-being. Its most obvious concomitants are a feeling of being at home in one's body, a sense of 'knowing where one is going,' and an inner assuredness of anticipate recognition from those who count."[7]

The opposite of identity is diffusion, in which you are spread out all over the place.[8] Like the woman at the well before she met Jesus, when you don't know who you are, both you and your effectiveness are compromised. Our identity is shaped around our core values. In understanding identity we discover God's unique giftedness for this church. When you understand your identity, it is conveyed to both members and newcomers. Sometimes a congregational gathering is held on core values and identity.

As the church looks at its identity, people develop a sense of trust, know who they are, and are able to affirm their strengths. The more the church has a sense of its identity, the more self-confidence it can develop. Identifying core values is a significant step in formulating the church's identity.

Discerning a biblical passage is also a significant step. Here a church can see itself in a biblical frame of reference and come to understand more clearly how God would use the church. Paradoxically, knowing all it can about its identity is a significant step toward discerning a biblical passage. The congregation will be drawn to a text that fits its unique identity.

Discern a biblical vision (fifth congregational gathering). Discerning a biblical vision is another way to regain energy for transformation. Usually this concept is introduced early in the renewal process by beginning to discern a specific biblical passage in step 3 (see chapters 2 and 5). You may hear people talking about such references from time to time. As the process moves along, the renewal team may begin this discussion and then take time at congregational gathering 3 to explore what guiding text can lead the church in renewal. In the usual schedule this may be further discussed at the fourth congregational gathering, though it may not be until the fifth that the results come in.

After discerning strengths, core values, identity, and a biblical passage comes discerning a biblical vision. This is usually during a fifth congregational gathering. This chart is repeated here for your convenience.

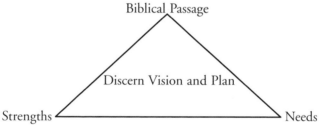

We have seen how to put strengths on the left corner of the triangle, the biblical passage on top, and the needs on the right corner of the triangle. We peer down the center to discern a biblical vision. We ask about the head and its practicality, the heart and the feeling portion, and the faith journey and the challenge to grow spiritually in this walk.

A creative vision is often only two to five words long, but it expresses the church's calling and mission. Being able to paint it on the side of a bus, which one church literally did, means the vision is crisp and focused and can be remembered. Such a vision is transformational in that it centers attention on where the church feels led by God, and it provides the path for the mission of the church in all it is and does. The church now needs to see things whole through the center of the triangle and to discern a vision and a plan.

✍

Transformation happens in a multitude of ways in the renewal process. Once a church has felt the thirst and encountered Jesus, it can move through experiences in which the power of the gospel is experienced. Corporate spiritual disciplines, calling and training a renewal team, and focusing on a Bible text begin the movement. Then the congregational gatherings are transformational as the church gains a vision and a plan. Transformation continues as special units of renewal are discerned and carried out through implementation of the renewal plan.

For Reflection and Discussion

1. Share your reflections on what Andrew found in the growing churches we visited. What do you think about the concept of hospitality "Andrew style"? Do you know of someone like him?

2. What advantages do you see in a church doing renewal together through spiritual disciplines and congregational gatherings that build on strengths?

3. Were there any outcomes of gatherings that particularly spoke to you? Where do you feel new energy can be gained and transformation occur?

4. Can you see advantages to handling difficult topics in the context of the momentum of a renewal process? How can such resolution help promote renewal?

5. In terms of using servant leadership, can you see how leaders plays a key role in helping a group discern a vision? What role do you see foresight playing?

6. Does anything in this chapter speak to you in terms of spiritual transformation of the church? Where do you feel God is leading your church in terms of renewal?

10

Transforming Pastoral Leadership

Being a pastor in the renewal of the church is challenging and exciting. In this chapter we will look at the ninth characteristic of a servant leader: leading in spiritual formation. Spiritual formation is at the heart of pastoral ministry. While others in the church certainly do spiritual guidance, the pastor's role is integral to spiritual transformation and the renewal process. Thirsty like the rest, servants lead people and go with them to drink by the same pools. All are refreshed by springs of living water.

The Ninth Trait of Servant Leaders: Leading in Spiritual Transformation
Servant leaders engage in spiritual leadership and spiritual formation. Christ the Lamb becomes the shepherd and leads us to the springs of living water. In turn, the servant invites others to share in the living water.

Many years ago, preaching from the lectionary in the Easter season, a time of renewal after the resurrection, I was struck by a defining text, Revelation 7:17: "For the Lamb in the midst of the throne will be their shepherd, and he will guide them to springs of living water" (RSV). In this interlude between opening the seals, Christ the Lamb becomes the shepherd and guides people to spiritual refreshment. God wipes all tears from their eyes. The servant becomes the leader and the leader the spiritual guide.

A consultation for churches. This passage comes after John gives his consultation to seven churches in Asia Minor. Unfortunately, their evaluation is not good. One by one they have become acculturated. Pergamum and Thyatira go along with the culture and its values. John's call to them: Repent. Then there is Laodicea, which is like lukewarm tea—neither iced for a hot day nor hot for a cold day. And John says that God will spit it out. John's appeal is for costly discipleship, to live Christ even if it calls for sacrifice. The call for the church is to be faithful, thereby vibrant and robust.

Those who identify with Christ are privileged to open the seals of scrolls. In that act, God's plan for defeating evil is revealed. Like an interlude that the organist plays before the last verse of a hymn, Revelation 7 is an interval of worship before the seventh seal is opened. Using the same word for *springs* as in John's Gospel, the author pictures how Christ leads the believers to living fountains that give not stale, cistern water, but water bubbling up to eternal life. This is living water that connects us to the life-giving reality of God. The faithful have a seal on their forehead and know the victory.

Being servants of Christ, servant leaders are transformed into leaders with a mission—to lead the faithful to living water. John, a church renewal specialist, lifts up characteristics of a vital church, a body transformed by the blood of the Lamb, led and leading others to the springs. The Lamb redeems.[1]

In Revelation 7:17 we have a key paradigm for the source of new life in the church. Christ becomes preeminent in the church transformed. The very Lamb, the meek and humble, becomes the shepherd and leads the faithful to the springs. What a Christology to ponder in relation to renewal of the church! Fear related to the decline of the church is countered by God, who will wipe away every tear and offer hope. Christ becomes triumphant in the holistic vision of church renewal.

The Role of Pastors

Drawing on their call, gifts, training, and experience, pastors are key in the renewal of the church. As spiritual leaders they have five crucial roles: servant leader, spiritual guide, facilitator of the renewal process, messenger of good news, and encourager of others.

One of the requirements for a church to be renewed is to have a pastor with a passion for renewal and who wants to grow spiritually.

While the pastor does not work alone, a letter from the pastor, which could be co-authored by a chair or co-chair of the renewal team, shows how the pastor can draw things together, keep things moving, and give practical expression of spiritual leadership. Here's an example of a letter to go with an agenda:

> Dear Renewal Team,
>
> First, let me thank you for the wonderful job organizing the congregational gathering on strengths and for your work as discussion leaders. The council (board) said this was the highest attendance ever reported at a congregational meeting—106 people, not counting children. The outcome for the church in terms of focusing on strengths of our church is marvelous. Now we turn to our next work.
>
> One of the most important things is to continue the spiritual journey. As you look at the agenda, you can see the spiritual focus. We want to affirm the commitment of 113 people to the spiritual disciplines with the folders. We now ask, What are our next steps? After four–and–a–half weeks into spiritual disciplines, how can we offer encouragement in the journey? Several people will share in worship how they do the disciplines, the challenges, and the outcomes. You have been praying for each of these 113 people. What else do you feel could help? Should we let them know who is praying for them?
>
> Also, we face the question of what we do next over the summer. Do we want to continue an emphasis on the disciplines and have a similar folder? I have spent retreat time studying and praying over the various Sunday morning texts through August. June 8 is Pentecost, and we enter a period of ordinary time. How do we live Spirit-filled lives in the ordinary of life? I asked both Church Council and Spiritual Council for their input about a folder. Both felt positive. Where do you sense God is leading?

We will look briefly at the Land Dedication on June 1. In a real way it ties into the renewal process. One aspect of renewal is discerning the originating mission of a church. This is one aspect of the dedication. We will be looking at the past, where we are at present, this time of renewal, and then at our vision for the future. Besides the spiritual focus giving energy, looking at the church's originating mission gives energy.

Much of our planning is for our next congregational event on Sunday, June 22. Our topic is being a healthy church in terms of interactions, relationships, and mission. I asked Church Council and Spiritual Council about the format and they liked the after-church potluck meal, the fun icebreaker by the youth, and discussion over the tables, with dessert! Again, we close at 1:30 p.m. Two members of our team are already at work.

For our next meeting, we will continue training for our team. We will have an exercise on team building. Team members will look at where their gifts can be used in tasks and draw in other people. Let me close by offering encouragement to you. The living Lord wants us to experience Deeper Joy [the title of the season's disciplines folder].

May that joy be yours!

Pastor Young

Pastors as Servant Leaders

Leadership theory can run the gamut from "directing what should happen" to "just let it happen." In the former case, whether implicit or explicit, the pastor has a personal program to implement. Some people talk of the pastor "whipping people into shape." On the other hand, some pastors use nondirective counseling, hoping that something will happen and an agenda will emerge. The former style is short on building ownership and motivation in a congregation. The latter leaves the church at sea without a rudder. Isn't there something in between?

Ministry means servanthood. In the Scriptures, ministry means servanthood. In 2 Corinthians 5:18, Paul speaks about the ministry *diakonia*, the service of reconciliation. Transformation occurs as someone comes to the other side, is with another person, serves with spiritual sensitivity, and points him or her to Jesus. Trespasses are no longer held against someone else. Pointing again to the initiative of God, forgiveness is involved. Transformation occurs.

In service, bridges are built and brokenness is overcome. Reconciliation happens as someone kneels before another in Christ's name. Something happens to both people in the process. Both are brought closer to Christ and to one another. Service is not just done on the human plane, but is a spiritual initiative pointing to the sacrifice and power of the cross. The ministries of the church are acts of service.

Staying spiritually grounded. Leadership is not something achieved by announcing one is the leader. Even before anything is done in renewal, a pastor needs to gain rapport and trust with the congregation. At the foundation of servant leadership is the fact that the pastor has the spiritual needs of people in mind and holds their interests at heart. Rather than operating out of their own agenda, servant leaders signal that they serve the good of the church. They have the heart of peace that Isaiah the prophet spoke about in the suffering servant songs (see appendix 7 for specific references). They are a nonanxious, nonreactive presence, as it is called. They see the power that transformation brings to lives and to churches and engage people as partners. Their enthusiasm and positive spirit set the tone of renewal.

Pastors stay focused as servants through the spiritual disciplines. The life of prayer strongly influences the work of a pastor as a servant leader. We cue into signals to determine when the right time has come. If there is anxiety or hesitation, we wait. If there is inner peace, we go. Acts of service become a spiritual journey of being guided by God. Thomas Kelly says, "I find He never guides us into the intolerable scramble of panting feverishness."[2] Growing in the manner of the servant is a spiritual journey for pastors. Renewal calls for growth in faith and in a sense of God's timing.

Traits of a servant leader. Pastors stand at a pivotal point as servants and servant leaders in a congregation. Leadership is a calling and a trust that is an energizing, creative, dynamic, and stabilizing force in a congregation. Leadership must be clearly defined in the pastor's mind, even as he or she enlists the teamwork of others in the purposes of the church. Pastors are called to be servants of Christ and servants of those in their care. When pastors serve, they connect the spiritual focus with the practice of ministry.

Pastoral leadership done in the style of a servant has a number of traits. Servant leadership is a very active style. Servant leaders have a clear sense of their own identity. They understand the call and claims of Christ and have a view of the body of Christ and the church. Pastors are spiritual leaders. Committed to the care entrusted to them, they know nothing happens if nothing is done. Recognizing this, pastors respect their own identity and that of others. They come to realize that God values them and all as partners.

Entering the dialogue. As servants, pastors listen. Pastors enter dialogue with people so they feel affirmed and get involved in the conversation. Assisting them to deal with inner conflicts and questions of faith, pastors help them get to know who Jesus is for their lives. Rather than telling people what to do or forcing the issue, servant pastors have a gentle manner. They have a sense of timing and peace. They sacrifice for others rather than trying to win a name for themselves. As servant leaders, pastors grow in humility and poise. Their ministerial practice takes on a form and a spirit of service as they fulfill their calling and help the church in its faith journey.

Lifting up all. Pastors as servant leaders lift up all other people. Rather than just serving those who seem to have something to offer, pastors kneel and serve all those present in the church. They assist as people discover Jesus for themselves and help them as they set priorities and discover their mission. Keeping their eye on spiritual formation, pastors seek to develop healthy relationships and a healthy church.

Listening to the inner voice. Servant pastors can sense that little voice of inner guidance. They then make that phone call or respond to that inner nudging of the spirit. Rather than being a voice of the privileged, this voice comes to the humbled. Pastors realize that all people who follow Christ and his calling have such leadings and promptings. The question is whether or not they follow the guidance, take the time to do something, and not override the inner monitor that gives direction. In renewal, pastors follow this voice of inner guidance that steers them in a certain direction. As they do so, the rightness of the activity will seem uncanny even to them. Furthermore, they will ascribe the honor to God and know the reward of such service is genuinely humbling.

Pastors as Spiritual Guide

During the renewal process, pastors play a unique role as spiritual guide. Pastors can help set the pace spiritually, attend to the movements of God in consolation, and help lead the congregation on a journey of faith. Jesus was spiritually adept enough to know what to say to the woman at the well and how to guide her in issues to resolve her inner conflicts. From there she drank of the living water, left her water pot behind, and went to share the Good News in her hometown.

Similarly, pastors serve in a spiritual role, helping people be attentive to God's grace. Pastors can walk alongside others in their discovery of Christ. They can assist people to grow in first-person faith and guide congregations in their corporate spiritual formation. Revelation 7:17 points to the role of pastors and spiritual leaders as one of service and humility. They gain the rapport to be the shepherd who watches over others and goes to the springs of spiritual refreshment with them.

The spiritual role. In renewal, pastors take initiative to grow spiritually themselves, realizing they are among others who also desire to grow. This gives them firsthand experience of spiritual growth so they can speak authentically. Developing their spiritual life through spiritual disciplines leads to creativity, spiritual hardi-

ness, and maturity. Shaped by prayer, the pastor's ministry has the
energy, love, and patience needed in renewal.

Called into being shepherds, pastors observe the spiritual
growth of others. They encourage people in their disciplines and in
a thoughtful manner ask how their disciplines are assisting them.
They might mention something to a musician about a solo or
thank someone whose silent act of service speaks of their faith.
Noticing little things and being attuned to God at work in people's
lives, pastors can become spiritual guides. People ask questions;
they seek counsel. Pastors in renewal are attuned and respond in a
way that guides people to the next step. People begin to feel their
pastor is walking with them in the spiritual journey.

Renewal pastors affirm the ministry role of all who are believers. Having the pastor work with a renewal team underscores the
team's vital role in the renewal process and also their role in ministry. The more pastors become attuned to the team's spiritual role,
the more they both lead others to the springs and model the shepherd. Servant leaders nurture people in being disciples, then train
them in their ministry as apostles—those sent like the woman at
the well. In fact, pastors themselves can be inspired by what others
are doing. So, what we say here about pastors holds for all God's
people in ministry, serving, going with, and leading others to the
springs.

Being attentive to God's movement. In the renewal process
we become attentive to the invitations of God's grace in our lives.
Renewal attunes us to grace moments. People ask, "How do you
know which way to go? How do you figure out the Scripture?
Where is God leading? How do I make a decision?" The answers
cannot be programmed or copied. The answers are God's gifts.
Seeking becomes part of the process of being renewed day by day.
As pastors immerse themselves in prayer and as others do the same,
attentiveness grows. As spiritual leadership grows out of their
prayer life and practice of ministry, pastors learn to follow those
inner nudges of the Spirit.[3]

God reveals the spiritual path as pastors gather with the

renewal team, church leaders, and in informal settings to discern things of a personal or corporate nature. Pastors help people be faithful to God's gifts and to act—as risky as obedience might feel—in the moment. In terms of discernment, pastors constantly ask how they can get the head, the heart, and the faith journey together (see chapter 7). In being attentive to God's movements, pastors can assist individuals to be conscious of inner promptings in their daily life.

Celebrating the first steps of the journey of faith. Pastors focus on helping a church understand that it is on a journey of faith. God reveals the spiritual path. Often that takes times of waiting. A pastor can help people see that such waiting is intentional, is a season of preparation, and is renewal in and of itself. So in the renewal process, the pastor works with the team to help the church talk about spiritual growth and readiness and paves the way for spiritual disciplines. Perhaps a spiritual disciplines folder is created just for this purpose—to learn about waiting and readiness.

In turn the pastor assists people as they begin to explore what renewal means. Paul's definition from 2 Corinthians about being renewed by God on a daily basis sets the tone for a continuous, lifelong process. As a spiritual guide, the pastor helps people become comfortable talking about spiritual growth and helps them see how to go about such a journey. Being sensitive to people, affirming their thirst, and listening to their discoveries so far, pastors assist people to take the next steps. Affirming spiritual growth is part and parcel of the renewal process.

Growing in the journey of faith. In renewal, pastors are sensitive as people begin to make first steps and discover both the effort and the rewards. A spiritual guide helps them explore what they are discovering. People may share with the pastor about complexities they experience. Why aren't things going faster? How do you trust in God when things seem out of your control? When you think you are making progress, why do roadblocks emerge?

As pastors become attentive to the spiritual growth of individuals and the church, they make plans for such things as classes, workshops, and small groups on spiritual growth. As people gain new energy and excitement for their faith, they want to grow more. They ask questions. That is the time for pastors to pause and provide ministry. In ministry we know that we learn as much as we give. Sharing in the excitement of growth is truly a gift to behold. A spiritual synergy develops that is life-giving in the church.

Pastors Facilitating the Renewal Process

Along with being spiritual guides and servant leaders, pastors have a crucial role in guiding the renewal process. With the renewal team having a facilitating function, a pastor works with other church staff, as well as church leaders, to guide the process. Renewal is labor intensive. While supporting other leaders, pastors serve in communication, organization, and administration. As the congregation works together, the work of renewal pays huge rewards as a ministry plan is put into place and is implemented in mission.

Communication role. One central role of pastors as servant leaders is communication. We saw that in terms of implementing dialogue throughout conversations. Communication begins with getting the word out. That can be done informally by word of mouth. With a renewal team, the circulated word is multiplied (the pastor is not the only one communicating). But communication also means building a formal system for getting the word out. This moves the church up the life cycle by including everyone. Both informal and formal contacts should be made repeatedly.

In a pastor's communications, the roles of spiritual guide and servant should be represented. The letter that appears earlier in this chapter is an example of how a pastor can both inform people of what is happening and build enthusiasm. At the same time, I was able to integrate the renewal process with other events in the life of the church and show coordination with the rest of the church leaders. Renewal takes a lot of encouragement. In the tone of a servant, the pastor needs to guide, not tell. The tone of all communications makes a big difference.

The pastor often has a lead article in the newsletter that references the renewal work. Then the pastor works on the renewal page with the renewal team to ensure that everything needed is included. In a similar way, the pastor can refer to the renewal effort in board reports, informal conversations, and congregational meetings. All settings become opportunities to keep people apprised. As servant leaders, pastors find which method of communication works best for individuals. It is important to note that emails generally need a follow-up personal contact, like a telephone call or personal visit, to ensure the communication is complete. When communication breaks down, people feel excluded and unwanted. Including everyone builds energy in the process.

Organizational role. Pastors are integral in the overall design and implementation of the renewal process. Being in the unique role they are as spiritual leaders, they can build on the trust of the congregation. Using all their training and experience, pastors can help tailor the design of the renewal process for their church. How will the church enter the spiritual journey? How will dialogue be taught? The renewal team called? The renewal team trained? And so on.

From there pastors are crucial in terms of setting up congregational gatherings by including people, communicating details, and seeing to the smooth flow of the process. The pastor's energy and enthusiasm makes all the difference and supports the efforts of other leaders as well. Part of the pastor's role is to draw others in—to participate, to grow, to become servants themselves. Having an organized renewal process makes everyone feel included; they can clearly see where they can get involved and what the next steps will be in the renewal process.

The administrative role. Administration is a crucial part of building a healthy church. Administration means balancing people and programs, budgets and resources, and the emphases of various ministries. In fact, renewal is as much an art as a science. Leadership in renewal is listening to God, discerning the movements of God, and letting God direct. Some administration is coordination, following up emails with phone calls, checking meeting agendas, and writing memos. While seemingly mundane, administrative work can become spiritual work as people talk about their interests and concerns and faith. In the artist's role, pastors shape a spiritual journey.

Now, pastors certainly do not do all this administration on their own. In fact, part of the faith journey is shaping teamwork with others and drawing resources together. In renewal there is a fair amount of detail work, such as creating spiritual disciplines folders, making an extra page in the newsletter, and doing follow-up phone contacts. As servants, pastors invite others to be servants. Sometimes, despite best-laid plans, things do not work out. Rather than rescuing everything, pastors try to find a way to turn failure into a growth experience. In this way, administration becomes a ministry in its own unique way and can bring renewal as people deal with the realities of what renewal means in a church.

Worship and Preaching in a Renewing Church

As Bush Creek Church underwent renewal, the worship event on Sunday morning became more central to the life of the congregation. As people invested in ministry, a greater need for worship developed. Affirming the ministry of everyone, the church found the effectiveness of the spoken word in renewal. In the second year of the plan for ministry at Bush Creek, worship was identified as a focal area to assist the renewal of the congregation. Let us look at the ministry of worship, the purpose of worship, our approach to preaching for renewal, and the anointing of the servant in the Word.

The ministry of worship. The spirit and climate of worship services is especially important. This can start as people arrive. A parking-lot ministry can be developed for greeting people. Churches can be coached not to do business on Sunday morning so members do not use fellowship time to "catch people" to ask them to do something. Emails or phone calls during the week are less intrusive on worship and more effective in getting things accomplished. With a focus on worship and building up the church, everyone can be attentive to others, offer encouragement, and welcome newcomers. Such items of atmosphere and context can be the focus of a worship committee working with the pastor. Excitement and intentionality increase in worship services as the church gives attention to renewal.

Pastors play a key role in worship. In worship planning the pastor can take into account each detail of the service so everyone can follow along easily. The pastor can work with a worship committee to set the tone of services in terms of hoped-for outcomes.

The purpose of worship. In renewal some churches have taken up the study of the purpose of worship and have made important discoveries. In Isaiah 6, the prophet experiences five elements of worship: praise, confession, pardon, challenge, and response. While studying praise, churches discover the need for those five elements. The order of worship can incorporate all five, maintaining integrity in worship. There is a flow of the faith experience moving from praising God to encountering the Good News to being renewed to leaving ready to move into mission.

The liturgy or a music team can move from praise to the Lord to asking God for forgiveness during a time of confession. Then the affirmation of God's grace and pardon prepares us to receive a challenge. At its heart, worship speaks to the dynamic of transformation. Worship moves to the challenge of the message and the people's response to go in mission. Training in the purpose of worship for all involved is helpful. Having one theme that emerges out of the biblical text and message adds unity and impact to the service.

Preaching for renewal. In renewal, preaching the Good News is important. Jesus set the tone of the inauguration of his own ministry by preaching good news to the poor, release to the captives, and freedom for the oppressed. Good news should be in the forefront of any sermon, particularly for a congregation desiring new life.

James Forbes, a master in homiletics, advises placing the power and hope of the biblical text early in the sermon.[4] He begins a sermon by reflectively repeating some words from the Bible text that cast the entire sermon in the biblical record. Then he develops the theme. While Good News does not mean everything is okay, it does mean there is hope in Jesus Christ and salvation from exilic despair. Preaching plays an important role in setting the tone.

Connecting preaching and the spiritual disciplines. Preaching in renewal is rooted in the spiritual journey of the pastor and the church. In *Spiritual Life and the Foundation for Preaching and Teaching,* John Westerhoff sums up how preaching is based on an active faith: "Prayer is our awareness of the movement of God toward us in which we open our hearts, minds, and wills to God by first listening and then responsively moving toward God so that we might grow in that relationship."[5] There will be a direct correlation between our prayer life as pastors and our preaching in the pulpit. The more we commune with God in prayer, the more creative, sensitive, and powerful are our sermons. The rewards of the disciplines are many in ministry.

Preaching grows out of disciplines like worship. Richard J. Foster speaks of heart preaching that goes on to enflame the spirit of worship.[6] Preaching grows right out of the ministry of renewal. Because one is growing in obedience and seeking to be guided by the Word, the great themes of Scripture come alive. Preaching speaks of God active in our lives. The energy and movement of renewal is felt in a spirit that communicates good news.

Preaching and dialogue. In renewal, there are a number of considerations for the pastor in terms of preaching. Preaching can never be done as a monologue. The renewal pastor gives special attention to engagement of the listener with the Scripture. James Forbes suggests asking permission. When preaching on the woman at the well, I ask, "Do I have your permission to draw a little closer to this text and come down to the well right now?" Certainly people will give such permission, and they become involved in the dialogue as if right at the well with Jesus. People become engaged dialogically in their spiritual journey. In this way, they can be transformed by the preaching moment.

With so much focus on dialogue, Reuel Howe wrote a book on preaching entitled *Partners in Preaching: Clergy and Laity in Dialogue*. Howe suggests that in preaching the pastor listen dialogically. Howe says we "find out what people bring to us in the way of questions, hypotheses, affirmations, and doubts; and our communication, whether formal like a sermon or informal like a conversation, should include these as part of its context."[7] Such engagement in preaching allows people time to answer the questions posed for response in the message. There can be well-placed pauses that invite the listener to engage in the message. This builds presence in communication.

Preaching and the renewal process. A pastor may wonder how preaching can specifically intersect with the renewal process. The pastor can preach a series of sermons that builds on the themes in the spiritual disciplines folder week to week. The planning will become evident and the daily Scripture readings will support the theme. Pastors can include discoveries of their own spiritual growth, as well as the spiritual growth of the church. They can affirm the way people are following their disciplines. Preaching for response, the pastor invites the church to take its next step in a deeper spiritual walk.

In a similar way, messages can include interpretation of what is happening in the renewal process. There is a tie between entering the spiritual journey of renewal and the way Abraham went out on a journey of faith and the disciples left their nets to follow Jesus. We can look at the parallel of the fruit of the Spirit Paul speaks about in Galatians 5:22 and the gifts of the church. The great commission expresses inclusion and involvement in renewal. Themes on agape love point to balancing people needs and program needs. The pastor can encourage people to catch the spirit of the early church, where people broke bread in their homes daily and were very active in their mission. Preaching is not an add-on to renewal, but integral to the transformation of the church.

The practicum of preaching. How do you go about the preparation and practice of preaching? The goal is to have sermons with a central thesis that speaks to a human need. From servant leadership and transformation, we are servants of the text and see how its message can transform us. We study the text, review key words, and explore the setting in which it was written. We ask what message we find in the text. What is the Good News? How did this apply to the readers at the time it was written?

In turn we study the text for its application today. How does the text speak to individuals and issues? How does the Good News in the text speak to this situation? What would people do if they said, "Lord, I want to follow in your path"? In preaching courses, Forbes has his students write in one sentence the message of the biblical text for the day.

Writing, practicing, and praying the sermon. When writing a sermon, my practice is to follow the techniques of Forbes, who says to begin by stating just one phrase of the Scripture, the central portion. Then pause and visibly ponder its meaning. Then I state the key points with one word each in a slow manner to give time for the listener to think. In the example from the John 4 passage on the woman at the well, I discerned four dynamics we've been discussing: thirst, encounter, transformation, and mission (see Introduction). Such a list gives pegs on which the listener can hang content. The Good News can be stated in an inviting manner with room for the listener to respond. Rather than starting with the antithesis, start with the thesis, state the outcomes if followed, and give the invitation of God's grace.

Just as important is the practice of sermon preparation. Early Sunday morning, I walk with the sermon. Something within the walking energizes the movement, shows what parts slow the sermon down and what parts need refinement. A last-minute touch-up helps. All this helps the sermon become a dialogue instead of a lecture. I become less tied to the manuscript and can enter the presence of the moment.

Prayer is effective preparation. Howe suggests prayer for the people, "putting them in God's hands, interceding for their cares, and pleading for their peace, asking God to love them through you."[8] Does the closing of the sermon invite response? Returning to the opening presentation of the gospel, the pastor can invite people to respond to the message of hope. With all this prayer, preparation, and practice, significant transformation can occur in the preaching and worship hour.

Being anointed. A special blessing available to pastors involved in the ministry of renewal is taking part in a service in which they are anointed to preach. In anointing there is intentionality, prayer, and urgency. Words prayed over the pastor usually include those of Paul to Timothy to preach the Word in season and out of season. Pastors in renewal understand the importance of proclamation in all seasons of renewal. Being anointed, preachers do not preach on their own power or prowess. Anointing comes as hands are laid on one's head and the messenger is lifted by God's Spirit in preparation and in the preaching moment. There is power in such preaching.

In *The Holy Spirit and Preaching*, Forbes writes, "If we preach out of the experience of the anointing such as is described in Jesus the Christ, and if we appreciate the nurturing that shapes our very lives, and if we experience the Spirit as a collaborator in the process of normal preparation, we can expect to receive the text and the message that is sent by God."[9]

Providing the Ministry of Encouragement

Congregations in renewal often need a lot of encouragement. Perhaps they have been through difficult experiences or have become discouraged by factors like people moving away due to change in employment. Maybe the congregation has been through rough waters of conflict or just stagnant for a period. Churches can feel bruised and vulnerable. They might ask what is wrong with them. Pastors can uphold them and look for what is unique and good in them. The ministry of encouragement affirms the priesthood of all believers and helps churches walk through the challenges in order to grow. There will be times that will call for spontaneous prayer or a follow-up call.

Pastors in renewal have the opportunity to minister on a personal level to those who feel hurt, frustrated, or alone. Renewal opens up relationships as people grow. People are often more receptive than you might imagine when they see there is a possibility of growth and a path to take. Decline of churches often results in outcasts who, like the woman at the well, feel alone. Such people need to be drawn back into the life of the church. They may need to be connected with others in a small group.

Pastors in renewal need to be positive, enthusiastic, and affirming. Time is needed to generate a climate for renewal. A pastor seeks to find small openings to encourage people. As people make new discoveries in their faith, the pastor can encourage them to share what is happening. Such inner development goes along with growth in the church.

Rather than be drug down by cycles of decline, the pastor can be realistically positive. Pastors in renewal need patience in order to stick with the process. In the life cycle of the church, any crisis can be an opportunity for new life. The spirit of the pastor is very important. Pastors help people as they deal with the challenges of life. As pastors believe in them, people are more likely to take up the renewal work.

Encouraging active leaders. Pastors in renewal have the opportunity to minister to a set of people that can easily be overlooked: the active leaders. Often they are shouldering a heavy load in the church. While they may seem to need little care, they have needs just as great as others and need support and encouragement and the pastor's permission to pace their efforts. Servant ministry can cause active leaders to be overextended, which does not serve them or the church well.

Pastors in renewal work right alongside active leaders. One of the great helps in the renewal process is that pastors do not work alone. They work with a renewal team. This gives not only pastors but also lay leaders the support and encouragement they need to accomplish the mission of the church. Often church leaders mention the joy in leading the renewal process and realize their pastor can't do without others who have a heart for renewal.

Encouraging participation from everyone. Pastors can also support others, both active and inactive, who catch on to the renewal process. As the renewal got underway at Bush Creek, I will never forget the day I walked into my Sunday school class when one of the newer members was teaching. I heard the class grappling with concepts I had never thought about. I felt I needed to be there as a student and catch up with the class.

When people begin to participate and bring their gifts, renewal gets exciting and challenging. New people feel included and interaction with others enriches everyone. Such growth is a real sign of refreshment at the springs.

❧

In this chapter we have looked at pastoral leadership as transformational and how spiritual leadership is at the heart of the pastor's servant role. While we do not underestimate the importance of others to the spiritual growth and renewal of a church, we do want to affirm the role of the pastor as an agent of new life. Throughout this chapter we have looked at how pastors can be spiritual guides and assist others in that role. We also looked at how they can help guide the renewal as they work with people and committees, such as the renewal team. Pastors help equip people for ministry. In all of this, pastors can find a rewarding role in renewal that is at the heart of what ministry entails.

For Reflection and Discussion

1. Pastors play a key role in the renewal of a congregation. Can you see the truth to this statement? How does the role of servant leadership impact the pastor's job?

2. The pastor as spiritual guide is a seemingly new but actually traditional function of leadership. What are your reflections on this role? Who have been the spiritual guides in your life?

3. We looked at the role of worship and preaching in a renewing church. How could your church use these two to aid the

204   Springs of Living Water

renewal process? What about the need for confession in services as well as pardon, challenge, and response?

4. Can you attest to the outcome of encouragement by pastoral leadership and others in the church? How can the renewal team join in this important endeavor?

5. Church renewal calls on every discipline of pastoral ministry. Reflect on this statement.

11

Developing Healthy Churches

Green Tree Church of the Brethren outside Philadelphia experienced dramatic spiritual renewal through the Springs process. Much happened in a relatively short time. Once the church began the spiritual disciplines folders, people began to find a focus. The church decided to call a renewal team, calling it the Green Team. Usually I like people to take time to think over things, but I found they were eager to commit on the spot to this endeavor. Sixteen people responded. A "Green Page" was established in the newsletter to carry notices of congregational gatherings, minutes of the Green Team, and results of the renewal effort (see appendix 9). The Green Team reported regularly to the board and asked for suggestions about upcoming direction and events.

As we moved to a second disciplines folder, this time on the spiritual disciplines themselves, the church felt more strongly than ever that things were heading in the right direction. This folder, entitled "A Closer Walk," had weekly topics built on the twelve classic spiritual disciplines explained in *Celebration of Discipline*. Daily Bible readings came from its study guide[1] (see appendix 10). Each worship service had a skit and a sermon on the discipline of the week. Four Sunday school classes studied the disciplines: junior high, senior high, young adult, and an elective class. Two congregational gatherings were held, one on strengths of the church and another on spiritual appreciation. Training was done for callers and small-group leaders. The Green Team did a wonderful job calling every family in the church, including all inactive families. There was excellent response.

The congregants sensed they were more together because everyone was united in their efforts of prayer and spiritual disciplines. This began to align the church in its spiritual journey. There was new energy and increased financial giving. The church affirmed its strengths in the first congregational gathering and was ready to begin the self-study part of the renewal process. The renewal team was a great help in creating the spirit of new life. As the process continued, the church gained the vision that it was called to be a faith center for the community. Intentionality developed; there was a mission to accomplish. A spiritual foundation had begun to be established for the work that was to follow with a permanent pastor.

Healthy Systems

The spiritual journey of transformation is the foundation for building a healthy church. How can a healthy church be fostered? Family systems work can help in this regard. A church functions as an emotional system. Rather than being machines to be fixed or computers to be programmed, churches are vibrant bodies with many dynamics at work. Systems that entail human factors are described in the work of Murray Bowen and Edwin Friedman, as well as George Parsons and Speed Leas. Ronald Richardson describes family systems for congregations in *Creating a Healthier Church*, which could be used for study.[2] Rather than thinking of individuals, we think of systems that have developed over a long period and take time to be transformed. It is not just individuals that need to be healthy, but also systems.

The body of Christ is more than just individuals and even more than the sum of the parts. Early in my ministry I heard James Glasse, president of Lancaster Theological Seminary, share about visiting a home for dinner. There he took a healthy portion of spaghetti noodles and put plenty of sauce on top. As he began to eat, he noticed that when he pulled on a noodle at one end of the plate, a seemingly disconnected noodle wiggled at the other end. The only thing in between was all that "mush." In a similar way, a church is a dynamic body. Because everything is connected, when bad decisions are made and unhealthy ministries are launched, everything is affected. Hidden agendas are at work. Transformation is needed to be true to Christ and be a healthy church.

Parsons and Leas encourage understanding a congregation as a system in this way: "Thinking systematically means that the parts of the whole take into consideration the needs of the other parts and the needs of the system as a whole. But there's more. Systemic thinking assumes multiple causes—not a simple cause; it assumes that there are many contributing factors to any given set of circumstances."[3] Unhealthy systems invite dysfunction, so factors must be addressed so that health returns. Transformation of a church takes time and concerted effort. In renewal, our approach is made at a multitude of levels in a spiritually focused way to create a healthy environment in which energy is utilized in a system that works in a positive way to accomplish its mission.

The role of anxiety. In church renewal work, one quickly becomes aware of the level of anxiety in a congregation. If there is decline, there is anxiety about where all this is heading. If the budget is not met and uncertainties such as changes in the community are present, there is anxiety. If there is a significant level of conflict, there is certainly anxiety. And anxiety provokes anxiety.[4] In systems work, all this is not the cause of one or two people but occurs within the system of the church. We don't always find out from where all the anxiety stems. What we know is that all human systems must process emotional energy. What is important is how we react to anxiety. Humans react either consciously or unconsciously.

Interim time is certainly an anxious period for any church. Congregations that have lost a pastor go through a grieving process that feels like being uprooted. What about all the fond memories? What about the pain of separation? How will we get a new pastor? Are we going to get the "right" pastor? Transitions are anxious times and remind us of aging. Whereas people note changes according to how many birthdays they have celebrated, churches often note their age by the pastor under which something happened. In his semi-nars, Loren Mead calls interim "prime time for renewal."[5] Anxiety invites us to God. As we pour out our hearts and release all to God, we open our lives to God and find we are guided into confidence.

Nonanxious through faith. How we respond to anxiety is impor-tant. In systems thinking, leaders are to be a nonreactive, nonanx-ious presence. How do we do that? If the renewal process shows anything, it is that, by going deeper in faith, pastors and leaders can turn over their anxiety to God and discover the peace of the servant. From the suffering servant songs in Isaiah (see appendix 7 for spe-cific references), the servant leads from a heart of peace.

Pastors engaged in spiritual disciplines will be more able and equipped to provide a calming influence through preaching and to provide a nonanxious presence through uncertainties that arise in a congregation. By drawing forth that same peace, a congrega-tion will become more able not to react, but to be creative in meeting the challenges that come. In fact, it will be able to dis-cern a vision and a plan of renewal and implement the plan. This is being proactive and transformational.

As a congregation enters a faith journey in the renewal process, it begins to find its way. Continuously the congregants ask, "Where is God leading us?" With that question asked and answers discerned, they begin to feel more of the presence of God. Their thirst begins to be quenched, and they feel the companionship of Jesus. Out of this experience they feel their own inner life trans-formed. They see people in a different light.

Through dialogue, new understanding develops. People become even more grateful for one another. As they develop a focus and mission, they gain a sense of purpose and direction. Peter Steinke talks about not becoming a host for anxiety by keeping our focus and mission sharp and by being mature and thoughtful.[6]

Responding to anxiety through renewal. Renewal is not just something a committee does in its work, but is a very important process to help churches be proactive and become transformed into healthy churches with an urgent mission.

Quite a number of factors determine how a congregation responds to a new anxiety. As we might expect, there is a mathematical equation at work: the greater the anxiety, the greater the chance of reactivity. In fact, anxiety can escalate not just arithmetically but exponentially. Anxiety creates anxiety.

A church can feel more vulnerable at times of change, even if the change is for new life. Situations handled in a calm manner are stored in one's memory. Unearthed, positive examples can lead to confidence in handling present problems creatively. Handling current anxiety is one place where knowing a church's history can be very helpful.

In one congregation I sensed there was something like birth trauma affecting them adversely. When I investigated I found that this congregation had a heritage of difficulty working at problems. At the first hint of controversy, one side would accuse the other side of heresy. However, the church also had a tradition of deep, abiding faith that helped their ancestors deal with strife, war, deportation, fraud, poverty, and relocation. It was going to take this same deep faith to lead the church to take the next step past their anxiety and conflict. Once the pain was named and the history reviewed, the congregation was able to heal wounds and choose to operate in a different way. There was new focus, and the spiritual journey flourished in the renewal process.

Triangles. Nothing can lead to entanglement in a church like a third party being drawn into a conversation between two people. Triangles are created when someone goes to a third party rather than dealing directly with another individual about a concern.

Triangles can be for good or ill. In negative triangles, a third party creates further anxiety by also complaining about the individual. Triangles become entangled when they interlock and more people talk to others about the situation.

Positive triangles are created when the third party tries to create understanding and points the person back to the individual with whom there is the concern. They practice the message of

Matthew 18, encouraging others to go to their brother or sister with a situation. They might also protect the person in question, such as mentioning that he has been under stress with a family illness that no one was aware of in the church. Approaching this person in the spirit of love could bring resolution. The anxiety is curbed. Such positive action builds up the Christian community.[7]

In renewal, the challenge is to enact the positive traits of the servant, such as love, and build up relationships. People soon realize that if someone will not join in the negative talk about someone else, this same person will not talk about them in a negative way behind their back. Trust is gained. The signal goes out that it is appropriate to go and talk with someone directly about a concern. Each such interaction affords the opportunity to reposition oneself in triangles by helping people focus on their own anxiety and thereby remove themselves from taking sides.[8] While triangles are a natural way to interact, the challenge is to create a calmer, less anxious, less reactive church. The love of the servant builds up the body.

Separate yet connected. Through dialogue, healthy churches attempt to keep building relationships. In systems theory, it is important to be your own person while also staying connected with others. How can we be our self, what is called self-differentiated, yet be connected? When a system is healthy, people's identities are built up and anxiety is not allowed to enter and destroy the body. In this way you can be your own person and still stay connected.

Dialogue moves us in the right direction. In dialogue we each have different ideas, but we stay connected and actually affirm that the outcome of discussion is a solution more right than either party brings to the table. Dialogue helps prevent triangulation. Rather than a pattern of going around another person, dialogue creates a model for people to engage directly. The third party can reconnect people and, using dialogue, help them focus on solutions.

Besides staying connected, servants stay self-differentiated in an unusual way. While at first sight we might think servants become fused with their master, actually they adopt a style that delineates them in a specific role. In a real sense, it takes a stronger person to serve. By rendering themselves up to God, they serve others through faith. The servant discovers a power and freedom that leads them to be effective. Being a chosen servant, they point themselves and others to the vision to which the church is called. By staying connected with God and others, they move everyone to greater strength and mission.[9]

A Special Unit on Conciliation

Once a church has gained sufficient focus and new energy, it may wish to focus on a particular topic. In the church renewal process described in chapter 2 and in appendix 1, there is time for special units—either in the self-study portion of the process or while a renewal plan is being implemented. Church leaders and the renewal team can discern when such a unit will be helpful.

Special units can play different functions by lifting up the faith journey, educating the congregation in a special area of ministry, creating understanding to build greater unity, and propelling the renewal process forward. For example, one church renewal team worked with the church on conciliation, which moved the renewal process forward.

Discerning a special unit. Before entering a renewal process, a church and the executive of its district need to look at the level of conflict to see what interventions need to be made. The church with the unit on conciliation had already had the help of consultants before it entered the renewal process. Because an even greater level of unity was desired, the renewal team decided to have a unit on conciliation and renewal, which led to deeper transformation.

The team decided to invite a conciliator who could teach more on this topic and also facilitate any remaining conciliation work. One rule of thumb for pastors is that it is tough to do the work of mediation and be viewed as neutral. Since pastors need to minister to all people, it is wise to call in a conciliator or mediator and do it early rather than let things fester. Much spiritual discernment goes into such an effort.

Designing a pattern for growth. With renewal well underway in this church, the renewal team sought a spiritually oriented person with a deep respect for people who also knew how to use dialogue. Along with having this guest preach, the renewal team decided to have two congregational gatherings, one with prayer and one on conciliation. The conciliator strongly supported setting the ministry of conciliation in the context of prayer and then having a gathering on the topic.

The congregational gatherings were tailored to fit the needs of the congregation on its faith journey. Michelle Armster, the conciliator consultant, had everyone look at various Bible passages in which conflict emerged so they could see how people worked through those situation. She had us look at conciliation in Matthew 18:15-20 and asked, "What is conflict? How do you go about resolving it? How do you apply this to the church today?"

Discovering holy ground through Scripture. Michelle also had the group look at the story of the woman caught in adultery in John 8:1-11. Jesus, by speaking truth and mercy, got the group to face the situation and resolve things in an extraordinary way. In Galatians 2:11-14, after noting, "He and others hid their true feelings so well that even Barnabas was fooled," Paul corrected Peter "in front of everyone" (CEV). In Acts 15 men came from Judea to the church in Jerusalem, teaching that believers had to be circumcised. With the trouble created, Paul and Barnabas and a few others were sent in as mediators.

Michelle talked about how conciliation in Scripture led to growth. Conflict can be constructive; it just depends on our reactions. Constructive conflict might mean acting differently than our emotions dictate. If we know we have only part of the truth and affirm that others have part of the truth, we can find the best solution with everyone being involved. In Acts 15, all were given opportunity to speak, then they were silent. God gave Peter a voice to speak, and after an agreement was forged, they went out and spread the gospel. Michelle said that conflict can be holy ground, with God in the midst.

Traits of a Healthy Church

When a church enters the growth side of the life cycle (see chapter 1) new vigor is evident. Entering the spiritual journey of renewal, the church begins the path to new vitality. People become excited about what is happening. They are amazed that it takes greater output of energy to be in decline than to be healthy. In health, energy is received, and the work is rewarding. We can identify a number of traits of a healthy church: strength at the center, healthy boundaries, ethics of congregational life, and being involved in urgent, Christ-centered mission.

Strength at the center. In the stage of gaining energy, building relationships, and starting program, a congregation develops a very important trait for a healthy church: strength at the center. *The Inviting Church* by Roy Oswald and Speed Leas defines strength at the center as basic integrity and vigor in the church's life. They discovered that growing congregations have a keen sense of identity and what is unique to them.

In these healthy churches, there was an invigorating spirit. "The message the church proclaims is central to this identity," Oswald and Leas write. "When it knows that its basic enterprise is to proclaim a message of faith, hope, and love to the world, and it is doing it, it feeds its people with bread and not a stone. No amount of propaganda or organization will cover a lack of substance at the core."[10]

How do you build strength at the center? As the spiritual focus is set, people begin to feel united through the spiritual disciplines. They speak of their growing spiritual journey. As the renewal team goes to work, dialogue is held up as premium, and people begin to communicate at a deeper level. That brings unity. Training leaders and the congregation in servant leadership and church renewal, churches begin to think about leadership, which brings inner strength. Strength at the center develops as the church moves through the renewal process. A new vigor is felt; a positive spirit grows.

In the revitalization process, we specifically discover core values and discern the identity of a church. Identifying core values helps a church to know what it believes in and works together to accomplish. What makes this congregation distinctive, and what has God uniquely called this church to be in this location? The steps of discerning a Bible passage, vision, plan, and implementing the plan bring unity at the core. This basic unity conveys that things are together, dialogue is happening, and something life-giving is stirring. There is hope, purpose, and living water!

Establishing boundaries. Establishing boundaries is a crucial part of establishing identity. A healthy church has a set of boundaries that are named. Some think that the more "anything goes," the more inclusion and diversity there is, but this does not prove to be so. There is a critical need for knowing that some things are acceptable and others are not. Violating other individuals is unacceptable, as is pulling down the body. Healthy systems develop boundaries, respect, Christian love, and positive relationships.

In the book *Boundaries*, Henry Cloud and John Townsend write that, most simply, "boundaries are anything that helps to differentiate you from someone else, or shows where you begin and end."[11] Rather than thinking about walls, Cloud and Townsend write that "property lines [need to] be permeable enough to allow passing and strong enough to keep out danger."[12] In fact, they argue that the concept of boundaries comes from God, who is responsible for the divine but limits what is allowed. In the story of the woman at the well, we saw how Jesus showed respect for the woman as a person who was of value rather than affirm the prejudices against her.

Boundaries are needed for a healthy church, and each church must decide on its boundaries. Expressing your own point of view in a respectable way is acceptable, as long as you listen to others and their point of view, treating them as equally valid.

Dialogue in the church renewal process is a great help in setting boundaries. People learn how to communicate with one another even if they have different points of view. The better the boundaries in the church, the stronger the center. Communication and respect flow back and forth.

The challenge in setting boundaries is to allow different points of view but still stay in relationship. Boundaries extend to all areas of the church's life, with everyone doing their part, following up, and being responsible with their calling. Once people have talked about matters of healthy relationships, they feel much better. Those on the outside feel they will be able to come to the inside. With appropriate boundaries, they feel they can be creative. They can be partners and be valued. A healthy church is blessed with such understanding.

Establishing congregational ethics. In the same vein, a church needs congregational ethics. Often a renewal team helps a congregation name the values by which it lives and operates. As people explore needed boundaries, they find they should have a set of standards by which to live. Just as pastors have ethics, so congregations can have a set of guidelines that name the values, boundaries, and procedures by which they operate. A church may specify ethics for types of interaction, such as emails, triangulating, and practical matters. One businesswoman in a church said there are rules about emails at work, but she never thought of them in church communication. She expressed how helpful such ethics would be for the church.

The renewal team can explore the possibility of developing a congregational ethics paper.[13] Such a paper explores the appropriate boundaries in every area of a church's life. The renewal team may well engage the entire congregation to write the paper. This will create ownership for the standards. Ethics need to be regularly reviewed and updated to be incorporated as part of the life of the congregation. Ethics are established to keep communication flowing and people respected. They ensure that the gospel is lived out in a healthy church that attracts people.

Ethics papers often use Matthew 18 as a model: a person feeling offended goes to the offender directly in a spirit that attempts to lead to growth. In this way trust is built and understanding is created. The discussion of ethics can take you in many areas around which dialogue can occur and understanding is created. The challenge is to have a transformed congregation in which relationships are held in high regard and people work together so that members are responsible for themselves and do not violate others. Framing such an ethics paper in a positive manner can show the spirit of renewal.

Implementing an urgent, Christ-centered mission. With all the above in place, one of the best ways to develop a healthy church is to be involved in an urgent, Christ-centered mission. As churches discover who they are and where God is leading them, they gain a clear sense of direction and can devote their energy to accomplishing their mission. This certainly takes leadership and vigilance. With the renewal team guiding the mission forward, all the official and unofficial leadership bodies of the church are needed to accomplish mission. By working together and continuing to grow spiritually, a church can reflect its mission and do its mission. Being fruitful becomes a wonderful way in which to gain health and vitality.

Becoming New Vessels—Shedding Old Water Pots

Through the process of transformation, a congregation becomes so involved with living water that the entire focus turns to being new vessels. They become the vessels for noble use of which Paul speaks: "If a man therefore purge himself from these, he shall be a vessel of honour, sanctified, and meet for the master's use, and prepared unto every good work" (2 Timothy 2:21 KJV). Such vessels are priceless, and we cherish them—us—dearly. We use spiritual discernment to test how we can carry the gospel in these new vessels.

In chapter 1 we discussed the life cycle of a church. Here again we will use this model to explore how the renewing church takes up the cycle of growth. You can't just reverse decline; it takes total transformation. In this section we look at both what we *take up* and what we *give up* in the renewal process.

Key: E—energy; I—inclusion; P—program; A—administration;

	EIPA	eIPA	
EiPa		eIpA	
EIpa			eipA
Eipa			eipa

Transformed maturity. *Being vessels of focus, we give up being presumptuous.* Focusing on Christ, a renewing church senses it is on a mission to introduce others to the Savior. This mission takes one's total heart. Faith formation needs to be constantly tended in all areas of the church. To keep gaining new energy and keep on its mission, a church needs to keep asking, "Where is God leading?" Energy and spirit need to be fostered regularly. God does the renewing, so to keep in touch with God we continue spiritual disciplines, find experiences that strengthen our faith, and connect spiritual growth to all ministries. The renewal process becomes a pattern of being renewed by Jesus day by day, year by year.

With our focus on living water, one water pot we leave behind, like the woman at the well, is presumption. The moment we presume something will just happen, we enter the cycle of decline. "What happened?" someone asks. "We had such a friendly church." "We used to work together." "We feel tired." The internal formation of faith has given way to the externals, and a toll is taken on the spirit and relationships in the church. Just as soon as you think you have it together—that you have health and vitality—you are on the way to losing it. Martin Saarinen writes, "Growth can be aborted by succumbing to the seductive forces of presumption ('that couldn't happen to us') and despair (burnout)."[14] To keep on the growth side of the life cycle, take nothing for granted; renew continually day by day.

Transformed aristocracy. *Being vessels that balance, we give up overextending.* From the standpoint of keeping on the growth side of the life cycle, new vessels do what mission calls for in each situation. We use spiritual discernment to balance all we do as a church. With the head we make sure the practical things are covered. With the heart we test God's leading before moving forward. We make sure the ministry will lead to the next step in our faith journey. And we follow through, which gives integrity to decisions. We artistically work to design programs that fulfill ministry while keeping the needs of people in mind. We evaluate ministries for their effectiveness and viability. As a vessel for noble use, we maintain a high, positive spirit in all endeavors.

With our focus on living water, we leave behind the water pots of doing it all. Churches that rush to build programs often lose sight of the needs of people and soon find themselves without energy.[15] No longer do they have people willing to do what it takes to accomplish what they used to do in the church. Or maybe they just don't have the people, period. Look into signs of inertia, which causes class sizes to drop and a youth group to falter. The pot of doing everything loses its sheen. Beware of overextending.

Become attentive to God's leading. Discerning God's call and following it gives focus to energies and leads to carrying out what it means to be a faithful vessel. Saarinen writes, "These tendencies to proliferate and perform invest the energies of the congregation more in starting up programs and services than in following through."[16] Establish the policy to do only what you can follow up on and consider that small steps will lead to larger goals. Refuse the short-cut that looks like a bargain. Focus on living water and the priorities set in the renewal process and plan. Become a vessel that carries a mission on your heart and do your part to see that it is accomplished.

Transformed bureaucracy. *Being vessels that invite, we give up being closed to newcomers.* In renewal we are vessels constantly reaching out to others. Partaking of living water invites a listening ear and offers the message of hope. In the dialogue process encouraged by Springs, everyone is included. The church listens to God to discern its mission together. Transformation occurs as people reach out to everyone to share the gospel and to build up the body of Christ.

In terms of leadership, experienced people in the church mentor others who have talents for the task. Newsletter pieces, bulletin announcements, information on the church website, and all communication become more inviting and positive. Signs of energy reflect the state of the church. The cues show a church moving with living water. You can't stop the enthusiasm and the joy from drawing others in.

Because we want to share living water with others, we give up water pots that exclude others, such as being friendly only with friends but never with newcomers. Give up the comfort of tightly formed groups that not-so-subtly exclude others. Let go of the "good old boys" club, only consulting with certain people when decisions are made. Widen the "in-the-loop." Eliminate discussions in the church hallways in which people confide that they are doing things because "no one else will do them."

Ask others; invite others. By entering a renewal process, ask where God is leading. Develop a vision and invite others to join in. By consulting with someone new, you can become excited when you hear what they have to offer. Enter into a new day with what is possible with transformation of human hearts and renewed churches. Take on momentum and inclusion in order to share the living water with others.

Resurrected from death. *Being vessels of hope, we give up despair.* Living water offers hope; Christ is reaching out. Realizing that, a church can be born again. Having a mission of hope is God's invitation to flourish. The turnaround for the woman at the well was dramatic. She internalized a faith that led her to throw off the old and take on the new. And she did it by going back to her hometown. We can only imagine that, when she went, she did not saunter or dally. She went with a mission and with a vision. Her steps were intentional. She carried good news in her heart.

Give up the water pot of hopelessness that causes us to do nothing. Hopelessness leads to malaise, inertia, and loss of vision. Give up the sense of defeat. Give up the idea that "everything we do fails." Give up the downside in which people feed off the negativity of "how bad things are around here." Let go of a failure identity. The water pot of hopelessness is one to let go of forever.

Yes, we *can* give Jesus a drink. This church has something to offer. This church can be healthy again. This church can be transformed! Experience shows that it takes just one person to respond to the thirst and begin the movement to new vitality. The invitation of Scripture to be a servant reveals that even the least likely one is called by God to be the light to the nations. The resurrection provides the hope that the gospel message is about new life—abundant life for individuals and churches.

∽

Throughout this chapter we have looked at how to build a healthy church. We see how anxiety and fear drive the system down but how the renewal process builds new energy and helps the church learn healthy patterns for growth. A church may even have a special unit to enhance the health of the congregation. Establishing boundaries and ethics can help in establishing strength at the center. A Christ-centered mission helps a church become a new vessel and keep attuned to factors on the growth side of the life cycle. In this we live in hope, partaking and sharing living water.

For Reflection and Discussion

1. Reflect on the transformation of a church and what happened at Green Tree. Can you see the benefit of total immersion in spiritual growth? Can you see how that would impact an entire congregation?

2. As you look at the concepts of a healthy church, which ones resonate with you? Can you see how the traits of the servant can help create a healthy church?

3. What are your thoughts about the suggestion that conflict "is

not the cause of one or two people but occurs within the system of the church"? How does this change how a church approaches conflict?

4. Can you see how the vigor of a church is connected with setting boundaries? What avenue could your church use to create better boundaries? What about drafting an ethics paper to assist you in having dialogue on being a healthy church?

5. What tools of renewal could be used to transform the anxiety and replace it with a heart of peace?

6. What do you think about becoming vessels of new life? Can you see how the renewal process helps a church be transformed into a healthy vessel of hope?

12

Experiencing Deep Transformation

As we reflect on the woman at the well, we see how she went from her encounter with Jesus to being drawn to living water to exploring the deeper implications of what her newfound faith would mean. In renewal, both individuals and churches discover what a deep transformation means. The woman discovered that the source of new life was found not in externals but in internals. The well bubbling up with living water was within her. Authentic worship is in spirit and in truth. In a similar way, deep transformation of churches is in the heart.

Renewal in Ohio

The Northern Ohio District of the Church of the Brethren is made up of fifty-three congregations in the northern part of the state, stretching from the Indiana to the Pennsylvania borders. The story that follows shows the culmination of three years of work there. The result was that one third of the district churches became involved in the Springs renewal process. How did this happen? What motivated these churches to begin the hard but gratifying work of renewal?

For years John Ballinger, the executive of the district, had been out visiting with the pastors and churches to which he provided oversight. He was constantly in touch with the needs of people and met with groups of pastors on a regular basis. John had been tilling the ground for church renewal for many years.

The Church Life and Growth Committee of the district is

responsible for starting new churches and revitalizing existing congregations. As a servant leader, John had worked with the chairperson, the committee, and the district board to address the need for renewal in the congregations of his district.

Not by chance, I was introduced to John at the church's annual conference in 2004. Immediately I knew we were talking the same language. At this same conference an article I wrote, "Brethren, Let's Renew," was in the denominational magazine found in every delegate packet. God was at work, and small steps were taken to get renewal to the Northern Ohio district.

In the fall of 2004, conversations began within the district about renewal. We sent the Springs notebook for consideration to the district's executive committee. They were very excited after their meeting. They said the biblically based, servant-led model spoke to their need for a positive initiative. Early projections were for four to five churches to get involved, though a wider scope was under consideration. By early May 2005, Springs was received with enthusiasm by the district as the initiative of choice. Arrangements were made for me to meet with the executive committee of the district in early summer of 2005.

At that executive meeting, I listened to the needs of the district and its vision for renewal. I shared about Springs and explained the spiritual focus and steps of renewal. I learned about the strengths of the district and its active work in communities. The district planned for the churches to be formally introduced to Springs in the spring of 2006.

But then a denominational program arose. Small groups across the denomination were scheduled to meet to discuss the nature of the church. Because this process would be a helpful background to a renewal endeavor, we decided that rather than attempt to do two programs at once, we would postpone introducing Springs for a year. Timing is critical in renewal. A general principle in Springs is that if two things overlap, both suffer.[1] So while this denominational work was done on the nature of the church, groundwork was laid for renewal. God was at work.

The Northern Ohio District conference committee invited me to hold an insight session at its annual meeting in July 2006, at which thirty people came to learn about Springs. I stayed to answer questions and to be part of the district gathering.

Meanwhile John had read all the servant leadership material and was excited about the concept. He took the initiative to visit clusters of pastors and teach servant leadership. Rather than reteach those concepts at an initial Springs event, I would be able to build on John's work. What a great example of renewal in the making!

The Church Life and Growth Committee set April 2007 as the time to invite churches to send their pastor and several other people who would be part of the nucleus of a renewal team to learn about the Springs initiative. To encourage churches to participate, they built in incentives: giving free summer camp scholarships for churches to give to their youth and distributing free copies of *A New Heart and a New Spirit and Servant Leadership for Church Renewal*, which cover renewal topics.

The day of the event arrived and, while it would have been a good day if twenty people came, more than twenty churches were represented by more than a hundred people. Walking out to the parking lot, I saw people streaming into the church and was filled with emotion.

It was a full day, and one important component was a testimony of Glenn O'Donnell, a member of a renewal team from Green Tree Church of the Brethren, which had gone through the renewal process. Glenn shared that never before had his church examined topics of spiritual renewal in such depth. He spoke of the positive spirit generated as they focused on the strengths of the church.

After that day in April, John and the Church Life and Growth Committee continued to encourage churches to discern whether renewal was right for them. An informal meeting was held during the summer, and by fall of 2007, eighteen churches—one third of the district—committed to a three-year process of renewal. The district made renewal a major initiative.

Deep Transformation

Deep transformation of individuals and congregations happens at many levels and certainly not all at once. In fact, it can happen in stages and can entail continuous new life. If we talk about deep transformation, we probably would not know what it really means because we have not yet experienced it. "Transformed into what?" we might ask.

When we talk about congregations and deep transformation, what do we mean by transformation, especially deep transformation? By the very nature of such a question, we identify that something new has taken place. "The old is gone, the new has come" (1 Corinthians 5:17).

Transformation is at the heart of the story of the woman at the well. She became a totally new person in faith with a new understanding of relationships, which translated to a new mission for her life. The author of *Deep Change* distinguishes between incremental change, which is limited in scope and reversible, and deep change, which takes risks and surrenders control.[2] In deep transformation God does the transforming, calling us into the people we are meant to be and calling us into mission. We have a changed heart, take initiative, are biblically guided, enter into ministry, and carry hope in our heart.

Inner motivation. Transformation means heart change and gives inner motivation for the work of renewal. Motivation is complex because it involves people and requires a change of individual hearts. Low self-image, one avid interest, and hostility toward God are factors that block significant involvement in the church. People differ in their needs and in the ways they fulfill them. Lack of excitement in the faith may result when people feel their faith does not speak to their concerns. Motivation is a complex issue stemming from individuals' personal life and their understanding of faith. Motivation also deals with each individual's self-centeredness. Leaders know that they have the human condition to honor and to deal with if transformation is to occur.[3]

At its heart, transformation is a spiritual journey. The spiritual disciplines folders have played a key role in churches to encourage a corporate spiritual journey. In filling out their commitment sheet in the folder and asking God's help as they dedicate it, people become intentional about growing. Facing our human condition, we need confession as a spiritual discipline. In *Celebration of Discipline*, Richard J. Foster talks about confession as a change in relationship to God. For him, confession is both a grace and a discipline: a grace because unless God gives it, confession cannot be made; a discipline because there are things we must do and action we must take.[4]

In *Spiritual Classics*, the companion volume to *Celebration of Discipline*, Adolfo Quezada says that God helps us let go of unfilled dreams and expectations and go on to dream new dreams and hope new hopes. Letting go of control, we surrender all to the love and mercy of God. Trusting more deeply in God opens the way for the future.[5] The renewal process helps by gently inviting people to become more mature in the faith. Motivation takes root in the hearts of people who are living for Christ and also changes the character of the church as people work together to fulfill God's mission.

Taking initiative. Among the many benefits of servant leadership is that it nurtures people in a way that leads them to take initiative. By being listened to and heard, by being affirmed and cared for, and by being nurtured and spiritually fed, people begin to feel that they can do something—and they do! Transformation cannot last when it depends on prodding people. When people are served, they are more likely to have their faith central to their lives and to take initiative to actively become involved.

People in church renewal projects talk about this kind of deep transformation. They begin to feel that they can do something. They see a vision for their lives and for the church. They carve out new areas of possibilities. The church in the background comes to the foreground. The energy level goes up. People in the community soon see the church in a new way. Deep transformation encourages people to take initiative and then supports them in newfound roles.

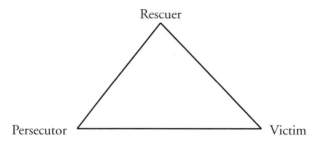

The Karpman drama triangle. The Karpman drama triangle helps us look at deep transformation.[6] In this triangle of human interaction, the rescuer in one corner becomes the persecutor in another corner, becomes the victim in the third corner. When things fail in renewal, we might be tempted to jump in and rescue everything. However, that sets up a dynamic in which we soon move to becoming the persecutor, putting pressure on others to do something. Finally, we end up as the "bad guy."

For transformation to really take hold, we must discover alternatives to rescuing things. This does not mean deserting the initiative. Rather, it means standing alongside people to help them look at alternatives. Many old patterns need to give way so that something new can come in their place. Being in the victim role is not helpful either and only invites dysfunction. Deep transformation is done by Christ and can be facilitated by placing things in his hands.

Deep transformation of the woman at the well occurred as Jesus stood with her and entered into dialogue, which helped her see that her life had value. In a real way she was caught at that time in the third corner of the triangle, a victim of circumstances and choices. As she responded to the spiritual thirst within her, she discovered living water, took it in, and had her entire life reoriented. In deep transformation we discover that Jesus is reaching out to us. By responding to him, we join as partners in his mission as the church. Our own deep transformation can lead to the deep transformation of others.

Being guided by a biblical text. A unique feature of the Springs renewal process is having churches discern a biblical text for renewal so they can see themselves in the Bible story and resolve their dilemmas in the light of God's grace. As explored earlier, churches find guidance for how to handle the present and move to the future through this guiding text. As churches discern a biblical text, they find a point of reference. They discover the very factors that lead to new life—I call them dynamics of renewal. Being a people of the book, the church discovers strength and freedom in following the wisdom of the text.

Deep transformation occurs as a church follows a text's guidance. The text is not just an add-on or something done and forgotten; in deep transformation a church comes back to the text again and again and becomes oriented. A church's understanding of the text deepens as it faces the challenges of living its message. The text leads to a vision and transforms the ministry plan from one that is built on human strength to one guided by the biblical message of promise and hope. Being guided by a biblical text is fundamental to deep transformation.

Ministry. The thrust of the work in renewal is to train all people—"saints"—to be in ministry. Ephesians 4:12 speaks of equipping God's people for the work of ministry so that the "body of Christ may be built up." Because Bush Creek needed an active church board with productive meetings, the renewal plan called for the pastor to meet with the board chairperson before each meeting to set the agenda and afterward to work with the board to implement decisions. The first agenda letters were signed by the chairperson and the pastor. Three years later, the chairperson formulated the letters, and the pastor was kept abreast of the board's work. People began to connect their faith journey with their ministry.

Wedding faith and ministry is Paul's vision in 2 Corinthians 5. In Christ, he says, we become new creations. No longer do we see people from a human point of view but from God's. The reconciled have a ministry of reconciliation. Paul understood spiritual transformation as active engagement in Christ's task of reconciling.

230 Springs of Living Water

We become servants of Christ. We become partners with Christ. When people discover and enact their ministry, deep transformation happens from within. They learn what being a servant entails. In fact, "service" (*diakonia*) is translated "ministry." To establish ministries we discern gifts and actively use people's gifts in ministry. (We will examine this theme in chapter 13.)

Resurrection hope. Our hope in the mystery of the gospel enlivens all our work. Even when the most defeating event occurs, we can step back and see the mystery in it. God raises to life what is painfully dead. We ask what the meaning of all this is. The Good News of the gospel is that God's love and grace surround us despite all the grief and pain we bear. Right within having it all figured out is the truth that nothing in the kingdom can be contained or programmed. God is at work taking the most human of efforts, the most unlikely situations, and the most unlikely people and making them what they can be for the sake of the kingdom.

My journals of renewal in local churches show many instances in which interventions of hope were made. Baptisms are one. One may wonder why people want to join a church still in formation. But it is getting into the spiritual journey that causes people to feel a call for their lives and makes them willing to be part of what is being born. The renewal process creates a readiness to take further steps, inspiring and motivating others in the church to take those steps.

Creating ministries for newcomers in the faith may not have been possible before renewal. Perhaps starting or invigorating the youth group, mission project, or personal spiritual growth would not have happened before the renewal process began. When people's attention and interest are focused, the mystery of the gospel brings new life. Churches begin to see that there are possibilities and that they have the tools for making them a reality. The renewal process also gives the training and guidance needed.

Transformation is evident as people experience resurrection hope. Renewal requires that we constantly stand on the side of hope, even when hope is challenged. When all is said and done, healthy life in a church is a miracle. Within the rules of consolation comes the wisdom to savor joy, express gratitude to God, and remember these moments and return to them often. Renewal is not an easy optimism, but is grounded in hope that the grave cannot hold what it cannot bind forever. The factors of renewal go deeper than developmental stages, church consultation techniques, and organizational development. The outcome of renewal is spiritually alive people. Renewal is a gift!

Transformed to New Life

Attending a youth work camp for Heifer International in Perryville, Arkansas, I discovered the library of Dan West, the founder of this worldwide endeavor to help feed the hungry. In his collection are materials about establishing training for the animal keepers, sending quality animals, and having the first offspring passed along to another family. One of the books that I found especially interesting described rebuilding the lives of men who had been in experimental projects of food depravation. When the study was completed, the men were offered food, but surprisingly, they didn't immediately start to eat. They didn't immediately resume their lives. They recovered only by rebuilding trust, receiving social support, and rediscovering life around them.

How can a church experience deep transformation? What does it take for a church to regain vitality prompted by God? Does it take a combination of factors to go through rebuilding? And what does it take for a growing church to offset the seeds of decline and continue the new life it has discovered? Transformation does not always come rapidly, although it might. As we see with the woman at the well and with illustrations throughout this book, once an invigorated spiritual journey begins, things start to happen. Let us explore rebirthing, a renewed infancy, a renewed identity, and re-entering prime.

Rebirthing. On a spiritual journey, rebirthing means hope is alive and a future is possible. Rebirthing is a gift. But before we go too far in our idealism and expectations, we probably will discover that new birth takes longer than we imagine and is more challenging than we like. The immediate benefits of spiritual disciplines are felt, but the greater benefits from the disciplines come only as we mature through the seasons of the church's life. The ups and downs of renewal test patience and endurance. Dependence on God challenges us in places we may never have been before. The rebirth stage will put to rest any false dreams that we can do renewal alone.

With renewed spiritual practices, a church experiences the excitement of rebirth. Servant leaders help the church enter a spiritual journey with intentionality. Like the woman at the well, we encounter Jesus afresh, and he becomes someone very important in our lives. With corporate disciplines like prayer, worship, and service, people know they are doing something together. The new energy and joy are like having a new birth in the family.

A renewed infancy. As the new energy from spiritual disciplines is felt in church life, attracting and including new people and new ideas comes easier and with greater joy. The renewal team is critical at this point. The team contacts all the members and friends of the church so the renewal process involves everyone. The team discerns the best person to issue invitations and how to most effectively spread the word about gatherings. The team may find that long-standing programs like Sunday school and small groups are an ally in getting everyone involved. Inclusion is part of a renewed infancy and is a fundamental factor in servant leadership. Servants include people, even the least likely.

Widening inclusion happens through the dialogue process. As people are given safe places to communicate, they are able to be present, to listen, to express themselves, and to be part of discerning the truth bigger than any one person holds. Some people need to work through hurt feelings or bad experiences to again cross the threshold of the church and become involved. Inclusion occurs as we reach out to others. Inclusion means working through various topics and schedules and preferences of people.

Having congregational gatherings increases inclusion. Rather than having just a few isolated attempts to discern God's will for the church, the process includes everyone. Experience shows that people need to be asked personally; very few will respond to a notice on a bulletin board. The renewal team's role of inviting others cannot be underestimated. Congregational gatherings are places where people feel welcome, dialogue occurs, and everyone's experience is called on as part of the process. Everyone matters! Everyone can contribute, even if it is bringing a casserole to the potluck dinner. That is a start and is using a precious, God-given gift. Infancy signals that something exciting is happening. Infancy is renewal in the making.

A renewed identity. As the renewal process unfolds, we identify the strengths of the church and how people in the church were shaped spiritually. Discovering a renewed identity becomes exciting. People see that their church's strengths are gifts from God, and they cherish the gifts and celebrate them. How nice to build our identity on affirmation! Servants become a servant body that takes on a special character.

In a similar way, in dialogue about core values, people discover beliefs behind the church. How helpful it is for a church to discover who it is before it tries to create a vision. And even more blessed is the church that discerns a Scripture text that helps it discover its faith journey and how God points it on the way. Using the dynamics of renewal from Scripture demonstrates that this is more than a management plan we are undertaking. The church's identity is rooted in the God's Word.

During this stage, the program of the church expands. Feeling renewed energy and vigor, the church looks to the needs that can be served. The Sunday school is built up, a youth ministry is expanded, and a kitchen is staffed. A time of discovering a renewed identity can be invigorating. However, to go through what Saarinen calls later adolescence, when a proliferation of programs takes place without sufficient work in their development, the church can become stretched in its resources. Saarinen says there is a "mesmerizing effect" in the high-energy and program combination.[7] Being attuned to its servant nature, the church is challenged to take a focused course and begin to come to terms with limits.

Through using servant leadership and dialogue, the church needs to remember to adequately negotiate the balance of people and programs needs. Support systems, such as childcare and mentors, need to be developed. Sensitivity is built in to meet conflicting schedules. Servant leadership reminds us that we are not just doing a program but engaging in ministry. Deep transformation occurs as a church comes to understand that all factors need to be balanced and that a church is guided by a purpose within.

Re-entering prime. We find that congregations realize they are re-entering prime at the very point in which they see renewal becoming real. In the renewal process, we are fortunate to have dialogue around a biblical vision to build on identity and give focus to our calling. Rather than trying to do everything, a church finds its unique call in one or two specialties. This means affirming God's gifts while also accepting limitations.

Deep transformation means excellence in what we do in ministry and what can be sustained. Servant leaders help people connect their spiritual journey and their activity in ministries. Ministries are supported and carefully guided. Ethics and boundaries are carefully guarded. Further energy is gained as mission is accomplished.

Rather than think a program or a new building will get it energized, the prime church knows that programs are started with energy. The dialogue process reminds us to have conversations with the people with whom and for whom a ministry is being created. Everyone is included.

Continued spiritual growth is the constant never to be given up. The renewal team uses creativity to chart the course of spiritual growth. It watches for signs that people are becoming presumptuous or taking for granted the factors that make for health and vitality. Growing churches continually work on all facets of renewal. They are aware of addressing the thirst, having fresh encounters with Jesus, being involved in transformation, and entering mission. They seek to be renewed by God day by day.

A Visible Presence and an Audible Voice

Out of the Springs process we have learned how the church can become a more visible presence in the community and have a voice that is audible locally and in ever-widening circles.[8] A church does not all of a sudden say that it wants to have its presence registered and its voice heard. Rather, like the spring, the water starts bubbling up, and you see evidence in the surrounding plants that begin to flourish. Churches voice the values identified in self-study and expressed in their new life and ministries. That is how renewal affects the wider culture.

A place of spiritual development. A value, a voice. People in churches using the Springs initiative say that the spiritual thrust is what has affected their personal lives and aligned their congregations spiritually. Through the spiritual disciplines they feel they have obtained workable tools for spiritual growth. They have seen evidence of new life for themselves. Having a mission deepens that new life and sense of reward.

Another level of spiritual development found in these churches is public expression of faith and witness to the community. This happened when Hatfield (Pennsylvania) Church of the Brethren marched in a parade with a church float that voiced Christian values. Ridge Church of the Brethren in Shippensburg, Pennsylvania, was part of the day of welcoming for students at the local state university. There was new vigor for their praise fest. Contributions were strong. Credibility grows for churches in renewal, and when they speak, there is authenticity and power.

Servant leadership. The results of those neighborhood visits by servant leaders at Bush Creek thirty-seven years ago are still being felt. On one such visit to Harry Swope, our conversation turned to the spiritual matters of life. The visits impacted people in the neighborhood, some of whom are vital members of the church today. Calvary Baptist, which learned from servant leadership to divide the load, had deacons visit different people and took the training a step further. After renewal was underway, Tommy Jackson held a training event for more than fifty community leaders in Chester, Pennsylvania. Servant leadership was the point of entry for churches in Maine, which in turn reached out to their communities. In Oregon a ministry to children of imprisoned moms spearheaded an endeavor that spread to include many churches.

Church executives at regional and district levels found satisfaction in working with churches that were being revitalized. This expression of servant leadership led some to be local coordinators, with striking results. One church in renewal put a banner over the street, proclaiming it mission statement: "being blessed to be a blessing." An inner-city church in Reading, Pennsylvania, brought street people into the sanctuary and ministered to them. Youth from Elizabethtown, Pennsylvania, went to the local service ministries office to assist the needy.

Not campaigns to becoming more prominent in the community, all these examples were part of the renewal process. Transformation has long-term effects that continue on and on. In the midst of discovering a new life, these churches started to do what came naturally. No longer did they hold their heads down— their witness was being expressed to others. Transformation and new life go hand in hand. The church's voice is heard and its presence known.

∾

In part 3 we have explored the third dynamic of renewal: transformation. The renewal process invites and leads to transformation each step of the way. As energy increases, focus is gained and deep transformation occurs. We have seen the pivotal role of the pastor, who stands with others as a spiritual guide and helps the renewal process unfold. We have also seen what it means to be a healthy church and to allow transformation to go deeper. Motivation becomes stronger, and the reality of new life is tested and lived. When a church is transformed to new life, it is ready for the fourth dynamic of renewal: mission.

For Reflection and Discussion

1. As you read the story about the Northern Ohio District of the Church of the Brethren, what factors do you see that helped this district get so many of its churches involved and committed to renewal?

2. In terms of transformation, what have been the motivating factors in your own spiritual life? What do you see motivating your church? What could be done to add a fresh spirit of motivation?

3. How do congregational gatherings lead a church in a spiritual journey and how do they build momentum?

4. Reflect on the Karpman drama triangle. Where have you seen this played out? Do you find it a helpful model for understanding deep transformation?

5. As you look at the process of rebirthing, what significant factors do you see? What next steps could you take to help your church to discover new life?

6. How might a church gain and express a new voice in its community?

Part 4

Mission

The woman left her water jar, went back to the town, and said to the people there, "Come and see the man who told me everything I have ever done. Could he be the Messiah?" So they left the town and went to Jesus. . . .

Many of the Samaritans in that town believed in Jesus because the woman had said, "He told me everything I have ever done." So when the Samaritans came to him, they begged him to stay with them, and Jesus stayed there for two days. Many more believed because of his message, and they told the woman, "We believe now, not because of what you said, but because we ourselves have heard him, and we know that he really is the Savior of the world."

—John 4:28-42 TEV

13

Implementing a Renewal Plan

Before beginning the first leg of its ministry plan, the leaders at Emmanuel Mennonite Church felt the church needed preparation. In fact, they called for a season of repentance—a whole month's worth! Out of a unit on worship that was part of their renewal process, the church discovered that confession is part of worship and wanted to put it into practice. Acknowledgment of sin moves us to receiving pardon and opens us to receive a challenge and then to respond to God's call. Confession becomes the opportunity to open our hearts for what God wants to do in our lives. What better way to enter the first leg of a ministry plan?

As pastor, the question on my mind was how to have a whole month on the theme of repentance in corporate worship. It was September, the time people usually return from vacations and start the school year. Where was I going to get materials for a season of preparation at this time of the year? I turned to the lectionary and to my surprise and joy, found those materials right in the Old Testament readings from Jeremiah 18:1-11, about the potter and the clay. From there complementary texts came to mind: Isaiah 64:8 and Romans 9:19-26. I began to study the texts and discovered the invitation to be molded by God.

Being transformed by God, as the potter transforms shapeless clay, took on new meaning. I began to explore how to make this imagery more real in the lives of people. I knew little about pottery, so I began to search for resources. Of all things, I learned there was a well-known potter, famous for his redware, with a shop just a few miles from the church. With a bit of trepidation

I went for a visit, but I received a wonderful lesson about pottery. The potter, Ned Foltz, is a Moravian with deep faith. He told me about the work of the potter and how the clay is shaped. He shared how he had once gone to a church and turned pottery during the opening of a service.

Getting up my courage, I asked Ned if he would turn pottery during an entire service at Emmanuel to help us envision how God is the potter and we are the clay. In back of his shop I saw a bin of old, broken pottery and learned that if moistened the clay could be shaped again. I began to imagine how cast-off pieces of clay could be used to enhance the faith experience of the people. My excitement built as I returned to the church leadership team to explore possibilities.

Others quickly caught this God-given imagery. What if during the month of September we focused on God as the potter and we as the clay? One Sunday we could hand out broken pieces of pottery, which people could use during daily prayer time. Making the pieces of clay moist, people could shape them in their hands during personal prayer time and reflect on letting God shape their lives to be vessels for God's use. We drew the worship committee and worship teams into the planning, along with others who set up and made preparations for worship. With so many people involved, word was getting out, and people did not want to miss any part of these corporate experiences.

This month of worship went way beyond our every expectation. A young adult prepared the spiritual disciplines folder for the month with a nice graphic of a pot to go along with the Scriptures and themes for Sunday worship and daily readings. The sermon topics included "Pliable to God's molding," from Jeremiah 18:1-18; "The anguish of God," from Jeremiah 4:1-12; and "There is a balm in Gilead," from Jeremiah 8:18–9:1. There was also Scripture on the potter from Romans 9:19-26. During worship, we confessed our resistance to the potter, placing our lives on the wheel. We explored having God draw us, cleanse us, and shape us—even if it meant pushing us down and remaking us. After worship, people were eager to receive pieces of broken pottery for meditation in their personal prayer time. We were being readied to be used as vessels of God in mission.

The Sunday with Ned was particularly meaningful. As he turned his wheel, the power of the visual message in action spoke to the congregation. Ned called the children up and explained how clay coming out of the ground is not very nice and needs unpleasant parts taken out. Then the clay is ground and water is added. The potter places the clay right in the center of the wheel. In the same way, Ned pointed out, we center our lives on God— we study the Bible, go to church, and listen to our parents.

As the clay moves on the wheel, the potter shapes it. Ned noted how easy it is for clay to "get bent out of shape." Then the potter puts the pot back on the wheel and reworks and reworks it. Ned said God keeps inviting us to be well formed. The potter really has to concentrate to shape the clay. Then the potter fires the piece so it doesn't fall apart. The visual and verbal images kept flowing forth.

As pastor I observed how our congregation was being prepared for mission and for looking at how our lives can be used in God's service.

The Dynamic of Mission

Mission is the fourth dynamic of renewal from John 4 and the woman at the well. Like clay, a healthy church is continuously shaped and transformed spiritually by God for mission. In this chapter we look at the dynamic of mission, how to prepare and plan for mission, and how to focus on a mission that further transforms a church and those touched by its ministries.

The woman at the well. When the woman at the well left her water pot behind, she took decisive action. New values took priority. Her life mission was focused—to go back to her hometown. In *Sacred Thirst*, Craig Barnes says she ran with "breathless excitement."[1] Back home, she said, "Come and see." She wanted those who shunned her to meet the one who changed her life.

She hid nothing. She admitted her past, but at the same time proclaimed new life.

Facing the challenge. Can we picture the challenge she faced? What led her to go back to her hometown on a mission to tell others about this one who told her all about her life? Where did she find the courage even to consider this option? How did she imagine that her hometown would receive her? They could have turned their backs and not listened.

Of course we cannot know what was going through her mind as she ran back to town, but we do know how she entered into mission. Rather than have all the answers and *telling* others what they should be doing, she approached mission as a dialogue, as Jesus had with her. She *invited* others to meet and know Jesus.

Effective ministry takes a confessional approach. We can say, "This is what I have found. Why don't you go and assess for yourself if this is the Messiah?" This approach shows deep respect, serving others by turning them to the one who can meet all needs. Servants point people to Jesus.

Clarifying her values. As we look at the story of the woman at the well, we can see how preparation for mission happened. Through her encounter with Jesus, the woman's values changed. Whatever had driven her to make the choices she had in the past was replaced by the hope and life in Jesus' invitation to drink living water. The woman had a new set of values as she ran off to tell others.

Mission emerging from the faith journey. Engaging in mission was an outgrowth of the woman's faith journey. Rather than receiving an add-on or an extra program, she now had her mission and purpose in life. Certainly it would have taken a lot of courage to go back to her hometown and tell people what she did. In confession, she acknowledged her past and invited dialogue with others as she told about this Jesus. She became a living example of one transformed in him. People could see that she was changed, that her faith journey had brought her to a new place. She was able to engage them to go and decide for themselves about Jesus.

This woman was empowered to do far beyond what she ever imagined. Her effectiveness is seen in the response of those who went on her word: "We no longer believe just because of what you said; now we have heard for ourselves, and we know that this man is really the Savior of the world" (John 4:42). The village then had Jesus stay two days. Many others put their faith in him.

Our congregations in mission. In the same way that Jesus prepared the woman at the well for her mission, he is calling our congregations to mission through renewal.

Facing the challenge. When congregations take up a ministry plan, they are decisively setting the way for a new future. Admittedly, they may not have done everything right in the past and face a challenge at present. All kinds of questions may arise in people's minds. They may wonder how they will be received. They may wonder if they have what it takes. They may wonder whether they can sustain this ministry for the long term.

The thirst they have felt, the encounter with Jesus they have experienced, and the transformation now in process leads them to take this step in mission. They may feel they don't have everything together or know all they need to know, or worry that they may not be the right ones to do this ministry. In other words, there is risk. Ministry takes courage. Much prayer is needed, with an absolute dependence on God.

Clarifying our values. In *The Leadership Challenge*, authors James Kouzes and Barry Posner speak of voicing our values: "Leaders must find their own voice, and then they must clearly and distinctively give voice to their values."[2] Otherwise they just reflect what is about them. Leaders develop an enthusiasm and passion for what they believe and that becomes a compelling force in transmitting their values to others. Here is where the church centers all its ministries on its core values and discerned vision.

Mission emerging from faith journey. As we saw in the opening illustration from Emmanuel Mennonite Church, people are more ready and able for ministry if they see their lives being molded by God and used as a vessel for God. Being pliable to God's molding, they can be more effective in what they are doing. Preparation helps us understand that we are not in this ministry alone, that we do not have to carry everything on our shoulders. Inviting God into our ministry can be the most important thing we do in implementing a plan. Renewal then comes from the heart.

Nothing is better than people inviting dialogue out of their own experience of personal renewal. People can share together. Whether the plan affects everyone, such as a family-night program, or only part of the church, such as a youth program, in renewal the entire congregation is part of the mission. In this way the ministry becomes part of the faith experience of everyone, and everyone's gifts can be used.

Discipline of confession. How can we go about developing the discipline of confession? Confession is one of the twelve disciplines that Richard J. Foster lifts up in *Celebration of Discipline* (see appendix 3 for a full summary of the spiritual disciplines). Emmanuel Mennonite developed this discipline as part of growth in the corporate faith experience. This happened quite naturally and showed how heart preparation can ready us for what is to come in the faith journey. In this case it readied both individuals and the church for mission.

The discipline of confession prepares us to be pliable vessels to be used by God in mission. Certainly the woman at the well went to people with a repentant heart. She approached her hometown with total honesty. She approached people who knew her and pointed them to the one who changed her life. She showed the heart of a servant, used the spirit of dialogue, and invited others to go and make a determination for themselves about Jesus. Out of her brokenness she was able to speak the heart of transformation.

What else is in this discipline? As Foster reminds us, God gives the grace, the ability even to confess our sins. Confession is a discipline because there are things we must do to carry it out.[3] First it is a grace. In confession we are reminded, as so often in this book, that God takes the initiative in renewal. God keeps trying to draw us back, renew our churches, and send us forth in mission. In confession we receive the abundant grace and forgiveness of God and grow in humility and in a winsome approach to ministry. We approach mission knowing our need for God and affirming the source of living water, which paves the way for implementing a ministry plan.

Confession is also a discipline that takes regular practice. It is an important part of our worship and prayer time. In the special renewal unit on worship at Emmanuel, the church discovered while studying Isaiah 6 that confession comes after praise. Seeing how high and lifted up God is, like the prophet we can see our humanity. This began to renew our worship in that we saw the pattern for drawing closer to God.

Acknowledging our sinfulness, we are ready by the grace of God to be pardoned and to hear the call of God, "Whom shall I send? And who will go for us?" With a renewed heart we can respond, "Here am I. Send me!" (6:8). Personal prayer can take on this same spirit of confession. Confession is an integral part of growth in faith and an integral part of preparing for mission.

Preparing for Mission

Preparation is a big part of the success of the ministry. With heart preparation in place, we see other needed factors. An action plan ensures sustainability. Defining a ministry, naming needs and hoped-for outcomes, looking at successful models, and discerning gifts of people are all entailed in establishing a ministry. Leaders need to be enlisted and trained in ministry. They need resources. Individual contact is important. Mentors, or some system of continual encouragement and guidance, need to be put in place. We need to ask, "What can keep the ministry growing?"

As we look at the specifics in preparing for mission, an example from one church's journey toward launching a youth ministry will be helpful and instructive.

Build spiritual energy. When Elizabethtown (Pennsylvania) Church of the Brethren discerned that a youth ministry was needed,

I was called to a one-year assignment to launch it. In this case, some form of renewal was needed to create the spiritual focus and energy for the new ministry.

For Lent I designed a Wednesday-evening follow-up to the Sunday sermons for feedback and small-group discussion. The response was far greater than I had anticipated. These midweek gatherings resulted in wonderful interaction and a deeper sense of faith for those who participated. Energy for renewal grew, and this spiritual focus became the launch pad for ministry.

Fitting ministry to needs. Whenever a church begins to plan for a new ministry, it must consider the actual needs to be met. Yes, a youth group is desired by all, but what kind of group? How will it function? What kind of leadership will it need? How can all the youth needs be met? The entire congregation needs to be involved in these discussions so all can feel invested in the ministry.

At Elizabethtown, we decided to call Walt Mueller, who was known for a keen interest in youth ministry and whose Center for Parent/Youth Understanding was located in the area.[4] With energy from our Lenten Wednesday-evening program, we decided to have a gathering of parents and youth to spur conversation. Both youth and adults freely shared about life from their vantage point in a spirit that invited understanding. Everyone drew closer and experienced a unity unknown before.

A youth ministry emerged from that evening. There were four groups, each with a different model and type of leadership. Coordinating all this was a youth council led by an older youth supported by adults. The youngest group had parent-driven leadership providing activities. The junior high group used advisers and youth to plan and implement activities. The senior high group used youth leaders with counselors who worked alongside of them. In this way, the youth were able to gain major leadership experience. The fourth group was a young-adult Sunday school class, which took over my office on the Sunday my assignment ended.

Obtaining resources. A spiritual focus and servant leadership style help us understand that, as leaders, we cannot shape ministry by ourselves. Getting resources is essential to begin to set the base for a successful ministry. Sometimes those resources are within the congregation. At other times, the church will need to go outside for help.

For instance if we say "youth ministry," what does that entail? How are youth shaped spiritually? Using materials from the Center for Parent and Youth Understanding website and the book *The God Bearing Life: The Art of Soul Tending for Youth Ministry*[5] can help set the pace for youth ministry. And there are many more resources to be found. Youth conferences provide a lot of learning, both at the event itself and through recommendations of resources and personnel.

Church denominational offices often have trained people who are glad to help or point you to the right places. The Internet also has a range of resources, which need to be screened for one congruent with your church's beliefs. By networking with other churches, you can locate resource centers that can assist you. Obtaining resources is part of shaping a ministry.

Learning the models. The next step is to create some kind of design for the ministry. Creativity can emerge in a number of ways. In the above case of the youth ministry that emerged out of a Lenten series, we see how one step often paves the way for another. In looking for a model, the leadership group that will be operating the ministry, as well as those profiting from the ministry, need to gather and dialogue about how the ministry should look.

It is important to fashion the ministry in a way that matches the vision and the need in a creative manner. For that we need to learn the possibilities. The church should look at various models and find one that suits it. There will probably be some adapting of the model so it can serve the church's purpose and not the other way around. Like any activity, whether painting a house or preparing a meal, the preparation stages are critical and time consuming. The more effectively the model is designed, the better the outcome.

Learning about models might entail a group going to visit a church with a specific program. Once there, they can inquire about how things are done and what is working or not working. How do they get people signed up? What kind of activities do they have in this ministry? How do they get organized? How do they enlist leaders? For a family-night ministry, one church went to visit a very vibrant Wednesday-evening ministry, asked many questions, and left feeling they had a much better idea of what was entailed. Observing a ministry in action will greatly help in establishing a solid ministry.

Keeping everyone informed. Through regular communication, such as through the special page in the newsletter, the church is kept informed about the enlistment process, finding resources, and training that is underway. Now is the time to interpret a mission. A congregational gathering could be held on a new or renewed ministry in order to educate and engage the church as a whole.

The more the church is informed and kept together during this period, the more the members will feel included when the ministry is launched. Communication needs to be in a variety of venues. This may feel tedious at times, but good communication is the work of renewal and a vital part of servant leadership.

In the same manner, communication needs to occur in a spirit of hope and joy. The word going out should convey that enough commitment is present for the ministry to go, but also that additional people can become part of the effort. There is nothing more discouraging than announcements that people are desperately needed. There is nothing more encouraging for a church than to know that a group is called, trained, and ready to go. On the other hand, people should know that they can sign up for the ministry and that their contribution is needed.

Part of good preparation communication is a clear and accurate description of what is needed. If a youth group is forming, what will a sponsor be expected to do? What is expected of the youth? What will parents need to do? Things as simple as picking up your child on time show respect for everyone's time and energy. The more that is specified from the outset, the greater the outcome.

Identifying gifts. Identifying gifts for leadership of ministries is important. In Acts 13:2-3, potential candidates go out in the field to tell the Good News in Gentile territory. At Antioch, four candidates emerge, including a close friend of Herod. As the disciples used the spiritual disciplines of worshiping and fasting, the Holy Spirit told them to call Barnabas and Paul for the work "to which I have called them" (NRSV). After everyone prayed and fasted a while longer, they laid their hands on Barnabas and Paul and sent them off. Acts goes on to recount the challenges they faced and how the discernment process carried them through many difficulties during which people came to belief.

In Springs we affirm that everyone has a ministry. In Ephesians 4:12, Paul writes that different people have different roles "for the perfecting of the saints, for the work of the ministry, for the edifying of the body of Christ" (KJV).

You can't do a ministry unless you have and identify the gifts. Gifts are God-given talents and capabilities. Some churches have a gifts discernment committee that updates the nominating committee. The committee might work with the pastor in preaching a series on gifts discernment, followed by a class or small-group meetings. As the committee meets it can begin to become excited about the strengths demonstrated in people.

The committee could use a resource to study the biblical foundation of gifts and have sessions using a spiritual gifts discovery tool along with an analysis of congregants' personality, passion, and experience. Sometimes a visit in someone's home or place of employment gives clues to interests and gifts. The outcome is a ministry profile. The biggest challenge is to use the outcomes of such instruments; gifts identification should be followed immediately by extending a call. Helping people use their gifts in ministry is crucial, both in their personal faith journey and in the ministry of the church.

A call process. In Springs we use a call process that entails prayer and then moves to discerning future leaders. First we have a united time of prayer with the leadership teams and with the entire congregation. We then call forth people with gifts. A variety of methods can be used, but if you use a gifts survey you will want to make sure to use the forms. The hope is to have everyone use their gifts and to have more people involved.

At the beginning of one church's renewal process, three people felt they were carrying the load of the church. The church began using dialogue to get the maximum benefit of everyone's thinking and leadings. It considered using gifts surveys, and these can be helpful, but in this case the church used a more interactive process.

An invitation was put out to have people meet together on a Saturday for a call process. It was thrilling to see fifty people respond and meet on two Saturdays. You could sense the interest and energy as people entered the building, even those who felt this was not quite the right time for them to serve.

In this case, the church was looking for members for six new positions on a lay ministry team that worked with the pastor on implementing the church's ministries. The facilitator asked the people who were nominated for these six positions to sit in the middle and talk. Because the team had to work together, the facilitator saw an advantage to having them all in one place. In a kindly manner people asked them about their time, passion, and availability to handle this ministry.

At the same time, some of the nominated people said that they did not feel led in this direction. When various questions, challenges, or issues arose, the facilitator served as moderator. Real dialogue occurred and an attitude of affirmation prevailed. Six members of the team were called, affirmed, and commissioned in ministry. The spiritual focus with use of discernment created a wonderful team that the body had called forth.

Whatever the process of discernment, people will feel they are operating out of their giftedness and therefore will be more effective, creative, and fulfilled in their ministries. People are helped when they name their gifts and then other people identify gifts within them. They feel included as the church opens its system and reaches out to new people.

Enlistment. Leadership means a lot in any ministry. The importance a church places on calling leaders matches the value people feel in being called. The intentionality with which enlistment occurs reflects the values of the church. The enlister rules out "catching someone after worship" or calling on the telephone or emailing to enlist the leader.

If we are asking people to commit a major portion of their time to a ministry, we need to sit down with them in conversation, which conveys the value we see in what they will do week in and week out to accomplish this ministry. The enlister asks what time is best for them and what location is preferable to talk. Enlistment can be seen as another step in the inclusion stage of the life cycle, in which people are invited into the church and can do their part in fulfilling mutual goals.

Preparing the heart of the enlister. Before going to a meeting, enlisters prepare their heart in prayer. In the style of servant leadership, enlisters search out where they feel a person's talents are and why leadership will fit into their faith journey. How will the enlister affirm their call, making them feel they have something to contribute, while also gaining something in the process? In prayer, an enlister asks for God's help in the finding the proper approach.

What will lead to consolation? To desolation? What practical barriers to taking on a ministry task are present (for example, having an elderly parent at home)? How can those practical barriers be dealt with (for example, would there be caregivers from the congregation who could help while this person is away from their responsibilities)? The enlister goes assuming no immediate decision will be made because this is an important calling and various factors need to be known for that person's discernment. With all the work done thus far in understanding the ministry, the enlister goes prepared.

Enlistment takes time. The enlistment process continues until all factors are worked out. The enlister must be prepared to listen to fears, objections, and other factors. Looking to the call process in Scripture, we often see how the prophets did not feel they had the words to speak or the credentials for the task.[6] Reluctance can be a positive sign that someone is really considering the seriousness of the call. Such consideration builds humility.

Often people need time to pray and to discuss commitments with their family and fellow members in the church. They need time to explore what this new role will entail. Sometimes they need to reprioritize their work or phase out another area of work in the church. That creates openings that will need to be filled, and they will probably be concerned about the void. Experience shows that committed people realize all the ramifications of taking up another ministry.

Further time for discernment. The best outcome of an initial visit is to have presented the call and set a time for another visit.

All these conversations are renewal. God is shaping a church. God is shaping people to use their God-given talents for ministry. Rather than being put-offs, such occasions are an opportunity to invite people into a new walk with Christ, just as they will be introducing others to Jesus. Real ministry can happen as people begin to open new doors in their life.

In the renewal process, people feel affirmed. If there has been a talent survey, someone has looked at the inventories and is following up on a person's sense of giftedness. Sometimes it is helpful for the enlister to tell the candidates that someone else has seen his or her potential. Not to flatter candidates, but to *call* them to ministry can be a privilege. Another valuable outcome is that a church is using people's gifts and they grow in their faith as they implement their ministry. Time spent in enlisting is time invested in renewal. The church gains energy. The church grows in mission.

Training needed. Preparation needs to take place at another level. Whatever the ministry, training is needed for its success. One option is to bring an outside trainer to the local site and build teamwork. The best training takes people where they are, helps them learn what is entailed, and teaches them how to do the ministry to which they have been called. We train not just those who are involved but also those who have an interest. This builds inclusion and helps the church to grow. More people feel affirmed in their talents and have the opportunity to grow into something they never could imagine doing.

The key will be to find the best training to match the objectives. The search for appropriate training can be an education in itself. Not all training needs to be at the front end; as leaders find they want to know more, training can be ongoing. Good training can be exciting. Building on the training of the renewal team, other training can be done in the style found most effective for the particular church. Training becomes an integral part in growing a ministry and is best done year in and year out. The joy and excitement of ministry are shared.

Mentors. A mentor can lessen frustrations and can be important to the success of a ministry. Mentors are people experienced in some form of ministry and can be trained for this specific task. Rather than telling people what to do, mentors use servant leadership to help people accomplish their ministry. Mentors adopt the listening part of dialogue and become partners in accomplishing the mission.

A sevenfold method of mentoring can be found in my book *A New Heart and a New Spirit* and in the Alban resource *The Calling of the Laity.*[7] In this model, the mentor helps people in ministry set and accomplish their goals so they know someone is coming alongside to encourage them. These steps in mentoring are listening, establishing growth areas, asking permission, discussing resources, developing an action plan, modeling, and growing spiritually. As in driver's training, the person in ministry is in the driver's seat with the mentor as the coach.

The mentor helps the person in ministry establish goals and find a way to accomplish them. The mentor also gains permission to help the one in ministry work on areas of growth. Finally, the mentor is there to help sort things out. Having an encouraging helper with some basic tools supports the new ministry.

✦

Mission takes preparation, the first of which is preparation of the heart. Moving from a season of preparation in the church to looking at the fourth dynamic of renewal—mission—we have laid the groundwork for a ministry. All this work is renewal; it is ensuring that all aspects of a ministry are carefully prepared and laid out for success. While time consuming, all these efforts bear fruit.

From preparation of the heart to preparation of the congregation to preparation of the endeavor, we see the time commitment needed by the church. When carried out systematically, the entire body grows. Corporate spiritual formation occurs as a church sees that it is being molded and shaped around its mission. Each person has a part to play, and the impact is greater than the parts.

For Reflection and Discussion

1. The opening illustration points to the need for repentance to begin a ministry. Can you see the merit of what this church discerned? What would it mean for your church to collectively practice the discipline of confession?

2. Looking at mission, the fourth dynamic of renewal, what does that entail for you and your church? Affirming how mission is renewal, what aspects of growth do you foresee in implementing your mission?

3. Can you see how gifts can be identified and used? What happens if gifts are identified but not used? How can an effective ministry of gifts discernment and implementation happen in your church?

4. Have your group do a Bible study on God's chosen and how they overcame their reluctance to be used in ministry. Study Moses in Exodus 3:11, 13; 4:1, 10, 13; Gideon in Judges 6:15; and Jeremiah in 1:6. Observe how God's assurance comes sometimes with a sign.

5. Groundwork was laid in terms of preparing a ministry. Certainly this takes a lot of effort and time. What challenges do you see in preparing for a ministry?

6. What do you think of the mentor idea? Has your life been impacted by mentors? How could an intentional mentor program strengthen ministries?

14

Launching Servant Ministries

Seven years after I helped two American Baptist churches in Maine implement renewal, I received a Christmas card from David Borger, a part-time pastor at one of the churches and a part-time area minister of churches in the region. In his card he said that we often do not hear about the good things we have done, so he wanted to share some exciting news with me.

You could hear enthusiasm in David's words when I called to learn more about the church he pastors at Buxton Centre and about Steep Falls, where Jim Key is pastor. Both churches continually received new members, a half-dozen members yearly for one and several members yearly for the other. Both churches were reaching out in their local community. Service both within their walls and in their community had led to new life.

Both churches once had weekly attendance in the thirties but were profiting immensely from the renewal process. David felt that the two biggest motivators of renewal were the spiritual approach by way of a scriptural passage and the focus on the churches' strengths, which caused them to gain confidence rather than continue to dwell on negative factors. Through renewal, the churches looked into their history and found why God put them there in the first place. Now, David said, they were stretching and seeking where God was leading.

Youth ministry was flourishing as well. At Steep Falls, a shared youth ministry was happening with other churches. Each year Steep Falls picked a new Scripture to follow. At Buxton Centre, David led a Bible study and was present at a social hour for residents at the nearby senior center. Buxton Centre was building an addition so they would be accessible, and instead of putting the office upstairs, they were planning to put it on the first floor, where the pastor would be available to the people.

Buxton Centre and Steep Falls were also reaping the benefits of cluster renewal work. By working together, these two churches, otherwise isolated in small communities, "re-infected" each other when something went right. Their collective renewal has spread into area clergy gatherings through the spiritual practice of prayer. David wrote that the emphasis on servant leadership was reaping benefits at the two churches; leaders were empathic, honest, and effective.

When people fall on their face, David wrote, the others help pick them up. No wonder the eight-year Scripture for Buxton Centre was Zechariah 4:6: "Not by might, nor by power, but by my spirit, saith the Lord of Hosts" (KJV).

The Tenth Trait of Servant Leaders: Entering the Drama of Reconciliation

Servant leaders enter the drama of reconciliation in the water basin and towel, experience the service of Jesus washing their feet, and so cleansed, kneel on behalf of Christ to serve others and are blessed. In turn, others serve (see John 13:1-17).

One important element of renewal in these New England churches was servant leadership. In chapter 4 we looked at the first eight biblical traits of servant leadership, and in chapter 10 at the ninth trait. Now we turn to the tenth trait: servants enter the drama of reconciliation (see appendix 7 for a full listing of all ten traits). At the beginning of the second part of the Gospel of John, the so-called Book of Glory, Jesus is in his crucial hour. Gethsemane and the cross are before him. Kneeling to take a towel, he depicts the nature of discipleship in the drama of serving.

Kneeling in ministry. True disciples *divest* outer garments, signs of success, pride, and selfishness and *invest* in the way of the cross, self-sacrifice, love, and compassion. In the Gospel of John, service is a key mark of ministry. In church renewal as we enter the fourth and final part of mission, we serve by taking basin and towel. What we do as the church is not programs, but ministries that convey Christ.

Serving, we become one with the Master. In service, we are the heart of the atonement, the self-sacrificial love of God reaching out to humanity to bring us together with Christ. Service is all about reconciliation and abiding with Christ. Servants participate as partners with Christ in the work of the cross. Service expressed by washing feet is a paradigm for godly action. God's glory and victory come through service. It happens as those who feel they have nothing to offer kneel and give of themselves.

The humble convey love. Jean Vanier, founder of L'Arche, where handicapped people live with their assistants, tells about a "paraliturgy" in their communities on Maundy Thursday in the United Kingdom and France. During the meal, people share about their past and the sorrows and joys of the year. Then they go in another room and have prayerful silence, sing a hymn, and read John 13. Then the house leader kneels down in front of the person on the right and washes his or her feet gently and tenderly. Then the one whose feet have been washed places hands on the head of the one who washed them and prays silently a prayer of gratitude.[1]

How touching it is, Vanier says, to see the handicapped wash the feet of assistants. What love and forgiveness is conveyed in this simple act that speaks of redemption. Vanier says, "By removing his garments Jesus is revealing his true glory, his deepest self, his heart's most intimate desire. He becomes smaller and smaller, more and more vulnerable, in order to communicate love." Elsewhere Vanier writes, "When love is given and received, a trust and peace enters the heart which the whole body radiates."[2]

Entering the drama of reconciliation. When Charlotte White participated in the closing communion at the seminary (see chapter 1), she felt the connection of foot washing to the eucharist and saw the change in herself; she returned to her church ready to serve. When going out to the community at Bush Creek with the image of basin and towel in mind, I saw how service transformed the people's lives as they felt valued and began to come to the church and use their gifts. When our son Andrew went to those growing churches and they served him by respecting him, he in turn was able to serve by holding the doors open for people.

In church renewal we enter the drama of reconciliation. We go through a process of growing closer to God and establish ministries that lead people to God. The church that takes on the very character of Christ in all it does is an agent of renewal for others. Moving from knowing to doing, from greatness to smallness, we are blessed: "If you know these things, you are blessed if you do them" (John 13:17 NRSV). Servant leadership begins with our spiritual journey and moves into serving, leading, and blessing.

Ministries Are Service

Servant leaders participating in the drama of basin and towel shape ministries of reconciliation. Ministries of the church, inside its walls or out in the community, are done as service to Christ and are literal expressions of him. We bridge the gap. In ministry we go across to the other side and are with people, becoming as Christ unto them. They can tell our love and authenticity. Service speaks to them of the manner of Jesus.

Let us turn again to the biblical text and the drama of Jesus washing his disciples' feet to examine a ministry (see John 13). Having seen the connection of the spiritual journey with leadership style and the renewal of the church, we see how ministries in mission are best shaped in the manner of Jesus. Rather than programs, ministries are service. Nowhere will style of leadership and shape of ministries for transformation be more important than in a church entering into mission and implementing a plan.

The ministry of all God's people. Affirming ministry as service, we see the authenticity of the priesthood of all believers. Renewal is all about the drama of all God's people joining in the work of reconciliation with Christ. People are turning faith into action. Each interaction is an opportunity to covey the love of

Christ and the nature of Christian love. In mission, people have a way to use their talents and grow in their faith.

Reconciliation happens by joining people to Christ and the church. People deal with their call, priorities, schedules, and the impediments that hold them back. Sometimes people need help dealing with self-esteem or old hurts. Taking basin and towel, servants kneel down in front of others, wash their feet, show respect, and invite them to newness of life. Implementing a mission is ministry to people.

Faith grows in ministry. People's lives literally blossom as they discover their ministry. In renewal we observe how people become new people. By using their gifts, they can give creative expression to their faith. They may find joy creating a worship center or participating in a dialogue on a discipline. In family-night endeavors I have seen person's talents in cooking used to reach out to others. Some have found joy in being youth counselors. Others have found joy in inviting a neighbor, who began to grow in the Christian walk. They themselves grew.

The faith walk of individuals is integrally related to discovering their ministry. Both those receiving the ministry and those who are serving in a specific role grow as part of the process. As people act in faith in ministry, they express their talents, grow in dependence on God, and walk further in their own faith journey. The purposes of God are being formulated and implemented and realized. Faith then grows not in a vacuum but through engagement in ministry in the name of Christ. Faith formation happens in real ways in the process.

The Servant Approach to Launching Ministries

In launching a ministry, there are many factors to keep in mind. One is acting in the name of Christ and entering the ministry of reconciliation. Hard work is ahead. The servant is one who can kneel down on the floor and serve the needs of those for whom the ministry is designed. The servant is very sensitive to the factors entailed.

Rather than operating from a superior position, the servant launching a ministry joins with people to make the ministry happen. Servants work to bring forth the gifts of others. The ministry, no matter its focus, demonstrates Christ and relies on his transforming power. While hard work, service is necessary for reconciliation, bringing people to Christ and to being the church.

Approaching challenges. Just as important in servant leadership is facing the practical details, the discouragement when things don't work as planned, and variables like illness in a family or bad weather for a church event. Like Jesus, servants face difficulties. You may be tempted to take a shortcut or overstep the leadings of God. But the call comes to stand in the abiding way of Christ. In renewal, challenges have a way of calling the church to greater God consciousness and obedience to Christ's will and way.

According to spiritual discernment, make no decisions out of anxiety or fear or self-centeredness. Listen to the inner voice. Wait. Pray. Act in the way of discipleship. Likely it will take longer to implement a ministry plan than hoped. Move forward. While facing many challenges, servants live the vision and reflect Christ, who, when faced with adversity, held up the model of the kingdom.

Spiritual formation. In *The Sacrament of the Present Moment*, Jean-Pierre De Caussade speaks of those depending on the divine will as given "mastery over themselves through habitual surrender of their hearts and, whether they obey it consciously or unconsciously, directs them to the service of others.[3] This is the very transformation of individuals and a church moving into mission.

Much spiritual formation happens in launching ministries. When ministries are shaped as service, the lives of all involved—those serving and those served—are molded as well. Launching a ministry is a major step in the life of the church.

Practical Items in Launching a Ministry

With preparation completed, people called and trained, and resources available, the ministry launch is ready to begin. Enlisting prayer support by the entire congregation is important. The church can have a covenanting service in which the entire church dedicates itself to the ministry, asks God's help, and affirms mutual support for the endeavor. Crucial to the launch will be the style of servant leadership used by all involved. Below we'll look at five elements in launching a ministry: announcing the launch, the need for personal contact, having an eye for details, praying, and celebrating.

Announcing the launch. With the help of leadership groups and the renewal team, the launch date of a new ministry is set. Often a new ministry announced in the spring is launched in the fall. Adequate information needs to be given. Since people learn in a variety of ways, three or four different means of communication ensure the message is heard. While official announcements can be made in bulletins and newsletters, a church may decide to find a creative way to introduce the ministry, perhaps with some of the very people who will be directly affected.

For example, a young-adult ministry launch could be announced by young adults doing a skit or reading, saying that now they will have a place to have discussions about their jobs and faith and life issues. This will get everyone's attention. Or perhaps something about the ministry itself can be advertised in a catchy way to get people's attention.

The Frederick (Maryland) Church of the Brethren advertised its new additional worship service on Saturday evenings as "5:38"—the time when the service would begin. Something creative can rivet attention and capture the essence of what the church has envisioned for its renewal plan. Being creative suggests something important is happening in this place at this time.

Need for personal contact. People often wonder about the need for personal contact. Shouldn't you be able to just say "y'all come" and people will come? In my hospice work, I learned that, while churches may wonder why people don't come to them, people in the community often wonder the same: why doesn't the church come to us? Using servant leadership, we can come to the side of others—we can be the ones to reach out, to be the first to get on the floor with a towel and make ourselves vulnerable.

In an Alban study of growing churches, researchers identified a factor they called "commitment anxiety." So many things have been offered in the church and have failed or been discontinued that people wonder if they should get involved. Servants are sensitive to the needs of those who may consider attending.[4]

In the spirit of servant leadership, those who initiate the new ministry can provide a listening presence and invite people to the event. In that listening, people can raise concerns or bring up practical issues that, if faced and dealt with, will make the ministry even stronger. Servants learn from others, especially from those the ministry is for.

For instance, a person invited to a worship service in the park may express fear that he or she won't be able to hear well. A sound system will not only help that person but others as well. This may take checking into, renting, and setting up equipment, but rather than wait several weeks "to see how things go," the need could be addressed at the outset.

Having an eye for details. Another critical factor for a ministry is to have all details in place well ahead of time. Servants see how critical this becomes. The appropriate committee, along with the renewal team, can work to get things organized. Using servant leadership, you can do a trial run of the event and go through the facility to see what will be needed and what can be provided ahead of time. Making adequate provisions is another example of the care and intentionality needed for a ministry to be established. With some creativity, you can build a welcoming space, have provisions for emergencies, and be blessed for the service.

Praying. Servants pray. Perhaps a certain group wants to take up a prayer vigil or lead the church in prayer for the endeavor. Such people become alerted to ways they can give general support. Nothing equals the support that prayer provides when something new is launched. A call from the prayer group to the leaders would be meaningful: "We have been thinking of you; we have been praying for you. While there are many challenges, we trust things will work out. Do you need anything?"

Celebrating. Celebrating is an integral part of starting a ministry. A service of celebration should be set. With all the work that goes into having a good launch, participants should have a time to thank God and people for arriving at this place. Launching a ministry is a high moment for a church. To be able to take a step of faith that has so much intentional planning and energy can build up the body. Testimonials can be given.

At this point those in leadership can acknowledge the ever-present help of the Lord, who continues to reveal things to us. This is no time to take credit; this is God's time. With a spiritual focus, servant leaders have a premium opportunity to acknowledge their faith and their appreciation for the people who have come to this place and this time. The focus needs to be on where the church is headed together. This is a time of great gratitude for how God is at work. Praise God from whom all blessings flow!

Servants Attend to the Movements of God in Ministries

While attempting to keep focused, getting all things ready for a renewal plan entails considerable energy. But in the midst of all this, it is critically important to attend to the movements of God. To what direction does the invitation of God's grace call us right now? Where is there consolation? We have covered the topic of the movements of God and seen how spiritual discernment is important in order to keep attuned to God and not override what God has in mind. We do not want to be fatigued by the panting feverishness about which Thomas Kelly warns us.

Listening to the presence of God. Amid all the activity of ministry, we can begin to find ourselves consumed in it all and forget that our overall purpose is to serve God. It becomes so easy to abbreviate the tending of our own thirst and let the ministry take on a life separate from nurturing the Christian inner life. The invitation of renewal calls us to sit back and reflect and tend to the thirst.

Thirst, encounter, transformation, and mission is the fourfold framework of this book. The movement of God will call us back to attend to our thirst. Rather than being an add-on, tending to thirst is central in keeping attuned to God. In a similar way, we keep attuned to encounters with God as we receive invitations to help others. Perhaps we will feel inadequate or like we do not belong. We may need to listen to where Jesus is inviting us for a drink in a quite unusual place.

In the midst of our inadequacies, we can listen to God speak. Some of our cooks for family night felt inadequate while preparing for seventy-five to one hundred people, especially after the spaghetti burned. We felt our building was insufficient for the number of children attending Bible school, especially with basement floors that were wet with humidity. We felt inadequate when the numbers who wanted to come to the Renovaré conference grew beyond capacity. We felt stretched to our limits in cluster work with renewal of churches. Real transformation begins at the limits of our adequacies and when we feel some greater power will be needed for all to be accomplished.

Renewal requires that we stay attuned to God's presence and build on the new life that comes forth. We depend on the presence of God to lead us into ministries. We see God at work as these ministries unfold, and we celebrate that God is helping these ministries to flourish.

Power in the towel. In renewal we keep remembering that the strength, power, and effectiveness of a ministry depends not on us but on God. Rather than being presumptuous that it all depends on us—or, on the other hand, being overwhelmed—servants lead others to living water. They go and get the towel. They kneel and begin the work. They go to the other side and do what leads to transformation and accomplishes mission. In being proactive, they rely not on their own strength, but carry Christ within them.

Servant leadership is an active, robust style that has humility within it but also the courage to face the challenge that Jesus' way entails. In ministry we too are an integral part of the redemption story and share that with others. Like Jesus, servants shape not just individuals, but also his kingdom on earth. That is why all efforts are grounded in prayer. Active encouragement is given at each point. Mentoring is established. Nothing is taken for granted. There is power in the towel.

Developing the ministry as part of the congregational mission. As the renewal team has worked to help launch a ministry, they can do a great service by having a congregational gathering to make this ministry a part of the church's mission. For example, Walt Mueller of the Center for Parent/Youth Understanding came to a church at which I was leading renewal to have a dialogue with youth and adults. This helped the entire congregation enter into one of the goals of youth ministry. With that focus, everyone felt they were part of something. While certainly there are differences between the generations, this large gathered group discovered through dialogue that both youth and adults faced problems with which they were attempting to deal. So the ministry became part of our church's life rather than being a side program.

Another opportunity to support a ministry is with encouragement. Attending a Missions Support Insight session at the annual conference of the Church of the Brethren, I thought I would learn how to support people in ministry locally. To my surprise and delight, I learned how a local church held a fair on foreign missions. People were encouraged to send notes to their missionaries and be an active part of the mission. I wondered about having a fair on ministries of the church, taking people to "lands" like the newly painted youth room, and sending the youth advisers monthly notes of encouragement.

Servants Are Aware of Size Transitions

Just as it helps to understand the life cycle of a church, understanding size transition can help a church in renewal. Aspects of size transition can be studied in the renewal team meeting and potentially in a congregational gathering as ministries grow. They can study how roles and relationships change, especially with the pastor. This helps newcomers to be welcomed, and members learn how to serve in churches of various sizes. Roles will change and plans will need to be made for growing. All this is critical for a healthy church discovering its mission.

Four size categories. In *Sizing Up a Congregation for New Member Ministry*, Arlin Rothauge defines sizes of congregations and how a true servant church can best serve the needs of people. Rather than thinking that one size church is better than another, Rothauge argues that each size has its own uniqueness and strengths. Bigger is not necessarily better, and neither is small necessarily better. Each size has a different character and mission.

The small church has up to fifty active members and is called a *family church*. The medium-size church, with between fifty and 150 members, is called a *pastoral church*. Here the pastor is the hub of communication and planning. The large church, with 150 to 350 active members, is a *program church*. The church of 350 to 500 or more is known as a *corporate church*.

The family church is one cell and has so-called matriarchs and patriarchs who are key to new members being adopted. Relationships are key in a family church. Establishing identity as a church, so important in the renewal process, is crucial for the small church. In the pastoral church are two or three cells with the same leader, the pastor, who relates to everyone in the church. The pastor plays a key role with newcomers.

In the program church, the pastor can no longer maintain contact with all members but will spend more time helping envision and coordinate various ministries.[5] People can be enlisted to welcome newcomers and help them find their way into the fellowship. Having a renewal process in place is important in any church, but certainly its merit will be critical in congregations of this size.

A renewal team plays a critical role helping a corporate church grow its ministries, maintain health, and reach out to others. Sizing up needs for new-member ministry in a corporate church, Rothauge says that this size incorporates many of characteristics of the other sizes but in magnified form. There needs to be a uniting purpose. If ever a continual renewal process is needed, it is in this size church.

Size transitions in renewal. Handling size transitions in renewal is critical for the health of the church. Building on Rothauge's four church sizes, Alice Mann alerts us to the spiritual path and the challenges of size transition. She likens dynamics of size transitions to dealing with fault lines in earthquake areas. In moving from family to pastoral, she says, key people may feel they lose influence. Renewal invites people to adjust and take new roles, which calls for growing in spiritual maturity. A church can take a season of prayer, dialogue as a body, and take up basin and towel as roles change.

In the pastoral-to-program transition, change happens in selecting and training program leaders. The group moves from being an organism to being an organization. How can everyone stay accountable? How do groups communicate effectively? With the pastor no longer the hub of communication, how does he or she stay informed and utilize church leaders in the ministry of the church? In the renewal process we saw how important the inclusion factor is for a healthy church.

In the program-to-corporate transition, program expectations are even greater. The pastor moves into a lonelier, more spiritually hazardous role. Staff may need to find adequate consultation and spiritual direction. Guiding the ship is a central task.[6] The call will be for growth in servant leadership, which requires significant time in prayer, guides corporate spiritual formation, and uses a servant approach in meeting situations calling for ministry. Certainly in the corporate church the administrative balance of all factors for health is critically important.

Dealing with a church in plateau can be quite challenging and is handled best with the renewal process. Mann puts it well: "Leaders find themselves in a lose-lose position because two competing sets of expectations are laid upon them. Confusion, anxiety and indecision often result."[7] Understanding size and size transitions is an important part of developing a healthy church with an urgent Christ-centered mission. In working with size transitions, the renewal team helps guide a church in renewal.

Facing Hardship

While implementing ministries, leaders are bound to face difficulty. In systems work, leaders are the most visible and the most vulnerable. When setbacks and conflict come, servant leaders can be heartened that their faithfulness speaks in any situation. As I noted in *Servant Leadership for Church Renewal,*

> By being servants and rubbing shoulders with people who are servants, we find that it is not the appearance that transforms, but rather the quality of the servant's life. Without even knowing it, servant leaders who follow their vision and embody faithfulness can have a tremendous impact on others. Their sincerity speaks; their loving service to others carries a powerful message. In time of difficulty and uncertainty, they can call upon others to augment a team. Perhaps unnoticed at first, the servant leader can speak a message that ultimately makes a tremendous impact.[8]

Growing through the challenges of implementation. While a lot of transformation happens in getting ready for one's mission, a lot of transformation can happen in implementing a renewal plan as well. In one church implementing a renewal plan, the work was going well. People rallied together, and the response was better than anticipated. Creativity was abounding. The church began to see all of ministry as service. A tremendous launch occurred without a hitch. What more could we ask for?

And then it happened—and all over coffee. Someone with an old memory about contention over coffee decided not to serve the beverage one evening. Emotions flared, and at first I thought all was lost. Everyone became very quiet and like a storm front that comes in and changes the atmosphere, people wondered how to proceed. We had worked so hard to help the church in renewal. How could not having coffee stir up a hornet's nest?

By the grace of God, the one offended used Matthew 18 and went to the offender. You could say the one went with a towel and washed the feet of the other. Transformation occurred. Together two people growing in Christ worked things out. Leaders evaluated and took responsibility for their side of the misunderstanding. The reconciliation was in and of itself a morale booster as it showed that renewal was at work and the ministry had accomplished its purpose. Here was a genuine experience of growth.

Holding to vision. With the servant helping turn around such a situation, there is another factor to remember: in the good times and the rough, the servant lifts up vision. That means both personally and corporately. In all times it is good to hold on to one's sense of direction and to the group's sense of direction. Here is where having a renewal team really helps. The pastor or pastors do not go it alone.

In renewal, the vision is not just ethereal; it has real substance and is practical. So we return to our strengths, to core values, and to our biblical passage. At all times we remember our calling. In reality we know that this is God's vision, not ours. Servant leaders project the vision again and again and recast the vision in new and creative ways.

In any slowdown or setback, we ask the question from servant leadership: "How can this be an opportunity for further spiritual growth?" When it is difficult to keep focused in the work, servants point the way to fulfilling mission. The commitment of individuals who sacrifice when the chips are down and go the extra mile in a ministry is the foundation on which churches are built. The early church was built by martyrs—witnesses who gave their lives. Drawing on their spiritual resources, churches can grow as they faithfully serve and implement their mission and ministries.[9]

Servant Structures

Churches often wonder if they can be more efficient in their work. Should we take the time to get things properly organized? While there might be some advantages to reorganization, and it may be needed in some cases, the drawback is the amount of time, energy, and stress that comes from reorganization.

In Springs we enter the renewal process, experience transformation, see ministries emerge, and strengthen the organization. If reorganization is needed, it can be done more effectively after the renewal process is underway. In that way it is less likely to become the focus of hoped-for renewal. In this section we'll look at helping the current structure to function, reorganizing as part of renewal, having form follow function, and creating servant structures.

Renewing old structures. In the process of renewal at Bush Creek, we found the current structure was not operational, but this was not the fault of the structure. The commissions with specific responsibilities were operating in a more or less productive way, but the board, made up of the chairpeople of the commissions, met only twice a year and without a prepared agenda.

So we developed a vision for the board to be an organ that pulled together and gave focus to the church's calling in ministry. Then we established our purpose, which was to have meetings with a clear agenda—in which we felt we were getting somewhere, in which people felt heard, decisions were implemented, people had a level of interest and attended, and efforts of various parts were combined and focused.

To do that, the plan called for the pastor to meet with the board chairperson before each meeting and help set the agenda. After the board meeting, the pastor and board chairperson met again for evaluation and implementation of decisions. Three years later, the board was functioning as a healthy unit. Attendance was good, members participated, and there was a sense of purpose. Trust was reflected in the more central place the board came to hold in the life of the church. In this case, energy was put into making the current structure work, and positive outcomes resulted.

Reorganization as part of renewal. Reorganization in and of itself does not bring renewal. But new structures can be part of renewal once there is sufficient momentum and energy in the church. At one church, there were three overlays of organizations. Through the renewal process two of these leadership groups realized that one often yielded to the other. No one was sure who was ultimately guiding the church. They also found they were operating with two different understandings of authority.

What made matters worse was that when people wanted something, they were confused about where to go, so they wound up going to the people who would give them what they wanted or needed. After the congregation articulated these breakdowns in communication and function, they felt that reorganization would be right for this church at this time. The church began a process of spiritual discernment, looked at organizational models, and ultimately called lay ministers and lay teams to accomplish its mission. In all cases, organization should serve the church in the mission and ministry of Christ.

Form follows function. In renewal we may notice that the structure is not serving the mission. While forms may seem outdated and lifeless, we know that just changing them will not bring deep spiritual transformation of the church. In fact, changing them without being in mission has inherent dangers, one of which is to have issues emerge that can only be dealt with once there is energy, focus, and a sense of direction. Once those elements are in place, a congregation can more readily see the kind of organization that can serve the mission. They can go about a process of reorganization, which takes considerable time and energy. Then the time frame for getting reorganized is shorter and the new system is in place and operating for the mission. Form follows function—to spread the gospel, which points people to Jesus.

Creating servant structures. Creating servant structures means that a church shapes its life in a way that embodies its mission. With each structure, whether a committee, a small group, or an informal gathering, a servant church can embody the drama of the water basin and towel and convey the redemption of Christ on the cross. The church takes on a spiritual, transformational nature and sees all things as part of the mission. Being in mission by nature, the church's intent in all it does is to introduce people to Jesus so that their lives will be transformed and they become servants who lead others to living water.

In *Servant Leaders, Servant Structures*, Elizabeth O'Connor tells of Church of the Saviour in Washington, D.C., founded by

Gordon Cosby, where each person was encouraged to live out his vocation. Mission was defined, and mission groups formed and discerned what mission they felt called to accomplish. "What were the structures of the church that would so nurture men and women in discipleship that Christ would always have first priority in their lives no matter what the circumstances?"[10]

The structure bears the identity of each member who makes the commitment: "I unreservedly and with abandon commit my life and destiny to Christ, promising to give him a practical priority in all the affairs of life."[11] Such a dedication, such an orientation is felt deeply in the climate of the church. The spirit of the church reflects, conveys, and supports its mission. A servant ministry maintains openness to new people and is part of the mission to reach out to others, pointing them to the living water.

The church then, even in its structure, is in mission to the core. Being in mission has the form of Christ, the one who defined his life by basin and towel and went to the woman at the well. Imagine the drama when such servant-led ministry is the very core of the church. Through examples in this chapter and throughout the book, we see the new vitality in individuals, churches, executives, and wider church bodies.

Servants and servant ministries are integral to entering the drama of the reconciliation of Christ. All ministries are service and demonstrate the basin and towel in their very character. Each aspect of a ministry, from launch to development to tending to size transitions to facing hardship, is the drama of basin and towel. Even new structures, if they grow out of ministries, can serve the mission. Here is transformation in Christ at work. Each ministry is part of the faith formation of both individuals and the body that speaks the message of Christ.

For Reflection and Discussion

1. What are your reflections on the churches in Maine? What

parts of their stories would serve as an encouragement to your church? Can you see how these churches helped each other?

2. How do you see servants entering the drama of reconciliation? What does that say about helping ministries thrive? How are ministries integral to spiritual formation?

3. In looking at the five elements of a successful mission launch, do you see things your church does well? How could a renewal team help in this process?

4. How do you see a servant approach helping in difficult times in mission? Are there examples from your life or the life of your church when this approach helped?

5. Do you believe that form should follow function? When and where have you seen the best examples of servant structures that help mission get accomplished? What did they look like?

6. Share about how each ministry can be part of the faith formation of people and faith formation of the church that speaks the message of Christ.

15

Nurturing Disciples

Cedar Hills American Baptist Church near Portland, Oregon, underwent significant transformation through the renewal process. As a renewal servant, I could tell something significant was happening, and their story illustrates how churches in renewal become active in mission and make new disciples.

As part of the original startup, a Sunday of exploration featured a continuously running slide show with lots of faces speaking of the church's history and ministry over the years. They had been asked what kept them coming back year after year. The pastor interviewed three people: one in a wheelchair with multiple sclerosis, a teacher of drivers for the handicapped, and a person who came to the church as a teenager. What moving stories they had to tell!

Cedar Hills creatively made the renewal process its own and continually had positive responses. The church wrote the strengths it discovered on large toy blocks and placed them on the platform in front of the sanctuary. Prayer began to emerge. People identified what nurtured their lives of faith. The churches developed a vision and a unique plan of ministry that took creativity and strength.

Three years later, I called Everett Curry, who had been integrally involved in the renewal at Cedar Hills. During the phone call I experienced the transformation myself. Out of the renewal endeavor, various ministries had developed, with people feeling empowered to do their ministry. With one, called Operation Baby Lift, Cedar Hills had become the organizing congregation of a program to assist babies of mothers incarcerated in the Oregon prison system. Rather than just meet their original goal of helping twelve babies, they assisted twenty babies and mothers. On the Sunday I called, a mother of one of the babies had just been baptized at Cedar Hills. Her life was totally changed in Christ through the efforts of this church. She had experienced the "arms of love wrapped around her."

The church became stronger within and more able to work together and with others. The theme that emerged was "being a new kind of family," and Operation Baby Lift was one way they lived out that theme. Renewal is happening now at Cedar Hills, years after the original process, as the church continues to share the Good News with others.

In this chapter we'll look first at cultivating disciples, becoming apostles, and sharing the faith. Then we'll look at being stewards of the faith in the use of time, talents, and financial resources. How do we go about growing a healthy church that is actively sharing the faith as its mission in all of life?

Making Disciples

Those who receive the living water from Jesus become disciples. They become vessels that carry the Good News.

Speaking practically, churches ask a number of questions: How do we help disciples grow in the faith? How do we train disciples as apostles to carry the faith to others? How do we go about the mission of spreading the Good News to others?

We see how Jesus met the woman at the well where she was and invited her to partake of living water. Her initial growth in discipleship came by being in dialogue with Jesus. She sorted out issues of faith and of her own life. Then she went out in mission. Her practice was to lead others to discover who Jesus was for themselves. Transformation happens in the lives of those we touch and also within ourselves, so let us look at cultivating disciples, becoming apostles, and sharing the faith.

Cultivating disciples. Growing disciples involves the training and growth of Christians. Both new Christians and those who have been in the church for many years need to grow. Growing as disciples does not happen overnight. In the rapidly growing church in Nigeria, new believers spend a number of years training as disciples. Churches in renewal have the opportunity to prepare people for baptism and help someone who has been baptized to grow as a Christian through all the stages of life.

What is entailed in training disciples? How would we design ministry and follow up with people who express interest—both new members and long-standing members? Along with listening to their journey of faith, how could such a ministry prepare them for their next step of using their gifts? Discipling means exploring these and other questions and spiritually discerning how to assist people to grow in faith.

In *Reclaiming the Great Commission: A Practical Model for Transforming Denominations and Congregations*, Bishop Claude Payne of the Episcopal Church speaks about the importance of the disciple-making process. Regarding preparing new disciples for baptism and teaching them to obey Christ's commands, Payne says, "[The] goal is changed attitudes and behavior—spiritual transformation—leading to a richer and more productive life."[1]

People cannot be left on their own to grow in Christ. Speaking of the need for discipleship training in *The Great Omission*, Dallas Willard says, "Spiritual formation in Christ is the process whereby the inmost being of the individual (the heart, will, or spirit) takes on the quality or character of Jesus himself."[2] Any church in renewal will carefully look at how it goes about training in discipleship. A renewal team could help the official bodies of the church establish ongoing teaching in basic Christian discipleship.

Developing a course for training disciples. In the Springs process we teach by learning objectives. Rather than wonder what we want to impart to others and how much we can cover, we begin with where people are. How can they move from where they are at present to a deeper spiritual walk? To do that, we need to decide on a context, on a structure, on a format, and other practical details.

So a renewal team, along with the pastor and other leaders of the church will ask, "What will assist inquiring people to experience the excitement of the Christian life? What are the beliefs of a Christian? How do you interpret the Bible? What are the beliefs of the church? What are the tools new believers will need to live a life in the spirit of the cross day by day?"

We also need to ask what format will best serve the purposes we have outlined. What role will prayer and spiritual disciplines have in training disciples? Will this be a presentation or include questions and answers? What will be the context? Will it be formal or informal? People like to get involved. Maybe a skit could be used to illustrate some point, with small-group discussion following. People may write or draw something in response to the skit or presentation.

In terms of the time and context of such training, we ask whether we will use the traditional routes, such as Sunday school and corporate worship, or an informal setting, such as a Wednesday-evening family night or small-group meetings in homes. Is it possible to have a retreat, even just for half a day, off the grounds of the church? Can everyday living be actively incorporated, such as having participants do a weekly activity and gather together to discuss outcomes?

Building a ministry of discipling. There are many resources on discipling, and while the Springs renewal process does not endorse any curriculum, I will mention a few that we have tested and found to be helpful.

The Alpha series from England is designed to introduce people to the Christian life. Alpha's opening invitation comes from Jesus, who invites all who thirst to come to him for a drink. Participants explore who Jesus is, how one prays, and how God guides us. The format for the series includes relationship building, often with a meal, teaching through videos, and discussion. Alpha is especially helpful for those who have never been to church before.[3]

The basic text for the course is *Questions of Life* by Nicky

Gumbel.[4] Alpha discussion groups can have long-established members and newcomers. We did the fifteen-week series at Hatfield Church as a follow-up for newcomers who came as a result of participating in the spiritual disciplines folder launched on Easter. Presentations are very upbeat, as exemplified by the first session, entitled "Christianity: Boring, Untrue, and Irrelevant." Sessions can be adapted according to beliefs of your church.

As a church answers these questions, it no doubt begins to think of the topics to be covered in other courses for training disciples. This can include a wide range of topics, such as introducing the Christian faith, understanding the Bible, learning beliefs and practices of the church, and walking in the Christian way. While it is always good to have some structure and format in mind, one way to establish disciple training is to ask participants what they would like to learn and how they would like to grow. The goal is to meet people where they are in their faith journey. Step by step, a well-rounded course of study and discussion can be designed.

Building relationships among the group is an important element in this experience. Learning is augmented as people get to know one another and learn how others face challenges in real life. This is one of the reasons encouraging long-standing members to participate is a good idea. The assimilation process begins as new believers meet other Christians who are excited about their faith.

Becoming members of Christ's body. Eventually, a new believer will probably desire to become a member of the church. As a church goes through renewal, it may choose to revisit its membership curriculum. If the church has none in place, it will need to select or create one. Denominations usually have what are traditionally called membership materials. These cover the basic tenets of Christian belief, as well as the denomination's history and unique interpretations of the Christian life. As believers contemplate membership, they want to know what it means to be a part of this church family.

In addition to specific membership issues, growing as disciples entails learning about the Bible. While most inquirer classes have ample references to the Bible, I have always found that people appreciate an overview of the Bible. *The Unfolding Drama of the Bible* and *The User's Guide to the Bible* provide helpful overviews. *How to Understand the Bible* by David Ewert is another good resource.[5]

Often people have questions about the Bible. Ample time should be allowed to answer them. This would be a natural time to introduce inquirers to spiritual disciplines like Bible reading and prayer, which may already be in process through the disciplines folders.

Having mature Christians sit in with the membership class can greatly benefit the presentation and discussion. These church members can share from their experience how rewarding the Christian life has been for them. They can serve as mentors to new believers, and mutually beneficial, lifelong relationships can form. These mentors may be part of a service of baptism or reception as members and then continue to walk beside them for a year or two to see that proper assimilation occurs.

Walking in the way of daily discipleship. Early Christians were known as "people of the way." The way of the cross calls for a life of obedience. There are so many choices to make. This is where beliefs turn into action (ethics), and practical support for new believers is essential. A regular series of such courses can be offered as part of an adult Sunday school class or a family night.

Again, there are many resources, so research and discernment are needed. Through Bible studies, people can see themselves in the biblical narrative and learn from God's people. My study resource, *James: Faith in Action*, is a practical guide to daily discipleship through practical decisions. There also are resources on daily discipleship within one's vocation, such as *The Laity in Ministry* and *The Calling of the Laity.*[6] *God's Story, Our Story: Exploring Christian Faith and Life* by Michele Hershberger, as well as *Take Our Moments and Our Days: An Anabaptist Prayer Book* are helpful as well.[7]

There is no greater arena of growth in daily discipleship than in nurturing the family. The renewal process gives tools to help in communication, in being transformed, and in establishing a mission as a family.[8] The dialogue process encourages positive and uplifting communication styles. Living in the way of the cross includes peacemaking, in which Christian love and forgiveness is learned and practiced.[9] By joining together, a family can have a mission with a tremendous impact.

Becoming apostles. In Acts 1:26 no longer are the people of the way called just disciples, or learners. Now they are called apostles—those who are commissioned and empowered to carry out the mission to which they are called. Not just spectators, the church is made up of those who own the faith, live the faith, and feel sent to share the faith. What training is needed for becoming an apostle who intentionally shares the faith, calls disciples, and helps establish new ministries in new settings?

Certainly the woman at the well had a mission. Water pot behind, hometown in front, she headed out to share living water. As we move with the story of the early church in the book of Acts, we see its dynamic nature. In the same way, the woman at the well carried unbounded enthusiasm into byways and villages.

Training apostles. Is it possible to train apostles? We know that those who become new disciples often have the enthusiasm and passion to share the faith. We know too that there are longtime disciples who have the same passion for sharing the living water. In the Springs process, I've seen people catch the spirit of renewal and drink of living water then desire to share their faith and invite others to become disciples. They do this almost as second nature. How like the woman at the well! Here are a few illustrations that could become part of your church's ministry plan.

The Oak Lane story tells of the renewal of a city church using a Monday-evening visitation program. This program was designed by Richard Armstrong and is described in his book, *Service Evangelism*.[10] Systematically, congregants would go out visiting every Monday evening and then gather for reflection and observation. The concept of service comes into play as the "apostle" goes to listen to someone rather than to unload his or her beliefs. An apostle who shows caring testifies to a God who loves. From there apostles wait for the moment to speak about their experiences and to relate it to their own faith assumptions. All this is done in the context of affirming that faith is a gift of God.[11] At Oak Lane, cards were kept on all visits with appropriate follow-up.

Another resource from Armstrong, Faithful Witnesses, is a helpful course for church members training to be apostles.[12] A prayerful approach prepares the congregation and the participants. Sessions move from biblical foundations to background understanding to actual practice of sharing the gospel with someone. The spiritual work of prayer is turned to active practice, and participants use servant leadership as they build relationships by active listening.

Gaining practical experience. The role of practical experience is so important in the training of apostles. Hatfield Church learned it could not take for granted that people knew the normal church terminology, much less what the Bible said. Showing one newcomer around the building, I mentioned that the next room was the sanctuary. "What is a sanctuary?" this person asked. I knew then that Hatfield was attracting people with little or no church background.

This led to establishing a greeter team. Members made themselves available at the door to assist visitors in finding their way. But the greeters also joined visitors in the worship service if they so desired. This led naturally to follow-up because a relationship was started. Then the church began using the Alpha program to introduce people to the Christian walk. Much transformation was happening as the church entered into mission as apostles, helping others grow as disciples.[13]

Sharing the faith. The woman at the well went out to introduce others to Jesus. We have explored her methods of dialogue and her servant style, included her confession and her moving profession of faith. She had Good News to tell, and she took it to her hometown. Then the hometown invited Jesus to stay. Out of that, others believed. Once the process of sharing the faith begins, it spreads. We can see how telling the Good News gives new life and energy both to the individual and to the corporate church body.

Personal faith sharing. The renewal process gives the spiritual energy for people to invite others to know Jesus. Rather than sharing an external experience, people should be encouraged to share what is happening in their life. Spontaneous, natural sharing is so important in witnessing to one's personal faith. Often there is a felt sense of risk, but that can be overcome. In home, in school, in the community—sharing of faith becomes natural.

Personal faith sharing is a very natural part of Springs. Whenever there is an opportunity or whenever there is someone who has made a faith discovery, we encourage people to share in the way most natural to them. This might be on Sunday morning, especially if the sharing fits the theme of the day. Or if people prefer, they may write a faith testimony for the newsletter or tell of their faith to a neighbor. Such sharing becomes a more natural part of their life, beginning in their home and with their family. Call it evangelism or simply call it telling others to go see for themselves who this man Jesus is and what he could mean to them.

As chimney sweeps, Bob and Lisa Smith share their faith as a natural part of their business. The couple took up the spiritual disciplines using the folders, and Bob became a member of a renewal team. He tells how his faith life began to change, that he discovered what he calls a "rudder" in his life. On the way to the job, Bob listens to disciplines tapes by Richard J. Foster. He says he has never felt so close to God as when he goes up a chimney to clean out soot. When he comes down, rather than meeting a "customer," he meets a family and shares about life and faith.

You can't prefabricate experience. Sharing the outcomes of the spiritual disciplines will set us on our way. Gaining some practice, people discover how to do it more effectively. People can share personally as part of worship and tell their experience with spiritual disciplines. For everyone, those who are reserved in sharing personal details, sharing faith in the safe atmosphere of a church family makes them feel affirmed and builds energy for going out and sharing with others.

Invite a friend. While it's important to welcome strangers, statistics show that reaching out to friends and inviting them to church is more effective and makes a deeper connection. One way to share faith is to have an invite-a-friend Sunday. This is an especially successful endeavor if it is part of the renewal plan and everyone in the church is enlisted to be a part.

A first step for such an event is preparing the church for what newcomers sense in the first thirty seconds. Training can be done in a congregational gathering to help people understand the importance of those moments when people first enter a church. In *The First Thirty Seconds*, Joan Hershey describes the basic concepts of hospitality for greeters and ushers but which the entire church can also practice.[14] The pointers include making eye contact, remembering the needs of single adults, and learning the names of visitors. Business is laid aside. The focus is set on hospitality.

A second step is the actual planning of an invite-a-friend Sunday. Having a thorough plan will be reflected in the response to the event and sets a pattern for follow-up. Using the detailed packet *Invite a Friend Sunday*, the renewal team, along with other leaders in the church, can help the congregation plan.[15] The packet includes a guide for congregational preparation, including a Sunday school and worship emphasis.

Such a Sunday may be part of a regular series of events in which a congregation reaches out with the living water. Follow-up is important and could include any of the discipleship training ideas in this chapter. Growing disciples, training apostles, and sharing the faith are all part of the fourth dynamic of renewal, mission. To that we add the stewardship needed to make renewal possible.

Being Stewards of God's Gifts

One of the most challenging questions in church renewal is money. In decline, local churches, regions, and denominations experience the strain of finances. Until renewal is a high priority and a budget line item, funding it will remain a challenge.

Renewal is cost-effective because churches in decline are like houses with wide-open windows in the middle of a cold winter. These churches are losing their most valuable asset: people. Wanting to keep them for their money will not work. Offering growth in the spiritual life is the key. Churches in renewal discover that, like the woman at the well, Jesus is inviting them to offer him a drink. Churches discover they have something to offer. The spiritual journey leads to a renewed spirit.

Most of the money needed for renewal is for training and resources. People who can bring the needed skills—pastors, renewal servants, and resource people—help a church through this period. When renewal becomes an ongoing goal, a healthy church builds it into its budget, investing in planning and growth. Church renewal does not take a separate office or a large amount of technological equipment. It entails communicating with people either by email or phone or visits, having training events, and following a renewal plan. Mostly what is needed is the commitment of time, which will probably utilize both paid and unpaid help.

An invitation to be stewards. Faced with funding a Springs initiative, a church development team met with Jonas Beiler of the Family Center of Gap, who is known for his faith and for building on biblical principles of stewardship. "If the Lord doesn't have your pocketbook," Jonas says, "he doesn't have you." With that challenge, he said an exciting part of church renewal is the giving piece. You do not ask what it costs but, How can we invest?

Faithful in giving, churches demonstrate what the apostle Paul wrote about sowing and reaping in 2 Corinthians 9:6-7: "Remember this saying, 'A few seeds make a small harvest, but a lot of seeds make a big harvest.' Each of you must make up your own mind about how much to give. But don't feel sorry that you must give and don't feel that you are forced to give. God loves people who love to give" (CEV).

Without applying force or engendering guilt, Paul invited people to give. The offering taken at Corinth was for the mission of the mother church in Jerusalem. Paul was relieved to learn that the church at Corinth was not angry with him after he felt he had talked sternly with them. In that context he spoke of giving. Paul lifted up how their giving made the church in Macedonia want to give.

Paul had one regret with the church at Corinth: "When I was with you, I was patient and worked all the powerful miracles and signs and wonders of a true apostle. You missed out on only one blessing that the other churches received. That is, you didn't have to support me. Forgive me for doing you wrong" (12:12-13 CEV). He regretted cheating people out of the blessing of being part of the missionary work.

Paul's regret speaks loudly today. How do church renewal and stewardship fit together? Jonas says, "Let us not cheat our people of the opportunity to experience the blessing of giving. Either we give meagerly or generously." Being part of the ministry by investing in it financially goes a long way toward building a healthy congregation. Our giving plants the seed, and we invest in renewal, see the results, and experience the blessing.

With a keen interest in family, the Beilers are dedicated to the revitalization of the church. They feel renewal of the church and of the family go hand in hand. When the Beilers talk, their faith radiates. You feel like you too would like to both give your life more deeply to Christ and give so that others may have life. Actually this is the story of the woman at the well, who decided to invest her entire life in faith.

Entering the growth side of the life cycle. Inclusion means not just inviting people to attend church, but asking people to come and do their part. Part of that invitation is giving and receiving the joy that comes from being part of a mission. Church renewal entails stewardship at its best, because we are connecting people with ministries. People will see the direct outcome of dollars invested. Energy grows in the church. Servant leadership provides the way to approach renewal from the standpoint of meeting the needs of people. How do we do that in terms of stewardship?

Do people really want to see how they can use their financial resources in response to Christ to spread the gospel? In the self-study portion of the renewal process, a specialist may need to be called in to look at stewardship in the life of a healthy church. This person could meet with appropriate leadership groups, offer a Sunday message, and assist at a congregational gathering. The gospel truth is that it is more blessed to give than to receive. Financing renewal is renewal and is critically important for churches desiring to be healthy. Stewardship is an expression of mission.

Becoming conservationists. Another major way to be cost-effective is to be much more careful with the money we do have in hand. Renewal can lead people to feel a part and see how there can be cost savings. Churches can hold an energy audit. Lights need to be turned off, plumbing needs to be checked, and thermostats need to be turned back. In decline, churches lose their sense of ownership and are not as attendant to such items. By everyone doing their part, churches can conserve natural resources and stop budgetary bleeding.

Because administration is the last to go in a declining church, people usually figure that those running the church take care of such tasks. Renewal brings a new sense of ownership and pride. At one church in renewal, members held a work day and removed the thistles from the flower gardens so they could see the plants again. What a beautiful symbol of new vitality!

In a similar way, everyone needs to be safety conscious in a church in renewal. Often due to lack of funds, but also lack of investment, churches overlook maintenance items. They hope to get by with emergency repairs. Broken things are left unfixed, and a sense of decay sets in. Churches that begin to keep up with maintenance not only avoid catastrophes but also help people feel they are keeping up God's house. Maintenance contracts are important so larger costs are avoided. A clean and well-run building builds energy and creates a positive atmosphere.

Time and talents. In church renewal we see how stewardship of time and talents is just as important as financial stewardship. In fact, our time and our talents can be seen as financial assets, because many of us are compensated for both. Since renewal is labor intensive, people need to be willing to give of their time to do all it entails. Rewards soon come for this effort.

If a church wants fruitful outcomes, it needs to look at what a renewal process will entail and what the work of a healthy church entails. I have learned from experience that once people become involved in renewal of their personal faith, they adjust other priorities and feel their life has purpose. The investment of time given to the church becomes a joy.

Stewardship also entails the use of talents. Often at the start of the renewal process, people identify who has talents to do what the process calls for. Certainly as ministries are established, people are called upon to offer their talents and fulfill the ministries. The entire servant leadership style calls for identifying talents and can yield growth in discipleship.

Stewardship Enlistment

Talking about money is difficult when people are discouraged and anxious about their church. Church budgets may be taxed by the rising costs of energy and of the pastor's insurance plan. The youth want to go on an overseas mission trip, but the nursery ceiling is falling in. Which is the priority? Which will help generate energy and new life? The greatest challenge to starting renewal may be the initial enlistment period. This will be especially true for districts and regions. It may take a year or more just to make the decision to invest financially in renewal.

Since there are no immediate results in renewal, there will need to be a lot of patience and perseverance. Staff will need to take extra time to work on logistics, coordinate volunteers, and pay for printing and postage and everything else that needs to happen to get the renewal process off the ground. Enlistment is just as labor intensive as renewal and is, in fact, renewal. How do you get that accomplished? How do you build the base for a healthy church?

Connecting budgets with ministries. In renewal we connect budget with ministries. That conveys that something is happening with the investment. People can see how their contributions are making a difference. They feel engaged in their faith journey and in the work of the church. So the challenge is to interpret budget in terms of ministries being accomplished. This can be done by featuring a ministry a month in the newsletter, by people sharing about a ministry during the worship service, or by a ministry fair with displays showing what is being accomplished. Perhaps the team involved can perform a skit that shows the work done.

People also like projects. What if we linked the budgetary figure for a traditional ministry like Sunday school with the dollar value for each one trained in discipleship? The challenge comes in getting people engaged in their faith journey so they will practice biblical stewardship and want to accomplish the mission of the church. Connecting budgets with ministries is part of the work of renewal.

Developing a stewardship enlistment program. There are no better people to spiritually discern the best approach to stewardship enlistment than the renewal team. Just as we learned of negative experiences in the history of a congregation, so can we learn from what has been tried and found successful. In open sharing, the church can review the need for stewardship education and how to creatively go about this endeavor. Again, rather than find out what is wrong and fix it, we find out what it right and build on it.

Lou George, who is active in Springs, has these words of wisdom:

> To carry out a successful stewardship program, a congregation must develop a clear understanding of the ministry or mission it is called to do within the community and around the world. The members of the congregation must be involved in the developing and implementing of the vision for ministry. The key is found in ownership. If members of a congregation do not own the ministry, they will never adequately support it.[16]

Resources on the full range of biblical stewardship (money, time, faith, talents) are available from Stewardship University.[17]

Helpful books from Stewardship University include *Money Mania: Mastering the Allure of Excess* by Mark L. Vincent, *Stewardship of Faith: A Christian View of Hospitality* by Michele Hershberger, and *First Fruits Living: Giving God Our Best* by Lynn A. Miller.[18]

Positive communication. Talking about money is hard in our society, and taking the wrong tone can quickly close doors of communication. The use of "urgent notices" is an example. Such notices often show a lack of positive identity as a church. The renewal team, working with the stewardship team of the church, can give good advice on what is appropriate and helpful. All efforts need to relay a positive self-image and give encouragement rather than guilt. Check whether zingers in the newsletter or someone standing up on a Sunday morning with an appeal about giving will help or hinder sowing generously.

Let us look at another approach in a newsletter. The announcement reprinted in the sidebar is from the Servant Leader School of the Church of the Saviour in Washington, D.C. The appeal contains what the organization is doing in ministry, how no one is excluded, and how support is needed to fulfill their vision and motivate people to commit themselves to the kingdom. Such principles could be adapted for any church.

A Call For Financial Support

The Servant Leadership School at the Festival Center is a 501 (c) 3 non-profit organization. We are building upon an extraordinary legacy of faithfulness, vision, and sacrifice of the ecumenical Church of the Saviour faith communities. We are called to be a "people's seminary," and we keep tuitions rates low so that no one is prevented from participating and sharing their gifts. We also provide substantial scholarships for lower income participants.

Your support is critical to our vision of providing challenging Christian education that motivates people from all walks of life to commit themselves to the Kingdom of God. Tax deductible donations may be made to Festival Center, Inc. For more information about how you might help, please call [name, number, email.]

Funding forward. "Funding forward" is another way to express stewardship. This phrase comes from Harry Swope, who became a member during the Bush Creek renewal process. Thirty years later, Harry stood up at the annual conference of the Church of the Brethren. (He and his wife work to advance the mission of the church, and I am indebted to his wisdom on this topic.)

The concept of funding forward comes from Jesus' parable of the master and the talents (see Matthew 25:14-30). The master gave the servants talents. He expected them to go forth and multiply the talents. Two of the servants complied and one failed, because of fear, to multiply the talents, and he was not blessed. This story shows that forward funding requires that we first overcome the fear of failure.

This story also reminds us that God has given each of us great gifts and talents that he expects us to use to bring others to him. God expects that we, through prayer and practice, discern what our gifts are and how they can be used to tell others the Good News. After all, that is really what his church is all about.

To do this, leaders need to go beyond the normal budget items and budget for the new priority. This approach challenges the congregation to step up and put God's financial gifts to work in his service. If the planning is done with dialogue and servant leadership, the congregation will have been part of the process and the increased or rearranged budget will not be a surprise.

Funding forward also says that the congregation is willing to take a risk and trust that God will help them find the resources it takes. Churches always budget not knowing if the dollars will show up in the collection plate. If the project is an exciting step forward, many people will become a part of it by voting for it with their dollars.

&

The challenge in being stewards of living water is linking together two activities: growing in discipleship and using resources in the mission. In renewal, stewardship is an active partnership.

Growth can be experienced as we encounter living water, undergo transformation, and become part of the mission of the church with our time, gifts, and our money. We can tell renewal is happening when people begin to take initiative in both their own growth and in mission.

For Reflection and Discussion

1. What have you found effective in the training of disciples—both new believers and long-time members?

2. When does one go from being a disciple to being an apostle carrying out the mission of making other disciples? Is there a way to make a clean distinction? How can we encourage such growth in the Christian life as we enter into mission?

3. What do you feel about allowing people to share in the blessing of giving? How have you been blessed by giving? What ideas do you have for growing the financial end of a renewal initiative?

4. What role does stewardship play in faith development? What do you think about the concept of funding forward?

5. What are the connections among a renewing church, a discipling church, and a giving church?

16

Claiming the Deeper Journey

For the Lamb at the center of the throne will be their shepherd;
he will guide them to springs of living water.
—Revelation 7:17

The affirmation of Scripture is that the Lamb leads us to the springs of life-giving water. As we engage in the mission of sharing living water, we need to keep growing spiritually both personally and as a congregation. Sometimes people find that the further they get into the mission the more they drift from the very energy that initiated it. Such an identified need opens the invitation to go the next incremental step spiritually—to live in that trust, to keep up our spiritual disciplines, to develop a vibrant faith, to let our lives speak of the living Lord. This is to claim the deeper journey.

In mission there are continual draws on our energy. We get those reminders to replenish the faith in our hearts, to offer our gratitude to God, and to grow as partners in Christ's mission. In mission we desire a closer walk with Jesus day by day. We seek to grow in Christlikeness, humility, and poise in order to convey this mission. Our desire is to be supple to God's leading, to follow the contours of the teachings of Jesus. This is the deeper journey that keeps tugging at our hearts as we guide others to the springs of living water. The very renewal we desire in our churches we also desire in our lives.

This is the invitation we have been considering throughout this book. We have looked at how to grow in our faith. Once into the renewal plan we ask, "How will we keep growing in Christ?

How do you replenish at the fountains and keep ministry flourishing?" So we run full circle, and we see again how the renewal we desire in our church begins with personal renewal in our hearts.

Could part of the way to replenish of our faith be in sharing the joy of renewal with others and training them in the renewal process? Training in the Springs process takes various forms, whether in seminary classes, in churches, or in clusters. We have even held Saturday-morning breakfast gatherings for interpretation and training. Here we take up topics of renewal and have testimonials of what happened for people and their churches. People from churches in renewal invite others to attend. Viewing a DVD of one event, I saw evidence of this deeper journey on the faces of people who came to share their experience of renewal.[1]

Testimonies

Remarks from those who had experienced renewal of their church were interspersed with presentations that Joan and I made on the topics covered in this book. The testimonies carried the day.

Michelle Armster spoke of the heart of servant leadership exemplified in Springs. She spoke of the Holy Spirit at work in the process, of it being powerful and God-inspired. As she read Scriptures about servanthood in Mark 9 and 10, she shared how, for churches to be renewed, leaders must be servants. Don Mitchell, of Harrisburg First Church, an inner-city congregation in Pennsylvania, told of a large, intergenerational renewal team. He noted how people are thirsty and seeking to do what God is calling First Church to do. In their sanctuary they have placed a fountain in which water flows from cup to cup to cup, reminding them of living water. The highlight of renewal thus far for Don was the first congregational gathering, at which the church named strength after strength. He said tears came to his eyes.

Rey Aviles, also of Harrisburg First Church, told of the inner thirst the renewal effort was quenching. His sense is that living water needs to flow through us and in renewal we help people know about Christ. Rey spoke about the power of God and the search for how the Spirit of God moves. His remarks spoke of the urgency and joy in renewal.

Attendees of the breakfast shared the strengths of their church in small groups. When I asked about their energy level, the groups said the level went up as they talked about the God-given talents in their church. Involvement by the groups made the presentations on renewal topics flow easily.

Then we heard from Rod O'Donnell, Bob Smith, and Glenn O'Donnell of Green Tree Church of the Brethren in suburban Philadelphia. Rod, a steel sales executive, spoke of his heart for renewal. He told about the church's renewal team, the Green Team. He also told of the energy that came through personal spiritual growth and how his young-adult children told him they were following the devotional folders. The church was finding energy through the disciplines.

Bob, a chimney sweep, talked about how the spiritual disciplines affected his life personally. He shared how every day that he went to work he felt that God was in his life. His life was more directed to God, he said, and renewal helped him stay focused daily.

Glenn, a schoolteacher, spoke of building on strengths and how that style motivated his students. His enthusiasm for Springs was evident as he shared from 1 Thessalonians 5:11, on encouraging one another. He spoke about the spiritual disciplines and how, as in physical fitness, the disciplines keep one spiritually fit. In this condition we can draw others to Christ.

Alvin Hathaway, pastor of Union Baptist Church in Baltimore, known as "the servant church," studied servant leadership and church renewal and identified the great need for spiritual growth lifted up in the Springs process.

At the close of the breakfast, we invited people to come forward and receive a cup of water served by deacon Ruben Deoleo. The invitation was for every person to partake of the living water of Christ in renewal and to replenish our own lives as we went out in service.

Claiming the Deeper Journey

Jesus' manner of dialogue is so important in claiming the deeper journey. Rather than imagine that we can do this on our own, we are reminded that Jesus comes to us. We have come this far, now we seek to go the further distance of faith as we engage in mission. Rather than approach us in a manner that creates fear, Jesus comes to us knowing the barriers we face, the fears that are present, and the reorientation needed. By grace we are invited to take the next step. If we are into a plan of renewal in the local church, we draw apart to consider that Christ is coming to us to assist us.

Like the woman at the well, we can explore questions of faith in dialogue. We can encounter Jesus and the living water in new ways. In times of confession we can face our lifestyle at a new level, where Jesus reveals that he knows all about us. When we are into our mission, we may face new questions like how to help people develop their faith. We may not see the way through misunderstandings or challenges that seem too great to overcome. In mission we may need to be reminded that Jesus is for us and with us. Through dialogue, he offers living water to us for new life ahead.

Thirst. When people search for a deeper faith, the very process that has helped them thus far can be a helpful path. We know when thirst appears and when we sense an encounter with Christ. We feel the call to transformation and see mission afresh. The process has become part of us. The very dynamics of renewal seen in the story of the woman at the well help people claim the deeper journey. Christ is inviting us to place our hand in his.

Thirst can be a positive factor in claiming the deeper journey. We remember how the apostle Paul spoke about being renewed day by day. The spiritual life needs continual renewal. This is true for both individuals and churches. We stay renewed by continually responding to the thirst. This keeps energy alive and growing. The thirst that we can feel while in mission invites us to the deeper journey.

The renewal process takes root first in individuals. Once we begin to experience personal renewal, we always have the faith that draws us back. If we lapse, we feel that same thirst we had before. Once we drink the living water, it is an integral part of our being. The deeper journey is living a life of prayer in action. St. Benedict said that our prayer becomes our work and our work becomes our prayer.[2]

Renewal also takes root in congregations. We have looked at what it means for a church to unite in spiritual disciplines and focus on strengths, and we've seen the positive outcomes of spiritual growth in mission. We may experience the inevitable setbacks, such as economic downturns that affect members of the church. Sometimes a ministry falters even with best-laid plans. How can we keep renewal going?

The thirst rises up and we identify it. The thirst invites us to enter the faith journey at an even deeper level. The thirst reminds us to reassert the spiritual disciplines and do so even more devoutly, knowing the time will return when we will experience God's presence. The importance of spiritual discernment becomes even more real and guides us through this time. Our thirst leads us to enter a deeper journey with God.

Encounter. Encounters with Jesus are integral to the deeper journey of renewal. By the divine MapQuest of God, Jesus keeps seeking us. In the deeper journey we come to know that it is time to refresh and to experience him again. In this chapter we will look at a number of ways to create a context for such encounters each day on a personal basis. Each of these enrich us in our faith journey. Later we will explore ways that can keep this encounter fresh, including observing divine hours, taking personal retreats, observing Sabbath, and entering a school of spiritual formation.

In the deeper journey we affirm ever more deeply what Rufus Jones means by the double search: "atonement—God's search for us—and prayer—our search for Him."[3]

Corporately we can keep returning to be renewed in regular patterns of worship, Bible study, and small groups. Being a part of a vital group of believers encourages us as we share with others on the journey. The very creativity of a church in renewal inspires us to go deeper. The worship of the saints inspires us as we focus on God.

Transformation. I had the privilege of sitting in the living room of Douglas Steere, an esteemed Quaker, who nurtured the interior life and engaged in missions around the world for the American Friends Service Committee. What struck me was the quietness, being with one so steeped in prayer and an active life. He gave me a little book, *Dimensions of Prayer*, which he wrote for United Methodist women, in which he talks of returning for reshaping.

Douglas tells of his great-grandfather, who lived in northern Michigan. In his village there was a smith's shop. To mend broken implements, the smith took the broken parts and put them in the hot furnace. When they were red-hot, he hammered them on the anvil to get them back in shape. Douglas writes, "At no less price could it be restored. All the great masters of prayer remind us of the necessity of returning for reshaping."[4] In renewal we find ourselves drawn up short and recognize our need for reshaping.

Transformation is part of the deeper journey of renewal. Services of self-examination and seasons of repentance, such the earlier illustration of the potter at Emmanuel, are part of a church's continued renewal. The theme of repentance is prominent not only in Lent, but also in Advent. What better way to prepare for the Savior than to look at the Scriptures of those seasons. In a similar way, other church services call for self-examination, such as preparing for the anointing or for the drama of basin and towel. In these, we experience God's grace extended anew.

Confession can be a positive part of claiming the deeper journey. Confession is a needed part of each prayer and each service of worship. As we come before God we see how needy we are. Such need creates an openness to grow. Steere notes, "The greatest pain comes from the tightness of our grip on that which holds us back."[5] Renewal is a process that calls for continued yielding, reshaping, and serving.

Mission. Every ministry calls us to grow. We see other people growing, and we see new opportunities before us. Our involvement calls us to claim the deeper journey. We do that by going where God is leading us in order to introduce others to Jesus. Following those leadings and promptings is important. Mission leads us to a deeper journey. We can only imagine the things we need to lay aside, the no-longer needed water pots, in order to take focused life journey.

In his *Church Dogmatics*, Karl Barth says, "The existence of the Christian is not an end in itself. As fellowship with Christ it is in principle and essence a ministry. It is a witness."[6] Our vocation is set. The ministry of the Christian community is to go to all nations and by Matthew 28:19 call them to discipleship.[7] People with interest in mission have said, "The church does not exist for itself, but for participation in God's mission of reconciliation. Mission is not just an activity carried out by special people in far-away places. Mission is the character of the church in whatever context it exists."[8]

When an individual and a church begin to focus on their mission, the outcome is rewarding. Rather than reacting to daily pressures and circumstances, they are guided by their vision. Energy is gained. The mission takes much effort. They work first for short-term goals and then longer-term ones. Being mission-driven means mission is being accomplished, and the outcomes and rewards are experienced.

To go deeper in renewal invites us to all aspects of Christian growth. Once you get into mission, it becomes more familiar to you, but at the same time you are stretched further than you ever imagined. The sacrifice and calls to discipleship are beyond what you foresaw, but the joy and hope are beyond what you imagined. The deeper walk of faith calls for increasing dependence on God.

Longevity and Sustainability

Seeing renewal as a long-term process, not a crash program, is integral to claiming the deeper journey. It is for the long haul. As we look at the dynamic of mission, I encourage you to consider how renewal can be sustained. At the beginning of the fourth year, the church can reassert the process by reactivating the renewal team and undergoing the process in perhaps an abbreviated form. (See appendix 1, of which steps 23 and 24 are the beginning stages of another four-year phase of renewal.)

Creating an ongoing process. As people get into the renewal process, they marvel at its simplicity. They are encouraged; they see a path; the outcomes seem so right; they see that they want to continue the process. Renewal is always needed. Sometimes at the beginning of the fourth year the church sees how it can build on what it has discovered. Like Steep Falls in Maine, a church may find a new Scripture and biblical vision that will continue to build it up.

The question becomes, where is God leading next? The nature of the church means it is always seeking to follow the will of God. The renewal team may be called into a more intentional period. In this ongoing process, the church needs a spiritually oriented path that everyone understands and feels a part of. Perhaps you will see from your experience the elements of what makes for new life and establish a second phase of the renewal process.

The use of spiritual folders. As spiritual disciplines folders become a familiar tool, the renewal team can continue to coordinate their use. Pastors can use the format of seasons of the year for regular seasons of growth. Preaching series can be fashioned along with special-guest series. Banners, worship aids, and dialogues can be added. Finding ways for people to share about their spiritual growth and how they face challenges adds to the richness of a spiritually alive church.

A worship committee that works with the total worship experience, including music, is vital for spiritual growth. Other areas—Bible school, small groups, Sunday school, family nights—are integral to ongoing spiritual growth. Some churches develop neighborhood Bible study groups. These endeavors can dovetail with service ministries that provide for needs in the community. Whatever ministry is in the making, people need to keep being sustained spiritually and grow in new ways.

Congregational gatherings on renewal. Perhaps again you will hold congregational events. You could plan one on the strengths of the church and see how the outcomes compare to the first gathering years ago. You could have a gathering on how people touch each other spiritually. And often people see the progress in the life cycle. New core values may have emerged as transformation and mission have moved forward. The biblical vision can be reviewed and revised and the next stage of a ministry plan discerned. Other congregational events could be held on the dynamics of renewal, to refresh the corporate memory.

Another format to use is the three themes of this book: spiritual formation, servant leadership, and being a healthy church with an urgent Christ-centered mission. The whole church or small groups can study the Scriptures on the servant in this resource (see appendix 7) or discuss topics from the book *Servant Leadership for Church Renewal.*[9]

Updating a biblical vision and plan. By now the church may have decided to stick with its biblical passage and dynamics of renewal or to discern a new passage. But entering the deeper journey might lead to an updating of the church's biblical vision and plan. In either case, the renewal team works to help the congregation refresh its vision. Part of this is to review how far the church has come and what next steps will build on the progress that has been made. Celebrating progress thus far and the hope of what God has in store next would be very appropriate.

Sticking with the renewal process. Renewal is never a straight line. What can defeat us most is bringing expectations to renewal, rather than just having gratitude for what is happening. Be prepared for surprises. Some things will probably turn out better than you expected. Other things may not meet your expectations. Servants of renewal keep awake for whatever may come. Renewal is dynamic rather than static. What makes the difference is the continual nurture of the faith journey. Depth rather than breadth carries us when the headwinds blow. And depth keeps ministries moving forward when the seas are calm.

Even in the spiritual life, there are ebbs and flows. We move through periods of consolation and desolation. Nothing, good or bad, lasts forever. What makes the difference is whether we follow the rules—that is, the rules of the disciplines. We do not presume that consolation will always continue. During those seasons we offer gratitude to God. St. Ignatius counsels us to make a memory note of consolation so that when desolation comes, we remember that life can be better.

When desolation comes, don't give into it, but reassert the spiritual disciplines. When the renewal process slows, perform the disciplines even more faithfully. Patience and faithfulness can be strengthened. Renewal means pushing forward when the way seems unclear. Renewal reminds us to turn control over to God, trusting in what God is doing. As Thomas Green says, "In some profoundly mysterious way, the flowers in the garden of the Lord bloom best in times of drought."[10] Staying the course, people and churches in renewal are sustained and rejoice when new life comes.

Christ Becomes Preeminent

At some point in the process, we discover a deep sense that Christ is present. We have prayed; we have discerned God's will. We have moved out in faith on a renewal process, not knowing what is ahead. Like those who discovered the risen Savior, we realize that the risen Christ is with us and that we cannot accomplish renewal on our own power or prowess. All of church renewal is Christ centered, dependent on a risen Savior. In renewal, Christ is lifted up and becomes preeminent.

Something more important than all the programs, all the efforts, and all the acumen becomes evident. The visible Christ emerges above all else. As the author of Hebrews says, you discover "he is the reflection of God's glory and the exact imprint of God's very being, and he sustains all things by his powerful word"

(Hebrews 1:3 NRSV). To claim the deeper journey means to place Christ in the center of all renewal.

Christ-centered. Being involved in renewal invites us to think of our theology, our basic beliefs about God, behind our renewal effort. With God reaching into our lives and transforming us as we encounter living water, Christ is at the center of all church renewal. Prayer and Bible study draw us to God our creator and Christ our Savior, seen and experienced in Christian community—the church. In *Life Together*, Dietrich Bonhoeffer says, "Christianity means community through Jesus Christ and in Jesus Christ."[11]

Bonhoeffer adds, "First, the Christian is the man who no longer seeks his salvation, his deliverance, his justification in himself, but in Jesus Christ alone." "Second, a Christian comes to others only through Jesus Christ." "Third, when God's Son took on flesh, he truly and bodily took on, out of pure grace, our being, our nature, ourselves."[12] A renewing church is Christ-centered. Only God in Christ can bring about the renewal we desire in the church and only through him can we become what we desire to be.

In the spiritual formation of the church, we keep Christ before us. As we converse with one another, we think of the dialogue of Jesus. Whether we plan worship, nurture studies, coordinate games for the youth group, or go on a mission project, we lift up Christ. The church as Christian community becomes intentional in its life and in its mission. Through Christ people are drawn together and come to know one another. Someone is shaping us. All our efforts are done in and through the living Christ.

Seeking God's will. Throughout this resource we have talked about seeking God's will. This is how we find which direction to take in renewal. Rather than just say what we want for the church, we ask where God is leading. So often, that very question has God's grace within it. For God desires us to be a spiritually vibrant body, a healthy church in its internal life, and one with an urgent Christ-centered mission. That means following where God leads, despite the cost.

Spiritual discernment—getting the head, the heart, and the faith journey together—is important in renewal. To be Christ-centered means to bring all things personally and as a church under that filter. Your rational sense guides you into the practicality of a ministry. The heart helps you sense when something has the feeling tone of what Christ would have you do. The faith journey tells you whether a direction will call you to greater growth, even though it is costly.

When you seek God's will, you claim the deeper journey. You embrace what God wants and let all other priorities center around that mission. Those ministries do not have to be that complex, just creative. I saw this at the Hatfield Church, which had a number of people with disabilities. The decision was made to have a rhythm choir using instruments. Who would have thought of such an idea? But as they played in worship, the congregation came to life and was in total worship of God.

Continuing to Grow Spiritually

As I've said, to claim the deeper journey means to keep growing spiritually; if we wish for renewal in our church, it must begin in us. In renewal it is important to set a plan for spiritual growth in year two and three. Every church needs to discern how to continue spiritual growth for a wide range of people. Besides using the personal disciplines folders, you may appreciate these additional practices.[13]

Observing the divine hours. In the divine hours, also called the daily office, life is lived between periods of prayer. In Acts 10, Peter had a vision of a descending sheet because he had gone to pray at the sixth hour—noontime. And it was in that pause that the vision came. In our pauses, we can remember again how God is reaching out.

The divine hours occur four times a day and provide anchors around which to live life. Phyllis Tickle's *The Divine Hours* contains prayers for morning, midday, evening, and compline. Such a resource is easy to use because it gives you a daily schedule of prayers adaptable to your own format. There are many other resources about this type of "fixed hour" prayer, including *Take Our Moments and Our Days: An Anabaptist Prayer Book* (Herald Press, 2007).

Taking personal retreats. Another way may be to go to a retreat center for a particular length of time. In renewal, people become attuned to their need to spend time communing with God. As a pastor, I often feel that it is time to draw away and renew my spirit. While sometimes only a few hours are possible, an extended time of a day or more leads to space for being attuned to God. In *Wilderness Time: A Guide for Spiritual Retreat*, Emilie Griffin speaks of stepping-stones from our "furious activity into God's calm and peace."[14]

In *A Place for God*, Timothy Jones includes a guide of 250 spiritual retreats and retreat centers, with a description of offerings, accommodations, reservations, points of interest, and location.[15] The first section, which tells about the author's preparations for a retreat, can be helpful. With a Bible and minimal resources, such as devotional writings and a journal, you will most likely find that the time in retreat quickly passes. Such a time apart renews us for spiritual work.

Sabbath rest. Rest is integral to renewal. In fact, we build a fallow time into the Springs process. Time taken to rest the body and inner spirit is well spent. In *Sabbath Time*, Tilden Edwards writes about taking from a day to a month or longer to focus on being present to God in prayer. He says this practice helps in transition time, a time of self-examination when we look at the "hidden footsteps of God in our lives and how we have responded to them."[16] Taking Sabbath time includes confession and assurance of healing and strength for new beginnings.

Sabbath time can be such a wonderful growth experience. One can really release all to God, signaling that one is available only to God and family, and focus on Scripture and spiritual growth. Even shorter times can give opportunity to withdraw. Setting aside just a period of the day prepares you to enter into the Presence. What you find is that you are much better able to draw on your inner spiritual resources and to proceed at a slower pace, be reflective, and be proactive.[17]

Entering a school of spiritual formation. Another way to grow spiritually is to enroll in a school of spiritual formation.

Shalem Institute is such a school, located near Washington, D.C., and founded by Tilden Edwards. It has been one of the recent forerunners in developing the contemplative life. It offers many options for spiritual retreats and extension programs in the contemplative life and spiritual direction. Its website lists extensive program options (www.shalem.org).

The Kairos School of Spiritual Formation (www.on-the-journey.org) in the Jesuit Center in Wernersville, Pennsylvania, comes out of the Anabaptist tradition and "seeks to deepen the life of prayer and to nurture contemplative living in the world." Monthly retreats are held in spiritual formation, prayer, and the contemplative life. Kairos gives a structure of spir-itual growth, a community of other retreat participants, and spiritual guidance for those seeking it. Other such schools provide steady spiritual growth and can be a real resource for the renewal process.

The Dynamic of Mission

An indelible picture of the woman at the well is one of her joyously going into mission. Can we imagine the change from when she was thirsty to when she was pointing others to a drink? So much transformation happens as we are involved in mission. As Robert Mulholland reminds us, "Spiritual formation is not something that we do to ourselves or for ourselves, but something we allow God to do in us and for us as we yield ourselves to the work of God's transforming grace."[18]

Going to the hometown. We cannot be church and not be in mission. Living churches witness to the one who gives life. In renewal we capture our opportunity to spread the gospel. Mission is in the reconciliation accomplished in each ministry. Time and again people are reconciled to God and each other during the renewal process, not by human effort, but by God's grace. Here is the church's great mission. People begin to witness to their faith in very natural ways. Not at all prefabricated, such faith sharing leads to life change.

Growing through the global community. Renewing churches

become aware of the world's wider social needs, such as poverty, as well as missions projects around the globe. Back in 1970, through the renewal process, Bush Creek became aware of world hunger and took up numerous projects to address it.

An opportunity came from Heifer International: there was need for an entire shipment of heifers to Guatemala. This led to a district-wide project, spearheaded by Bush Creek to raise money, purchase animals, inoculate them, and escort them to a country in great need. This project became part of the renewal of the church because the congregation felt it could make a difference. The message sent to Guatemala was that these cows came in the name of King Jesus. In turn, the church grew deeper spiritually.

Us? In Mission?

Like the woman at the well, Jesus is inviting us to give him a drink. Is it possible that the next illustration for this book might be written by you? Quickly the impediments might appear before you. Could this be possible? This brings us back to the beginning of the book. Who would have thought in any of these churches that renewal was possible?

But the invitation is out. The path lies before us. We may have been blessed with the thirst that more is possible, but perhaps we held back not knowing how to go about responding. We might even wonder if we understand every aspect of the process. Do we have it all? Do we have what it takes? But now, yes, Jesus comes to ask us for a drink.

If John 4 provides any message, it is that God can take those who wonder whether they are adequate and show them that their lives can be used. The discoveries we make lead to life change as we are guided by the passion to share in God's mission. By asking where God is leading and following the answer, we discover the way to go.

Your own unique path. You will be creating a story uniquely your own. You may want to turn to other resources to learn more and find extra helps along the way. Discover what is unique in your own situation and find other resources that match your situation.

The examples given in this book are not just to copy. Even though you may be drawn to the same Scripture texts other churches chose, lay them aside and discern your own. The same is true for each topic in the book. Perhaps some examples can be adapted, but only after thorough discernment. Some illustrations give models but then need to be modified for your use. You can creatively discover your own ministries.

As we enter mission, we are invited to claim the deeper journey of faith. Rather than becoming worn out, we are refreshed by the fountains of living waters. Renewal is a vibrant faith journey of individuals and congregations. The very dynamics of renewal that get us started lead us to the deeper journey. These dynamics assist us to continue on the journey and to extend it for the long haul. Christ becomes preeminent. The outcomes are changed lives, active witness, and service to Jesus Christ. The fruit of the spirit of renewal, the blessed outcome, is joy in Christ. All praise and honor to God.

For Reflection and Discussion

1. What thoughts come to mind when you hear someone say, "Christ is preeminent"? Can you see how the renewal process leads individuals to claim the deeper journey?

2. What in this chapter did you find helpful in growing deeper spiritually and for the long haul? Can you see how important this is for sustained renewal in the church?

3. What is your opinion of Sabbath rest? What kind of preparation do you see as needed before you enter Sabbath rest? Could shorter periods of rest be built into your ministry?

4. Have you had the experience of growing deeper spiritually while you were in mission? How can the church collectively grow through its mission?

5. Jesus said to the woman at the well, "That water that I give will become in [you] a spring of water gushing up to eternal life" (John 4:14 NRSV). After reading this book, what do those words of Jesus say to you?

6. Us? In mission? Where is God leading? What is the next step God is inviting you to take in ministry?

Postlude

The Deeper Joy

Ho, everyone who thirsts,
come to the waters;
And you that have no money,
come, buy and eat!
—Isaiah 55:1 (NRSV)

That's it! During my weekly Saturday prayer time I read Isaiah's call. That is the invitation of renewal. When individuals, when churches, are thirsty, God invites them to come to the living water. Just as Isaiah gives the invitation of deliverance to the Israelites to return to their homeland, we are invited to claim the deeper joy.

As I delved into this text, I saw the great themes of renewal—of deliverance of a nation, of a servant people in formation, of renewed covenant, of seeking and finding, of blessing, and of joy. The context of Isaiah 55 is homecoming for the Israelites, who are to be defined as a servant people, a light to the nations. This is a time of hope and victory.

Proclaiming a Resurrection Hope

What is amazing about this text is its use in the early church. The early church is a symbol of the church alive. This text was used in the longest service of the year, the Easter Vigil. The night before Easter, the church gathered by a bonfire and read the Scriptures of hope and deliverance. Among them was Isaiah 55.

If church renewal teaches us anything, it is that Christ is alive. Churches, even those for whom little hope was held, have been renewed. Individuals just lumbering along in life have discovered a vibrant faith. Churches have found a path to renewal that people can become excited about. The church faithful is the church victorious.

New beginnings. Church renewal is about new beginnings. The Easter Vigil proclaims that we can leave the old behind as God's grace reclaims and restores. There are new beginnings; there are new possibilities. Throughout the renewal work of the church, we live in confidence that God is making all things new. Pervading the Springs process is this fundamental affirmation of faith. What a deeper joy we can claim!

The Easter Vigil and the Great Fifty Days that follow were a time of great joy in the early church. It was a season of baptisms and recommitment to baptism. It was a time of celebrating the sightings of the risen Lord. Throughout the renewal process we encourage such celebrations whenever new life is evident. The church that sees how fundamental renewal is day-by-day sets its claim on the deeper joy.

A service of rededication to baptism. A symbol for a renewing church would be a service of recommitment to baptism, which can be a time of celebration of the new life that God gives. Rather than being an obligation, such a service is marked by joy in the new birth that has come.

Some denominations encourage a yearly service. Personal preparation can take place and vows be reviewed. The service can include the laying on of hands by the corporate body.

The joy of resurrection pervades in Christian life. Even though renewal comes more slowly than we want, even if there are seeming defeats, there is the confidence that God is making all things new. In the long run, positive reversals come and you know the joy of persisting in faith. This sure and often quiet confidence is part of faithfulness in renewal. And you will be blessed by a deeper joy.

Claiming the Deeper Joy

As we claim the deeper journey and practice spiritual disciplines, we can claim the deeper joy. Once we begin the spiritual journey of renewal in a church, we have a change of outlook. We develop a sense of gratitude in our heart. People speak of the radical reorientation that happens when they look at strengths. They establish ministries in their personal life and in the church. Their entire life and ministry is changed. What about a baker's dozen of joy?

1. **The joy of prayer.** One outgrowth of renewal is the joy that comes through prayer. You can take all of your life to God in prayer and commune using Scriptures, quiet reflection, devotionals, and periods of contemplation. While not every time of prayer will yield the same growth, the more steadily it is done, the more the outcomes provide release, peace, thanksgiving, and joy. The sense of refreshment and guidance is amazing.

2. **The joy of spiritual discernment.** A direct outgrowth of prayer concerns decision making. To have a life guided by prayer rather than just by impulse is such a blessing. When people like young adults discover that they can find help in making decisions, they feel joy. Imagine getting the head, the heart, and the faith journey together in minor and major decisions of life. When things turn out better than you could imagine, you feel joy.

3. **The joy of a new climate.** Like a weather front that comes in and changes the temperature and humidity, so renewal changes the climate within individuals and churches. People find a better balance in life. Even with great obstacles to face, renewal changes attitudes. You may see someone redecorating a bulletin board or greeting a newcomer. The climate in churches changes as people start to feel better and see that hope is possible.

4. **The joy of giving.** In renewal giving often increases. People report new attitudes in the budget-building process. The kinds of material used in a stewardship emphasis changes. We have observed churches with very tight budgets enter renewal and after sufficient hard work and sacrifice begin not just to make budget but to move over ten percent ahead of current needs.

5. **The joy of celebrating.** Churches in renewal celebrate. Times of rest and rejoicing are built into the process. After you have

gone through a stage of self-study and the summer break comes, the renewal team pauses and plans a celebration. More thank-you notes appear in the newsletter. People do things for one another. The church begins to feel that it is making progress and has something to offer.

6. The joy of everyone with a ministry. People report that they begin to feel more enthusiasm and purpose in their life. In Springs, we affirm that everyone is in ministry. People discover in renewal that their life opens up and they have new energy with a purpose. This means that their life can be more fully used by God. They share an excitement. What has been amazing is how people in all walks of life have had their work flourish, including those in the trades, business, sales, and other professions.

7. The joy of a calling to the ministry. Though it's not a specific part of the renewal endeavor, people often feel a call to a "set apart" ministry. This may be a pastoral call or in a range of ministries. One apparent reason is that people begin to see the newly defined role of the pastor; they experience the excitement it brings, and they sense a call to use their lives in service in the church. Also, people in the church become more attentive to extending the call to others.

8. The joy of youth work. As already mentioned, often during renewal, youth work is either renewed or taken up. A church being renewed wants to share the faith with others. Often this entails stretching across the generations, which the dialogue process reinforces. Youth ministry takes youth willing to take responsibilities, advisers who will work along with them, and a church to discover the faith in all its dimensions, including having fun.

9. The joy of new believers. One thing about entering mission is that people are more intentionally called to faith. The joy of newfound faith is exciting for everyone. It shows that the church is alive, that people are both sharing and discovering the living water, and that the body is being fruitful. The challenge is to support and grow these new disciples, who also rejuvenate the faith of long-term believers.

10. The joy of renewed believers. Often in the renewal process, long-term believers experience a renewal of their faith. They make discoveries through a newfound life of prayer and meaning in worship. As they learn more about the Bible, their familiarity with the faith can be a real asset. They may find unbelievable growth as they become involved in a mission of the church. Sometimes renewed believers want to recommit themselves in a service of rededication.

11. The joy of mission. In renewal, people discover or rediscover their mission in life. The woman at the well found her mission in her hometown. Churches open a home missions department and find where they can help others discover Jesus. The range of these missions varies as each is tailored to the strengths of individuals and the church, as well as to the needs and context of the community.

12. The joy of renewed families. Missions can start in your own home as you dialogue about faith and living. So much love is created and regenerated through the life of prayer. The church becomes a laboratory of love and forgiveness. The family together can make a witness even greater than the sum of the parts. The family has a mission. The renewal we speak of in our lives is regenerated in the home and in the church.

13. The joy of the unexpected. In renewal there is the joy of the unexpected. You can never predict or program renewal, nor should you try. As renewal happens you just marvel, "This is not of us, but of God." The creativity is astounding, and the outcomes are greater than anyone would have expected. You step back and say, "I never imagined this could have happened." God is at work.

The Joy of the Lord

In Isaiah 55, we find a beautiful promise for our churches:

> For you shall go out with joy,
> And be led back in peace;
> The mountains and the hills before you
> shall burst into song,

and all the trees of the field shall clap their hands (55:12 NRSV).

The greatest joy is the joy of the Lord reflected in the faces of people who have discovered living water and whose church has new vitality. The way of peace is paved in a renewing church. And the effect all around is felt in the mission that is performed. Our towns and counties, nations, and world will be transformed by the church alive.

Closing Prayer

O Lord of the empty tomb and resurrection joy,
    we pray for the renewal of thy church.
Stir our hearts afresh as you come to seek us
    in the heat of the day and ask us for a drink.
Pour thy fresh waters upon us, Living Water,
    Life-Giving Water, Jesus Christ our Lord.
Give us the confidence, fresh courage, and
    stamina to receive the new life you give.
Transform our hearts and lives so that we
    may be supple to thy leading.
Renew thy Church with a sense of the gifts
    you have given us for thy service.
Equip us, train us for the work of being
    your apostles, servants in word and deed.
Send us forth in mission—with a divine
    vocation to spread the Good News.
      In Jesus' name, Amen.

Appendix 1

Steps of Renewal

The steps below are guided by spiritual discernment. Steps 1-10 of the spiritual journey and self-study take twelve to eighteen months. Steps 11-22 are implemented for three years to establish or reestablish ministries that fulfill the church's vision. Steps 23-24 are the beginning stages of another four-year phase of renewal.

Phase One

Step 1. Enlist congregation, asking, "Where is God leading?"

Step 2. Call a renewal team that works with leadership of the church. Train the team in the renewal process, spiritual guidance, servant leadership, dialogue, and the life cycle of a church.

Step 3. Begin spiritual disciplines: Entire congregation invited to take the next step in their spiritual disciplines. Use of disciplines folders.

Step 4. First congregational gathering, on strengths.

Step 5. Second congregational gathering, on spiritual appreciation.

Step 6. Third congregational gathering, on interventions of servant leadership in the life cycle and new energy in renewal. The renewal team tells of originating mission of the church and demographics in which God is inviting ministry.

Step 7. Optional congregational gathering if a special topic arises that would propel the church forward.

Step 8. Fourth congregational gathering, on identifying core values and spiritually discerning the identity of the church.

Step 9. Fourth congregational gathering can include discerning a biblical passage to guide the church in renewal.

Step 10. Fifth congregational gathering, discerning a biblical vision, a three-year plan, and the first steps to implementation.

Rest and Phase Two
At this point the renewal team may work with regular committees of the church to turn vision into reality.

Step 11. The renewal team begins to shape the plan and first steps and help the congregation celebrate vision and plan and rest.

Step 12. The renewal team works with church leadership to gather people to start the first ministry or renew an existing ministry.

Step 13. The renewal team helps the church to identify and call leaders to commence new ministry or renew old ministry.

Step 14. The renewal team works to provide ongoing training and resources for leaders.

Step 15. The congregation may have gatherings to learn of a new ministry or take up special topics vital to the church.

Step 16. The renewal team works with congregational leaders to launch or relaunch a ministry. A service of commitment is held.

Step 17. The renewal team works with congregational leaders and appropriate committees to provide mentors for leaders.

Step 18. Potential congregational gathering on appreciative inquiry to determine when and how things work at their best.

Step 19. The renewal team works to assist the congregation with ongoing spiritual disciplines and spiritual growth.

Step 20. The renewal team works with the congregation on the assimilation of new members and care of leadership.

Step 21. The renewal team helps the congregation take periods of rest to evaluate and celebrate gains.

Step 22. As time comes for new ministries or the vision to be updated, say the third year, the renewal team helps with this process.

Step 23. Reevaluate progress, enter the process with spiritual disciplines folders and congregational gatherings.

Step 24. Reaffirm or find a new biblical passage and vision, and next three-year plan. Begin the process of implementing the plan.

Appendix 2

Covenanting of a Local Church

A local church takes an important step with the commitment to enter a renewal process. Doubly blessed is a congregation that decides to make a covenant, calling on God as it shapes its agreement and asking God for help and strength. Such congregations see how they do renewal together with each one's help and see how they become partners with Christ in the work.

As you undertake a time of renewal, making covenant is a visible sign that you want to be intentional partners, respond to God's invitation to new life, ask God's help to be faithful in the renewal process, and seek God's will in each step. Discerned calls for renewal invite opening our selves to what God wishes to do. This entails clarifying your relationship with God anew and establishing your understanding of what renewal will entail. A covenant will also clarify your focus on your purpose and plan for ministry as the church. As part of the Springs process, each church creates and signs a covenant affirming God's active role and the church's active response. The covenant is an expression of the desire to be part of what God is doing in renewal of the church.

As you strike a covenant with God, have a service during which you formally make a commitment. There can be some visible sign such as a banner or communion table runner. A large candle representing the light of Christ may also be a part. This service may occur during a Sunday-morning service with an atmosphere of celebration. The banner, cloth, and candle can be used again at significant times of celebration. Here are some suggestions that might help you in planning your service.

1. Designate a Sunday as Covenant for Renewal Sunday. You may wish to invite your executive or conference minister and a representative of the denomination.
2. This Sunday could be the culmination of a series of messages or services on renewal. Biblical passages of renewal can be lifted up. There can be teaching on being intentional about your covenant with God and the blessing it can be for the church.
3. Along with worship aids such as litanies and dedicatory moments of response, people can participate in signing the cloth and committing to the covenant of renewal.
4. Some churches may wish to celebrate communion at this point, symbolizing their covenant with Christ and the greater church. Depending on the size of the congregation, people may actually want to gather around the communion table or the sanctuary.
5. Appropriate singing will add greatly to the service. Some hymns lend themselves to such a renewal time, such as "Spirit of the Living God, Fall Afresh on Me." The song could be sung a second time replacing the word me with us.
6. Often a covenant service is followed by a fellowship time, such as a potluck meal. At the meal, it is appropriate to display pictures of positive experiences of the church and share positive testimonies.
7. Make this day a positive experience for all age groups in the congregation. Let everyone share in their own way and feel that they are an important part of what is happening. In servant leadership, God can use even the least likely one.

Covenant for a Local Church: A Litany of Renewal

One: "The water that I will give will become in them a spring of water gushing up to eternal life" (John 4:14 NRSV).
All: We desire life-giving water.
One: Forgive us, Lord, for times we have relied on our own resources

and have been empty vessels because we failed to recognize our need for You.

All: We come before You, Lord, confessing our brokenness and desiring to be reshaped by Your hands and to renew our relationship with You.

One: As individuals we desire to renew our covenant with Jesus Christ and to give our lives anew to him for God's work in the world.

All: I reaffirm my belief in Jesus Christ as personal Savior and Lord of my life.

One: In order to grow, let us give our lives to a new season of prayer, study of Scripture, experiences of worship, and opportunities for Christian growth.

All: With God's help, I desire to grow into the fullness of the stature of Christ and be all that I was created to be as a vessel for his service.

One: As a congregation, we desire to open our corporate life to the movement of God and see where God is leading our church.

All: I desire to give myself wholeheartedly to the renewal process and to work with others to discover the new life God promises.

One: We affirm the blessing of our church and desire to work together as a body to follow God's leading and affirm the value and the gifts of each member.

All: We are grateful for our church. We desire to be vessels and work diligently in Christ's service in order to be a witness in our community and our world.

One: We now want to celebrate this covenant. We are so grateful to be partners with Christ in the work that God is placing before us.

All: We express our joy. The life-giving water of Jesus refreshes us. We are grateful that this joy can overflow in our lives and give hope to others.

Appendix 3

The Twelve Spiritual Disciplines

The Inward Disciplines

1. Meditation: Meditation is spending time hearing God's voice and becoming aware of God's presence in our lives. We may meditate on a passage of Scripture or ponder a truth of the gospel. As Thomas à Kempis says, it can lead us to "a familiar friendship with Jesus." Meditation affects our actions. We gain perspective and are led by Christ.

2. Prayer: Richard J. Foster writes, "Prayer is the central avenue God uses to transform us." Prayer involves listening as much as speaking. Prayer engages us in five areas: thanking God for blessings, asking forgiveness, receiving pardon, listening for God's challenge, and responding with our lives. In prayer we communicate with God, and we intercede for others by bringing their needs and ours before God.

3. Fasting: Fasting is refraining from eating for spiritual purposes. Fasting helps one focus on God and listen to God. Fasting is a powerful experience that attunes us to other people and to the heart of a situation. Foster writes, "More than any other discipline, fasting reveals the things that control us." Proper precautions and medical safeguards need to be taken before fasting.

4. Study: In the Christian life, we study the Bible and time-tested authors of the Christian life. Fosters observes that study entails four steps: repetition, concentration, comprehension, and reflection. We learn the great truths of the Christian life and apply them to our lives. We can study such classics as Thomas Kelly's *A Testament of Devotion* or Dietrich Bonhoeffer's *The Cost of Discipleship*.

Disciplines

ty: Simplicity means to be so focused on Christ
secondary. Foster writes, "Simplicity is freedom.
dage." With so many materials we can strive after
s. We easily lose the real focus of life through Jesus
Christ. We look to Jesus, who lived simply, and we can strive to
live Christ-centered lives and simplify our wants.

6. Solitude: Often Jesus went apart; he spent time alone with
God. The Christian life calls for taking time apart, at least to pause
in order to be still and know God. In these moments we can refresh,
reorient, and sense God's presence. Solitude allows one to pray with
à Kempis, "As thou wilt; what thou wilt; when thou wilt."

7. Submission: Foster writes, submission "is the ability to lay
down the terrible burden of always needing to get our own way."
In submission we explore the act of self-denial; we take up our
cross and follow Jesus. Voluntarily we follow Paul's advice to "consider others better than yourselves" (Philippians 2:3). Living in this
way of consideration of others revolutionizes our relationships.

8. Service: Service calls on us to model the way of Jesus, who
came not to be served but to serve. This defined his leadership and
authority. Thus we find the joy of Brother Lawrence, who found
Christ in the midst of serving among the pots and pans. Ministry
literally means service. As we serve in the name of Christ, we
become an expression of Christ to others.

Corporate Disciplines

9. Confession: In confession we bring our lives before God,
seek God's forgiveness, and seek to forgive others. Confession gets
to the heart of the redemptive process of the cross. Foster speaks
of confession as growing into the mature Christian of which the
apostle Paul wrote, "attaining to the whole measure of the fullness
of Christ" (Ephesians 4:13).

10. Worship: In worship we express the worth of God. In
Isaiah 6, we see five aspects of worship: praising and adoring, confessing, receiving pardon, listening to a challenge, and responding,

"Here am I. Send me!" (v. 8). Foster speaks of the discipline of worship as the human response to the divine initiative. Worship is vital to the renewal of people and of the church.

11. Guidance: Guidance can be on an individual or a group basis. Listed as a corporate discipline, guidance is working at discerning God's will as a group. This incorporates the discipline of dialogue. Together we work at what Foster calls a "Spirit-directed unity." Transformed by the will of God, we become Christ's expression of the kingdom and make a united witness to the world.

12. Celebration: The Christian life is joyful. In this discipline we remember the life-giving breath of the gospel. Obedience brings us joy, not a somber life. For Foster, "Joy produces energy. Joy makes us strong." As we perform the disciplines we discover the song of our heart. What a joy. We experience God transforming our lives and know his goodness and mercy.

Summarized from Richard J. Foster's Celebration of Discipline *(San Francisco: Harper & Row, 1978).*

Appendix 4

Core Values Audit

Please indicate what you feel are the core values of our church by rating each item below from 1 to 5, with 1 the lowest and 5 the highest.

_____ 1. Using servant leadership
_____ 2. Being relevant in today's culture
_____ 3. Financial stability
_____ 4. Inspiring worship
_____ 5. Making new disciples
_____ 6. Careful stewardship of resources
_____ 7. Strong learning program/classes, for all ages, like Sunday school
_____ 8. Denominational heritage
_____ 9. Consistent intercessory prayer
_____ 10. Smooth running organization
_____ 11. Christian service among the poor
_____ 12. Evangelism—reaching people with the gospel
_____ 13. Teaching peace
_____ 14. Experience of Christian community
_____ 15. Theology of denomination
_____ 16. Sustained excellence and quality
_____ 17. Spiritual growth/spiritual disciplines
_____ 18. A grace-orientation to ministry
_____ 19. Life change
_____ 20. Mobilizing all spiritual gifts in the body
_____ 21. Achieving consensus in decision making

_____ 22. Giving a significant portion (tithe?) to God
_____ 23. An attractive, well-maintained facility
_____ 24. Creativity and innovation for all ages, like Sunday school
_____ 25. Proper order and process
_____ 26. Bible-centered preaching/teaching
_____ 27. Using of spiritual discernment in decision making
_____ 28. Teaching the responsibilities and duties of the Christian
_____ 29. Nurturing a personal relationship with Jesus
_____ 30. Shaping ministries around needs in the community
_____ 31. Addressing issues of injustice
_____ 32. The lordship of Christ
_____ 33. _____
_____ 34. _____

Two areas have a similar core value that serves as a check and balance. You may wish to reduce this to one and/or add definitions to each core value on separate pages. Then circle core values that received a 4 and 5. Then prioritize with 1 as the highest.

Name:

_____

Please fill in so that your form can be returned after compilations are completed.

Adapted from an audit by Walter Sawatzky, Associate Conference Minister, Franconia Mennonite Conference, who built on an audit by Aubrey Malphurs.

Appendix 5

The Gift of Dialogue

Dialogue is tied directly to tending spiritual thirst. The four-point dialogue process described below can be implemented with two people or in a group setting. Spiritual disciplines are key to any dialogue, which should be cherished as a gift.

In monologue, one person speaks and the other listens. In dialogue both people listen and speak, seeking the truth among them. Jesus initiated dialogue with the woman at the well. He invited conversation, asking her for a drink, and empowered her to engage and seek truth. Using dialogue Jesus gave what he had to offer—life-giving water. Growing spiritually and growing dialogically go hand in hand.

The process of dialogue can be introduced at the beginning of any endeavor in church renewal and be part of the training in servant leadership. Guidelines for dialogue may be written on a card and put in a prominent place during all discussions. See the example on the next page.

Elements of the Tent Card on Dialogue

- Becoming grounded spiritually takes discipline. Rather than entering conversation out of anxiety, we should enter with the peace of God.
- Listening takes discipline. It takes discipline to really listen and not to think about what you want to say while the other person is still speaking.
- Speaking entails discipline. It takes discipline not to speak in a manner that conveys that you have all the answers.
- In discernment, we wait for understanding to emerge. It can never be forced. Discipline is needed not to push but to "wait upon the Lord."

Dialogue

1. Becoming Grounded Spiritually
   - Get in touch with the living Christ.
   - Release anxiety and be open to what is possible.

2. Listening
   - Set aside my agenda and listen to the other person(s).
   - Suspend judgment and be open to be influenced.

3. Speaking
   - Speak the truth in love, using my understanding.
   - Be able to reflect on the assumptions of others.

4. Spiritually Discerning
   - Seek God's will and truth together.
   - Get head, heart, and faith journey together.

Holding a Group Dialogue Session

The dialogue process can take place between individuals but also in groups. Learning dialogue moves us into group discernment. The following steps can help establish clear boundaries so that each person in the group can speak and be heard.

- The agenda needs to be adequately announced so people feel included in the discussion and know the boundaries around topics to be considered.
- The moderator reviews the four-fold dialogue process described on the tent card.
- The moderator may ask, in the midst of listening, whether someone has something to offer.
- The moderator needs to clarify that, while opinions are always welcomed, in dialogue we suspend judgment in order to look at something from all sides.
- Over time everyone becomes more comfortable with the dialogue process.

The Gift of Dialogue

Dialogue is seen as a gift because it cannot be forced or manufactured. Something beyond us has occurred. The understanding that emerges between people is cherished and is coupled with creative insight and greater understanding. These elements should be noted:

- Dialogue yields growth because we grow stronger as others grow stronger. Dialogue is essential for a healthy church because people communicate.
- Servants begin by listening. Dialogue is integral to key themes from servant leadership such as acceptance and empathy, all of which build trust.
- Dialogue helps churches build strength and gain energy as they communicate about basic matters and build on common core values.
- To build a healthy church and discover new energy, churches need a process of communication that builds understanding and negotiates critical factors.

Appendix 6

When Should a Church Enter Renewal?

A participating church should have a number of characteristics that make it a candidate for renewal. Like marriage enrichment and marriage encounter programs, which are not designed for marriages on the rocks, so church renewal is not designed for churches at the level of decline where drastic interventions are needed. However, some congregations in severe decline have used the process to great success.

The prime candidates for renewal are relatively healthy churches that see the need for new clarity of focus and know that more is possible. Below are some characteristics evident in participating churches.

1. The church should have a hunger and eagerness for renewal.
2. The church should have pastoral leadership that has a passion for renewal and a willingness to grow in the area of spirituality.
3. The church should be able to identify five people who are eager for renewal and may form the core of a renewal team.
4. The church may be on a plateau in terms of attendance and giving.
5. The church should desire to work closely with its district and denominational leadership.
6. The church will look at renewal as a longer-term process rather than a quick fix.

7. The church has a workable level of conflict. Highly con-
flicted churches should first seek intervention before entering the process.

8. In terms of pastoral leadership, the church may be in an
interim period. If so, the renewal process helps clarify the
very type of pastoral leadership needed.

9. The church should have the potential for renewal.

10. The church is able to work about a year on the spiritual
journey and is willing to explore its strengths and develop
a biblical vision with a three-year incremental plan that it
will commit to implementing.

What a Church Can Expect

It is important to understand how critical the enlistment period
is. Renewal is never imposed on a local church. Gaining a broad base
of ownership is vital. The church must take the time needed to ignite
a spark of interest and discern a sense of call to enter such a process.
In fact, it might well be said that once a church decides to enter
renewal, it is halfway there. These factors should be taken under consideration:

1. A congregation should enter a period of renewal only
after a considerable period of prayer and spiritual discernment. To be renewed is not a light matter and calls for
great commitment and involvement.

2. Church renewal is labor intensive and cost effective. It is
labor intensive because it is not the kind of program you
can purchase and then put into practice one Sunday.
Many people need to get involved in a very natural way.

3. Church renewal is cost effective. Churches that are in
decline and not taking initiative are losing material and
personnel resources. It takes a lot more money to shore up
something in decline than to invest energies in new life
and growth.

4. A congregation entering a time of renewal is entering a

deeper spiritual walk. This will not be accomplished overnight but will involve such things as taking the next step in spiritual disciplines, creating spiritual growth groups, undertaking spiritual growth efforts like retreats, and using spiritual discernment in meetings.

5. In a congregation there is a change of mood, a new level of confidence, energy, excitement, and a spiritual focus. Churches begin to grow in more ways than expected. Often they begin to see new people and need to be prepared to reach out to them.

6. Renewal is never a straight line. It might seem like the church is taking two steps forward and one back. Those involved in renewal need to maintain a positive outlook and rely on the strength promised to those called to do the work.

7. The discerned vision may be shorter in number of words than the group imagined. Someone has said that you should be able to paint your vision on the side of a bus. The process lends itself to crispness and clarity.

8. Because the process moves the church to understand who it is and what it has to offer, the discerned identity may not be like that of the church down the road. People will see what they uniquely have to offer.

9. The goals a church develops and the ministries it renews or initiates may not seem all that different or spectacular. But these goals and ministries use people's talents to fulfill the church's discerned mission. Renewal is about basics and may lead to unique ministries.

10. Churches adopt a flexible, bite-sized plan that is achievable and "right" for them. Sometimes they ask why they did not do this before. They may note that their plan is more right than they ever could have known, but this is the outcome of discernment.

Renewal Is Integral to the Work of the Church

A period of renewal is not be a sideshow or an add-on. As the process unfolds, all members of the church are an integral part. Each age group is important. Each committee is important. Each event is a step. Renewal takes deep root and affects the long term.

Renewal touches the life of each member and friend of the church; it touches the life of the church as the body of Christ. Everyone is needed. In fact, in servant leadership we learn that often the least likely person is the very one who has the key to the solution. Here are some ways in which renewal becomes the work of the church.

1. Rather than the pastor working solo, the church forms a renewal team.
2. This team facilitates the work of renewal, and this work is embodied in the meeting of the church board.
3. In the true sense of servant leadership, when something happens, no one exactly knows what individual is responsible. All have been an integral part.
4. If some aspects of the church are thriving, the plan of renewal builds on them rather than discards them.
5. The church may find it needs to focus meetings and perhaps have fewer regular meetings, perhaps doing follow-up work on the phone and by email. This allows time for the work of renewal and the congregational gatherings.
6. New leadership may well emerge with people who usually are on the sidelines but now want to get involved. This is the time to include people.
7. Be ready for excitement. With the pastor involved, the renewal team modeling renewal, and people beginning spiritual disciplines and looking at their God-given gifts, a new unity and spirit begins to emerge.
8. All the work in what we call self-study is saved. It is an integral part in shaping the vision and implementing a plan.

Appendix 7

Ten Biblical Traits of Servant Leadership

1. **Called and strengthened.** Servant leaders feel a call to serve God, assured that God will provide the strength for the task and that they will be blessed (see Isaiah 42:1). As servants they are to be a light to the nations, taking God's saving power to everyone (see Isaiah 49:6).

2. **Spiritually centered.** Servant leaders lead from a heart of peace. They lead from within—from the center—are attuned to healing, and sacrifice unselfishly to bring wholeness (see Isaiah 53:4-5).

3. **Listening.** Servant leaders listen first to God, who opens the servant's ears each morning. In like manner, servants listen to people. This is an outgrowth of their spiritual life and a hallmark of their efforts (see Isaiah 50:4-5).

4. **Manner of love.** Servant leaders lead in a kindly and humble manner. Rather than overpower people, they respect people and treat them with love (see Isaiah 42:3).

5. **Mission.** Servant leaders have a clear vision and use foresight to see things whole—to bring justice near and far. Using the wisdom of discernment, servants act as God's appointed with an urgent mission (see Isaiah 42:1, 49:5).

6. **Paradoxical expectation.** Servant leaders at first sight may seem to be the least likely people to make an impact, but God uses them in a role beyond what their appearance seems to warrant (see Isaiah 53:2).

7. **Paradoxical outcome.** Servant leaders trust that God brings dramatic reversals through their efforts. In suffering and sacrifice they act redemptively and believe God's will is accomplished (see Isaiah 53:10-11).

8. **Joyful.** Servants leaders carry joy in their hearts. There is a sense of surprise, victory, and peace. They go out in joy (see Isaiah 55:12).

9. **Leads in spiritual transformation.** Servant leaders engage in spiritual leadership and spiritual formation. The Lamb becomes the shepherd and leads us to the springs of living water. In turn, the servant invites others to share in the living water (see Revelation 7:17).

10. **Enters the drama of reconciliation.** Servant leaders enter the drama of reconciliation in the water basin and towel. They experience the service of Jesus washing their feet, and so cleansed, kneel on behalf of Christ to serve others and are blessed. In turn, others serve (see John 13:1-17).

For more see David S. Young, Servant Leadership for Church Renewal: Shepherds by the Living Springs *(Scottdale: Herald Press, 1999), 23-66, 157-58.*

Appendix 8

How to Lead a Discussion

Using listening skills from the gift of dialogue and servant leadership skills, group leaders lead discussions with productive outcomes by using the following principles.

1. Begin by reminding the group of the four points of dialogue and how the purpose of discussion is to first listen to the viewpoints of others and then express your own opinions in love, seeing that the outcome can be new insights through this time of interaction.

2. Then introduce the topic for discussion by saying something about the presentation or question. Express the hoped-for outcome of this time together. Invite people to take some quiet time for reflection and to begin as they feel led to offer a thought.

3. Use listening skills and make sure you understand what people are saying. You might even say, "If I understand, what you are saying is . . ." Then repeat what you think the person said. Or you might ask, "Is that right? Did I get it all?"

4. To take the conversation to another level, you might say to that person, "I am curious how you came to that point of view. Do you want to say more?" Remember you are moderating here, not forming a rebuttal but attempting to enhance the discussion.

5. Or you may turn to other members of the group and ask, "What does someone else think about this matter?" Try

to get the group members to interact with one another and not just with the discussion leader.

6. Some may respond spontaneously, and you can affirm each one's contribution by saying, "Thank you for your contribution." Then you can ask, "Would anyone else like to share?"

7. If a number of people share about a topic, you might choose to try to summarize what you are hearing by saying, "I hear some people saying . . . while other people are feeling . . ."

8. Try to prevent one person from dominating the discussion. Try to draw other people in by saying, "We have heard from a number of people; does anyone else wish to share?"

9. Be comfortable with silence; it gives people permission to think.

10. Keep the discussion on track. If people veer off, draw them back by saying, "Our question for discussion is . . . I wonder whether we can direct our comments to this subject?"

11. You may wish to observe how one member's thoughts build on another's comments. Affirm this and lift it up.

12. Keep the discussion moving and on track by restating the discussion question, by expressing hoped-for outcomes, and by encouraging participants when they make a helpful contribution.

13. Attempt to summarize where the group is so far. For example, you may say, "If I have heard us right, we are saying . . ." If there is another question, you may then say, "Perhaps we should move on to the next question and see what you have to share."

14. You can close by saying how the outcomes of the discussion will be used and what further steps will be taken in the process for which their input has been invaluable. See that this information is then recorded and put to use.

Appendix 9

Green Page

Celebration of Disciplines
The basis of the renewal process is spiritual practices and we can learn them and live them over the winter at Green Tree. We will celebrate.

How can we talk about celebration of spiritual disciplines? A book written over twenty-five years ago called *Celebration of Discipline* by Richard Foster is a classic.

In 2000 Richard Foster spoke at Elizabethtown College, where 850 people filled the chapel to learn how spiritual practices lead to exciting growth.

A Sunday Morning Series
Beginning Sunday, Jan. 15th there will be a preaching series to cover the disciplines one by one. We will have a dialogue each Sunday.

A Disciplines Folder
There will be a disciplines folder for daily Bible reading, meditation, and prayer on Scriptures on disciplines. We will grow daily.

An Adult Elective Class
The adult elective class has decided to use *Celebration of Discipline*. A video on the disciplines and reading resources are available.

(The effort keeps growing)

What Are the Disciplines?
The Inward Disciplines
Meditation, Prayer, Fasting, and Study

The Outward Disciplines
   Simplicity, Solitude, Submission, and Service
The Corporate Disciplines
   Confession, Worship, Guidance, Celebration

The Church Renewal Process

We will walk slowly step by step in a very spiritually oriented process that is easily understood.

Your input will be extremely valuable as our church discerns where God is leading.

The approach is very positive, as we attempt to discover our strengths and God-given talents.

Congregational gatherings will provide time to share strengths.

We will discover a Bible passage for Green Tree to discern a vision together and a plan.

Seven Steps

1. Deepening the Spiritual Walk
Each person is invited to take the next incremental step in disciplines.

2. Calling the Green Team
Eight to ten people are called and trained to facilitate the process.

3. Discerning a Biblical Passage
Meeting together, the church will see where we are in the Bible and how we can gain guidance.

4. Discerning Our Strengths
Meeting together, the church looks at its strengths, originating mission, demographics, and core values.

5. Learning Servant Leadership
From the Scriptures we will study the style of the servant and learn to lead in a serving fashion.

6. Discerning a Vision and Plan
Will discern a crisp biblical vision and a plan to carry out ministries.

7. Implementing the Plan

Appendix 10

Spiritual Disciplines Folder

The spiritual disciplines folder is a basic tool in the Springs renewal process. It lists weekly worship services and Bible readings for daily devotions. By uniting together in a corporate effort, individuals and churches experience spiritual growth in an intentional walk of faith.

The material that follows is a sample folder and can be used as a model. English and Spanish versions are included. The folder itself looks like a traditional worship bulletin when photocopied and folded on 8 ½-by-11-inch paper. The folder theme appears on the front page, in this case "A Closer Walk." When the folder is opened, the left side has a few paragraphs of explanation of the theme, and the worship services and Scripture portions for each day follow. If the folder needs to cover a longer period of time, an insert with additional Scriptures can be added.

The insert at the end of the folder encourages people to make a commitment to practicing spiritual disciplines. One copy is kept by the individual making the commitment, and the other is kept at the church.

In making your own spiritual disciplines folder, you may also list events related to the spiritual growth of the church.

Week 10: *The Discipline of Worship*
Message: "When You Worship: Five Elements of Christian Worship
        Isaiah 6:1-8
Monday: Communion: the essence of worship / John 6:52-58, 6:63
Tuesday: The life of worship / Ephesians 5:18-20, Colossians 3:16-17
Wednesday: The Lord high and lifted up / Isaiah 6:1-8
Thursday: Sing to the Lord / Psalm 96
Friday: Worship of all creation / Psalm 148
Saturday: Worthy is the Lamb / Revelation 5:6-14

Week 11: *The Discipline of Guidance*
Message: "Led by God" Acts 15:28
Monday: The guidance of divine Providence / Genesis 24:1-21
Tuesday: The guidance of Justice and obedience / Isaiah 1:17, 18-20
Wednesday: Led into all truth / Proverbs 3:5-6, John 14:6, 16:13, Acts 10:1-35
Thursday: Closed doors, open doors / Acts 16:6-10, 2 Corinthians 2:12
Friday: Listening or resisting? / Acts 21:8-14
Saturday: The family likeness / Romans 8:14, 28-30

Week 12: Palm Sunday and Bible readings

Week 13: Easter Day and Bible readings

Week 14: *The Discipline of Celebration*
Message: "Joy"—Galatians 5:22
Monday: The Joy of the Lord / 2 Samuel 6:12-19
Tuesday: Bless the Lord / Psalm 103
Wednesday: Praise the Lord / Psalm 150
Thursday: Hosanna! / Luke 19:35-40, John 12:12-19
Friday: Walking and leaping and praising God / Acts 3:1-10
Saturday: Hallelujah! / Revelation 19:1-8

Credit: The daily readings and themes are adapted from Richard J. Foster's *Study Guide for Celebration of Discipline* (San Francisco: Harper, 1983).

Permission is granted to photocopy this resource.

A CLOSER WALK

SPRINGS OF LIVING WATER

A Closer Walk

This spiritual disciplines folder covers the seasons of Epiphany, Lent and Easter. In Epiphany we celebrate Jesus' birth, receive the light and share the light. Lent is a period of preparation for Easter. Easter and the season to follow is a time of great celebration of the Risen Lord.

This folder is designed to help us in our spiritual lives to grow closer to Jesus. We will be exploring time honored practices which lead us to place ourselves before God so God can work in and through our lives. Our desire is for a closer walk with God.

Pondering this thought, we realize this theme of a closer walk came forth repeatedly in our Brethren heritage. The desire of early Brethren was to ponder the scriptures and use them as a pattern for faith and action. What a worthy goal today!

As a congregation, we will be exploring a discipline week by week in our Sunday messages which will be followed by a daily reading from scripture on that discipline. This is to develop a deeper walk of faith.

All this sets the stage for the renewal process in our congregation. Rather than once and forever done, renewal for the Apostle Paul is from God day by day. We are excited to lay a spiritual base as we consider the strengths of our church and move to a vision and implement a plan.

Let us be in prayer for one another as we seek to take the next incremental step in our walk of faith and for our congregation as we set in the New Year to have a closer walk with Jesus Christ. Below are topics for worship and daily Bible readings for your time of prayer.

Section I: Inward Disciplines

Week 1: *The Discipline of Meditation*
Message: "Keeping Our Mind on Christ, So We May Not Lose Heart"
    Psalm 1:2, 19:14; Hebrews 12:2, 3
Monday: The friendship of meditation / Exodus 33:11
Tuesday: The blessing of meditation / Joshua 1:8-9
Wednesday: The object of meditation / Psalm 1:1-3
Thursday: The comfort of meditation / 1 Kings 19:9-18
Friday: The insights of meditation / Acts 10:9-20
Saturday: The ecstasy of meditation / 2 Corinthians 12:1-4

Week 2: *The Discipline of Prayer*
Message: "Lord, Teach Us to Pray"—Mark 1:35; Luke 11:1;
    Luke 11:2-13, 1 Thessalonians 5:17
Monday: The prayer of worship / Psalm 103
Tuesday: The prayer of repentance / Psalm 51
Wednesday: The prayer of thanksgiving / Psalm 150
Thursday: The prayer of guidance / Matthew 26:36-46
Friday: The prayer of faith / James 5:13-18
Saturday: The prayer of command / Mark 9:14-29

Week 3: *The Discipline of Fasting*
Message: "Fasting Is Feasting" John 4:32, 34; 2 Cor. 11:27; Acts 13:2, 3
Monday: God's chosen fast / Isaiah 58:1-7
Tuesday: A partial fast / Daniel 10:1-14
Wednesday: A normal fast / Nehemiah 1:4-11
Thursday: An absolute fast / Esther 4:12-17
Friday: The inauguration of the gentile mission / Acts 13:1-3
Saturday: The appointment of elders in the churches / Acts 14:19-23

Week 4: *The Discipline of Study*
Message: "Study to Show Thyself Approved" 2 Timothy 3:16, 17
Monday: The source of truth / James 1:5, Hebrews 4:11-13, 2 Timothy 3:16-17
Tuesday: What to study / Philippians 4:8-9, Colossians 3:1-17
Wednesday: The value of study / Luke 10:38-42
Thursday: Active study / Ezra 7:10, James 1:19-25
Friday: Study in the evangelistic enterprise / Acts 17:1-3, 17:10-12, 19:8-10
Saturday: The study of Scripture / 2 Timothy 3:16, 17

Section II: Outward Disciplines

Week 5: *The Discipline of Simplicity*
Message: "'Tis a Gift to Be Simple" Matthew 6:25-33
Monday: Simplicity as trust / Matthew 6:25-34
Tuesday: Simplicity as obedience / Genesis 15
Wednesday: The generosity of simplicity / Leviticus 25:8-12
Thursday: Simplicity in speech / Matthew 5:33-37, James 5:12
Friday: Simplicity and justice / Amos 5:11-15, 24, Luke 4:16-21
Saturday: The freedom from covetousness / Luke 12:13-34

Week 6: *The Discipline of Solitude*
Message: "Alone With God" Matthew 26:36-46
Monday: Prayer and solitude / Matthew 6:5-6, Luke 5:16
Tuesday: The insights of solitude / Psalm 8
Ash Wednesday: "The dark night of the soul" / Jeremiah 20:7-18
Thursday: The solitude of the garden / Matthew 26:36-46
Friday: The solitude of the cross / Matthew 27:32-50
Saturday: The compassion that comes from solitude / Matthew 9:35-38, 23:37

Week 7: *The Discipline of Submission*
Message: "The Cross Life" Philippians 2:1-11
Monday: The example of Christ / Philippians 2:1-11
Tuesday: The example of Abraham / Genesis 22:1-19
Wednesday: The example of Paul / Galatians 2:19-21
Thursday: Submission in the marketplace / Matthew 5:38-48
Friday: Submission in the family / Ephesians 5:21-6:9, 1 Peter 3:1-9
Saturday: Submission with reference to the state / Romans 13:1-10,
        Acts 4:13-20, 5:27-29, 16:35-39

Week 8: *The Discipline of Service*
Message: "The Towel Life" John 13:14, 15
Monday: The sign of service / John 13:1-17
Tuesday: The commitment of service / Exodus 21:2, 21:5-6, 1 Corinthians 9:19
Wednesday: The attitude of service / Colossians 3:23-25
Thursday: Service in the Christian fellowship / Romans 12:9-13
Friday: The ministry of small things / Matthew 25:31-39
Saturday: Service exemplified / Luke 10:29-37

Section III: The Corporate Disciplines

Week 9: *The Discipline of Confession*
Message: "The Lost Discipline"—James 5:16, 1 John 1:9
Monday: The promise of forgiveness / Jeremiah 31:34, Matt. 26:28, Eph. 1:7
Tuesday: The assurance of forgiveness / 1 John 1:5-10
Wednesday: Jesus Christ, our Adequate Savior, Mediator, and Advocate /
        1 Timothy 2:5, 1 John 2:1
Thursday: A parable of confession / Luke 15:11-24
Friday: Authority and forgiveness / Matthew 16:19, 18:18, John 20:23
Saturday: The ministry of the Christian Fellowship / James 5:13-16

A Closer Walk

(Commitment copy)

God leads us to our next disciplines of growth. Rather than trying to do everything, we seek the next incremental step in practices that lead us to a greater sense of being close to God.

Below are some such disciplines of practices to grow in faith. Perhaps you will have another to add. We will place this insert in a basket at the church.

Let us be in prayer for one another as we seek to be faithful and receive the gift of Jesus.

1. Weekly participate in worship

2. Daily read and meditate on scripture and have prayer

3. Weekly participate in Sunday school

4. Enter the discipline of service and weekly help someone in need.

5. Enter the discipline of sharing your faith and invite a friend to worship during this season.

6. Other discipline of God's leading _____
_____

I am asking God's help as I make this commitment

A Closer Walk
(Personal copy)
God leads us to our next disciplines of growth. Rather than trying to do everything, we seek the next incremental step in practices that lead us to a greater sense of being close to God.

Below are some such disciplines of practices to grow in faith. Perhaps you will have another to add. Please keep this copy in your Bible for when you do your spiritual disciplines.

Let us be in prayer for one another as we seek to be faithful and receive the gift of Jesus.

1. Weekly participate in worship

2. Daily read and meditate on scripture and have prayer

3. Weekly participate in Sunday school

4. Enter the discipline of service and weekly help someone in need.

5. Enter the discipline of sharing your faith and invite a friend to worship during this season.

6. Other discipline of God's leading _____
_____

I am asking God's help as I make this commitment

Semana 10: *La Disciplina de la Adoración*
Mensaje: "Cuando Adoras: Cinco Elementos de una Adoración Cristiana"
Isaías 6:1-8
Lunes: Comunión: la esencia de adorar / Juan 6:52-58, 6:63
Martes: La vida de adoración / Efesios 5:18-20, Colosenses 3:16-17
Miércoles: El Señor alto y sublime / Isaías 6:1-8
Jueves: Cantad al Señor / Salmos 96
Viernes: Adoración de toda la creación / Salmos 148
Sábado: Digno es el Cordero / Apocalipsis 5:6-14

Semana 11: *La Disciplina de la Guianza*
Mensaje: "Guiados por Dios" Hechos 15:28
Lunes: La guianza del la divina Providencia / Génesis 24:1-21
Martes: La guianza de Justicia y obediencia / Isaías 1:17, 18-20
Miércoles: Guiados a toda verdad / Proverbios 3:5-6, Juan 14:6, 16:13, Hechos
    10:1-35
Jueves: Puertas cerradas, puertas abiertas / Hechos 16:6-10, 2 Corintios 2:12
Viernes: Oyendo o resistiendo? / Hechos 21:8-14
Sábado: La semejanza de la familia / Romanos 8:14, 28-30

Semana 12: domingo de Ramos y lecturas Bíblicas

Semana 13: Día de Pascuas y lecturas Bíblicas

Semana 14: La Disciplina de Celebración
Mensaje: "Gozo"—Gálatas 5:22
Lunes: El Gozo del Señor / 2 Samuel 6:12-19
Martes: Bendecid al Señor /Salmos 103
Miércoles: Alabad al Señor / Salmos 150
Jueves: ¡Hosanna! / Lucas 19:35-40, Juan 12:12-19
Viernes: Caminando y saltando alabando a Dios / Hechos 3:1-10
Sábado: ¡Allelujah! / Apocalipsis 19:1-8

Crédito: Las lecturas diarias y temas fueron adaptados de Richard J. Foster's *Study Guide for Celebration of Discipline* (San Francisco: Harper, 1983).

Permission is granted to photocopy this resource.

UN CAMINAR MAS CERCANO

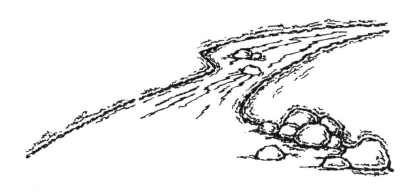

¡RIOS DE AGUA VIVA!

Un Caminar Más Cercano

Este folleto de disciplinas espirituales cubre la temporada de Epifanía, Cuaresma y Pascua. En la Epifanía celebramos el nacimiento de Jesús, el recibimiento de la luz y el compartir la luz. Cuaresma es el período de preparación para la Pascua. La Pascua y la temporada siguiente es un tiempo de celebración del Señor Resucitado. Este folleto está diseñado para ayudarnos a acercarnos a Jesús en nuestras vidas espirituales. Estaremos explorando prácticas honradas por el tiempo las cuales nos guiaron a ponernos delante de Dios para que el pudiera moldear dentro y através de nuestras vidas. Nuestro deseo es un caminar más cerca con Dios.

Reflexionando sobre este pensamiento, nos damos cuenta que este tema de caminar más cerca con Dios surgió repetidamente en nuestra heredad de la Iglesia de los Hermanos. El deseo temprano de las Iglesias de los Hermanos era de reflexionar sobre las escrituras y usarlas como un patrón de fe y acción. ¡Que meta digna hoy!

Como congregación, estaremos explorando una disciplina semana por semana en nuestros mensajes del domingo, los cuales estarán seguidos de nuestra lecturas diarias acerca de esa disciplina. Esto es para desarrollar un caminar más profundo de fe.

Todo esto abre el escenario para el proceso de renovación en nuestra congregación.

En vez de darse por terminada de una vez por todas, la renovación para el Apóstol Pablo fue día a día de parte de Dios. Estamos emocionados de exponer una base espiritual de forma que consideremos las áreas fuertes de nuestra iglesia y nos movamos a una visión de implementación de un plan.

Oremos los unos por los otros a medida que busquemos tomar los próximos pasos en incrementos en nuestro caminar de fe y para nuestra congregación conforme exponemos un Año Nuevo para tener un caminar más cercano con Jesucristo. Seguidamente se dan algunos temas para la adoración y lecturas Bíblicas diarias para su tiempo de oración.

Sección I: Disciplinas Internas

Semana 1: *La Disciplina de la Meditación*
Mensaje: **"Manteniendo nuestra Mente en Cristo, Para no Desmayar"**
    Salmos 1:2, 19:14; Hebreos 12:2, 3

Lunes: La amistad de la meditación / Éxodo 33:11
Martes: La bendición de la meditación / Josué 1:8-9
Miércoles: El objeto de la meditación / Salmos 1:1-3
Jueves: El comodidad de la meditación / 1 Reyes 19:9-18
Viernes: La percepción de la meditación / Hechos 10:9-20
Sábado: El éxtasis de la meditación / 2 Corintios 12:1-4

Semana 2: *La Disciplina del Poder*
Mensaje: "Señor Enséñanos a Orar"—Marcos 1:35; Lucas 11:1;
Lucas 11: 2-13, 1 Tesalonicenses 5:17
Lunes: La oración de adoración / Salmos 103
Martes: La oración de arrepentimiento / Salmos 51
Miércoles: La oración de dar gracias / Salmos 150
Jueves: La oración de guianza / Mateo 26:36-46
Viernes: La oración de fe / Santiago 5:13-18
Sábado: La oración de mandato / Marcos 9:14-29

Semana 3: *La Disciplina del Ayunar*
Mensaje: "Ayunar es Banquete" Juan 4:32, 34; 2 Cor. 11:27;
Hechos 13:2, 3
Lunes: El ayuno escogido por Dios / Isaías 58:1-7
Martes: Un ayuno parcial / Daniel 10:1-14
Miércoles: Un ayuno normal / Nehemías 1:4-11
Jueves: Un ayuno absoluto / Ester 4:12-17
Viernes: La inauguración de una misión gentil / Hechos 13:1-3
Sábado: El nombramiento de ancianos en las iglesias/ Hechos 14:19-23

Semana 4: La Disciplina del Estudio
Mensaje: "Estudia para Mostrarte Aprobado" 2 Timoteo 3:16, 17
Lunes: La fuente de verdad / James 1:5, Hebreos 4:11-13, 2 Timoteo 3:16-17
Martes: Que estudiar / Filipenses 4:8-9, Colosenses 3:1-17
Miércoles: El valor del estudio / Lucas 10:38-42
Jueves: Estudio activo / Esdras 7:10, Santiago 1:19-25
Viernes: Estudio en la empresa evangelista / Hechos 17:1-3, 17:10-12, 19:8-10
Sábado: El estudio de la escritura / 2 Timoteo 3:16,17

Sección II: Disciplinas Externas

Semana 5: *La Disciplina de la Sencillez*
Mensaje: "Es un Regalo el Ser Sencillo" Mateo 6:25-33
Lunes: Sencillez como confianza / Mateo 6:25-34
Martes: Sencillez como obediencia / Génesis 15
Miércoles: La generosidad de la sencillez / Levítico 25:8-12
Jueves: Sencillez en el discurso / Mateo 5:33-37, Santiago 5:12
Viernes: Sencillez y justicia / Amos 5:11-15, 24, Lucas 4:16-21
Sábado: Liberación de la codicia / Lucas 12:13-34

Semana 6: **La Disciplina de la Soledad**
Mensaje: " A Solas con Dios" Mateo 26:36-46
Lunes: Oración y soledad / Mateo 6:5-6, Luke 5:16
Martes: Comprendiendo la soledad/ Salmos 8
Miércoles de Ceniza: "La noche obscura del alma" / Jeremías 20:7-18
Jueves: La soledad del jardín / Mateo 26:36-46
Viernes: La soledad de la cruz / Mateo 27:32-50
Sábado: La compasión que viene de la soledad / Mateo 9:35-38, 23:37

Semana 7: *La Disciplina de la Sumisión*
Mensaje: "La Vida de la Cruz" Filipenses 2:1-11
Lunes: El ejemplo de Cristo / Filipenses 2:1-11
Martes: El ejemplo de Abraham / Génesis 22:1-19
Miércoles: El ejemplo de Pablo / Gálatas 2:19-21
Jueves: Sumisión en el mercado / Mateo 5:38-48
Viernes: Sumisión en la familia / Efesios 5:21-6:9, 1 Pedro 3:1-9
Sábado: Sumisión con referencia al estado / Romanos 13:1-10,
Hechos 4:13-20, 5:27-29, 16:35-39

Semana 8: *La Disciplina del Servicio*
Mensaje: "La Vida Toalla" Juan 13:14, 15
Lunes: La señal de servicio / Juan 13:1-17
Martes: El compromiso de servicio / Éxodo 21:2, 21:5-6, 1 Corintios 9:19
Miércoles: La actitud de servicio / Colosenses 3:23-25
Jueves: Servicio en el compañerismo Cristiano / Romanos 12:9-13
Viernes: El ministerio en cosas pequeñas / Mateo 25:31-39
Sábado: Servicio ejemplificado / Lucas 10:29-37

Sección III: Las Disciplinas Corporativas

Semana 9: *La Disciplina de la Confesión*

Mensaje: "La Disciplina Perdida"—Santiago 5:16, I Juan 1:9

Lunes: La promesa del perdón / Jeremías 31:34, Mat. 26:28, Efe. 1:7

Martes: El certeza del perdón / 1 Juan 1:5-10

Miércoles: Jesucristo, nuestro Salvador Adecuado, Mediador y Abogado/ 1 Timoteo 2:5, 1 Juan 2:1

Jueves: Una parábola de confesión / Lucas 15:11-24

Viernes: Autoridad y perdón / Mateo 16:19, 18:18, Juan 20:23

Sábado: El ministerio de Compañerismo Cristiano / Santiago 5:13-16

Un Caminar Más Cercano
(Copia de compromiso)

Dios nos guía a nuestro próximo crecimiento de disciplinas. En lugar de tratar de hacer todo, busquemos nuestros próximos pasos en incrementos de prácticas que nos encaminen a un sentir mayor de estar cerca de Dios.

En seguida se presentan algunas de dichas prácticas de disciplinas para ayudar a crecer en la fe. Quizás usted tendrá alguna otra que agregar. Incluiremos este inserto en la iglesia en una canasta.

Estemos en oración los unos por los otros, de manera que busquemos ser fieles y recibir el regalo de Jesús.

1. Participar semanalmente en la adoración.

2. Leer y meditar diariamente en las escrituras y orar.

3. Participar semanalmente en la Escuela Dominical.

4. Entrar en la disciplina del servicio y ayudar semanalmente a alguien que lo necesite.

5. Entrar en la disciplina de compartir su fe e invitar a un amigo a adorar en este tiempo.

6. Otra disciplina que sea guiada por Dios_____

_____

Pidiendo la ayuda de Dios a medida que hago este compromiso.

Un Caminar Más Cercano

(Copia personal)

Dios nos guía a nuestro próximo crecimiento de disciplinas. En lugar de tratar de hacer todo, busquemos nuestros próximos pasos en incrementos de prácticas que nos encaminen a un sentir mayor de estar cerca de Dios.

A continuación se brindan algunas de dichas prácticas de disciplinas para ayudar a crecer en la fe. Quizás usted tendrá alguna otra que agregar. Por favor mantenga este folleto en su Biblia para cuando haga sus disciplinas espirituales.

Estemos en oración los unos por los otros, de manera que busquemos ser fieles y recibir el regalo de Jesús.

1. Participar semanalmente en la adoración.

2. Leer y meditar diariamente en las escrituras y orar.

3. Participar semanalmente en la Escuela Dominical.

4. Entrar en la disciplina del servicio y ayudar semanalmente a alguien que lo necesite.

5. Entrar en la disciplina de compartir su fe e invitar a un amigo a adorar en este tiempo.

6. Otra disciplina que sea guiada por Dios_____
_____

Pidiendo la ayuda de Dios a medida que hago este compromiso.

Appendix 11

Bible Study Guide

As a church looks at its strengths, it often becomes drawn to a Bible text. This guide is designed to assist you to look deeply into a text and find the spiritual dynamics of renewal. As a church seeks where God is leading, these dynamics can serve as a spiritual guide to new life.

Study

What is the background of the text?

What is the setting in life?

Look at translations and nuances of meaning.

What are key words and concepts in the passage?

Message

What is the good news in the passage?

What progression to new life is found in the text?

How does the passage speak to you personally?

How does the passage speak to your church?

Guide

In spiritual direction, a text can serve as a guide. Not only do we study the text, but we spend significant time meditating on its message and how it speaks to us.

Pray over the text, asking God to reveal the truths of the gospel. Take time to listen.

What message do you see arising out of this text?

How might that message guide you spiritually?

What dynamics of renewal do you see that would lead to new life?

What practical applications do you see for your church?

Appendix 12

The Gift of Spiritual Discernment

Discernment is a real gift and is linked directly to encountering Jesus. Decisions made by spiritual discernment lead us to the heart of God.

What Is Spiritual Discernment?

- Some people call spiritual discernment reading the face of God. In discernment we seek to know and live the will of God.
- God wishes to reveal his will to us. With prayer we can discern getting our head, our heart, and our faith journey together.
- Through spiritual discernment we encounter Jesus as we come to know that he is inviting us to partake of living water.
- Discernment is rooted in one's prayer life, pausing for time to get in tune with God. To have a discerning church you must be a praying church.
- The desire of discernment is to be in communication with God and do God's will. The hope is to get into the flow of God's will.
- We need not feel we are in a game of hide and seek; God wishes to help the church to renew and flourish.
- God needs us to be partners in order to do his work. God needs colaborers. God will guide us as partners to accomplish ministries.

Getting the Head, Heart, and Faith Journey Together

- Affirming the validity of rational thought, we use the head, weighing factors for something on one side of the ledger and those things against on the other side.

- With a decidedly feeling or affective tone, the heart in discernment is sensing the movements of God—desolation or consolation, that is, anxiety or peace
- The faith journey is the way of costly discipleship as well as hope. Decisions that call us to grow in faith are more in tune with God's will and way.

How Do You Practically Go About Discernment?

- Some discernment arises because you take a problem to a place of prayer. At other times it arises in unexpected moments.
- One good way to enter discernment is to enter one's style of prayer and spend significant time in communion with God.
- As the time in prayer lengthens, a person in prayer will sense a deeper stillness and sense the movement of God in consolation.
- In discernment, be ready to entertain the unexpected. A new perspective may arise. You may feel the tug for immediate action.
- When you are alone and faced with uncertainties, stray thoughts may come into your mind and distract and disrupt you from seeking and doing God's will.
- Spiritual discernment will take longer than you wish, but not as long as you fear, and the outcome will be more right than you could ever know.

What Is Group Spiritual Discernment?

- Discernment speaks of the faith journey not only of individuals but also of churches. With our discerned Scripture we build on our identity as a congregation, discern a vision that becomes our vocation, and discover a plan of ministry (See Schemel).
- The convener keeps the process moving, at points slows it down, and at points sees where the opening for resolution lies.

- Arrange an appropriate environment for corporate discernment using something to remind everyone of the presence of Christ and the activity of God.
- Discernment needs "interior freedom, sufficient knowledge of self and the world, imagination, patience, and the courage to act responsibly" (see Boroughs).
- The convener lays out a format, beginning with prayer and reminding the body of the various aspects of discernment: head, heart, and faith journey.
- Sometime during discernment, the group can specifically look at the head, that is, the rational part of this decision.
- The groups looks at its collective "heart." When we prayerfully consider going in one direction, what is the outcome in terms of what we sense is the movement of God?
- The group considers the faith journey. If taking a direction, will we be just comfortable or will we be stretched to grow in faith?

How Does Discernment Lead to Mission?

- As we wait in fasting and/or in prayer, we become focused in acting. Just to discern is not enough. Discernment leads to action. Discernment means obedience.
- Decisions made by spiritual discernment will take a little longer than we would like but not as long as we might fear and are more right than we ever could have known.
- While in desolation, make no decisions. Rather we give ourselves to more prayer until consolation returns.
- Having a purpose to fulfill, we move to our vocation as individuals and as a church. We move to the grace we experience and proclaim though our mission.

Notes

Introduction

1. Raymond Brown, *The Gospel According to John* (Garden City, NY: Doubleday, 1966), 169.

2. Annotation on John 1:10, *The New Interpreter's Bible* (Nashville: Abingdon Press, 2003), 1914.

3. Jeffrey Bullock, review of *Servant Leadership for Church Renewal: Shepherds by the Living Springs* (Scottdale, PA: Herald Press, 1999) in *Congregations*, November—December 2000, 21.

Chapter 1:
Getting to the Well

1. See Richard J. Foster, *Celebration of Discipline* (San Francisco: Harper & Row, 1978), or the Spanish translation, *Ababanza a la Disciplina* (Nashville: Betania, 1986).

2. Rufus Jones, *The Double Search* (Richmond, IN: Friends United Press, 1906).

3. Carlo Carretto, *Letters from the Desert* (New York: Orbis, 1972), 13.

4. This insight is from Graydon Snyder, New Testament Professor Emeritus at Bethany Seminary and biblical scholar specializing in the Gospel of John, and John David Bowman, pastor from Lancaster, PA.

5. Raymond Brown, *The Gospel of John*, vol. 29, The Anchor Bible (Garden City, NY: Doubleday, 1966), 506.

6. For a fuller exposition connecting the story of Lazarus with church renewal, see David S. Young, *A New Heart and A New Spirit: A Plan for Renewing Your Church* (Valley Forge, PA: Judson Press, 1994), 2-5.

7. For further description of these four "genes" and stages, see Martin Saarinen, *The Life Cycle of a Congregation* (Bethesda, MD: Alban Institute, 1986).

8. See "Interview on Springs of Living Water!" in *Renovaré Perspective* 17:2:4-5, which describes some of the journey of entering spiritual renew-

al for local churches. http://www.renovare.org/documents/
perspective_17_2.pdf.

Chapter 2:
Engaging in the Seven Steps of Renewal

1. Similar processes are used in intentional interim ministry. See Roger Nicholson, *Temporary Shepherds: A Congregational Handbook for Interim Ministry* (Bethesda, MD: Alban Institute, 1998), and Alan Gripe, *The Interim Pastors Manual* (Louisville: Geneva Press, 1997).

2. Roy Oswald and Speed Leas, *The Inviting Church* (Bethesda, MD: Alban Institute, 1987). See especially 51-77. Presentation of the study was done at Pendle Hill in Wallingford, PA.

3. Martin Saarinen, *The Life Cycle of a Congregation* (Bethesda, MD: Alban Institute, 1986), 22-23.

4. From a conversation with Saarinen.

5. See www.perceptgroup.com. See also the work of Alice Mann. Resources on the demographics of your church can often be obtained from your denominational office.

6. Gray McIntosh, *Look Back, Leap Forward* (Grand Rapids, MI: Baker Books, 2001), 77.

7. Ann Hammond, *The Thin Book of Appreciative Inquiry* (Plano, TX: Thin Books, n.d.), 7.

8. Ibid., 24.

9. Ibid., 31.

Chapter 3:
Discovering the Gift of Dialogue

1. My interest in dialogue began with a conversation with Gary Looper at a Servant Leadership Conference. His consulting firm was helping Southwest Air develop dialogue throughout the organization. Knowing Gary was a church planter, I asked if dialogue could help a church. This led to my study on dialogue from a Christian perspective, focusing on strengthening churches in renewal.

2. Robert Greenleaf, *Servant Leadership: A Journey into the Nature of Legitimate Power and Greatness* (Mahwah, NJ: Paulist Press, 1977), 31.

3. Reuel Howe, *The Miracle of Dialogue* (Minneapolis: Winston Press, 1975), 66.

4. Ibid., 81.

5. William Isaacs, *The Fifth Discipline Fieldbook* (New York: Doubleday, 1994), 362-63.

6. Howe, *Miracle of Dialogue*, 11.

7. Kerry Patterson, et al., *Crucial Conversations: Tools for Talking When the Stakes Are High* (New York: McGraw Hill, 2002), 1ff.

8. A sixty-page handbook that features each aspect of enlisting a cluster of churches is available. Go to www.churchrenewalservant.org.

9. A full description on the calling and role of the local coordinator is explained in the Springs notebook. Copies are available by contacting us at www.churchrenewalservant.org.

10. See appendix 6 in the Springs notebook, which describes having a local church become renewed: www.churchrenewalservant.org.

11. A full description on the calling and role of the local coordinator is explained in the Springs notebook. Copies are available by contacting us at www.churchrenewalservant.org.

12. See chapter 10. Important areas to cover are growing in the spiritual walk, learning the renewal process, learning to rest, being a spiritual guide, servant leadership, and guiding the renewal process. Three or more such sessions could be held before the process begins or during the process.

13. For a thorough treatment of using this style of teaching that is consistent with servant leadership, see Robert Mager, *Preparing Instructional Objectives* (Atlanta: Center for Effective Performance, 1997).

Chapter 4:
Leading with a Basin and Towel

1. Such an emphasis on service has led to projects like Heifer International. See www.heifer.org.

2. A project submitted at Bethany Theological Seminary in partial fulfillment for the Doctor of Ministry, Oak Brook, IL, May 1976, located in the historical archives of the Church of the Brethren at 1451 Dundee Avenue, Elgin, IL 60120.

3. Robert Greenleaf, *Servant Leadership: A Journey into the Nature of Legitimate Power and Greatness* (Mahwah, NJ: Paulist Press, 1977), 21.

4. E. Herman, *Creative Prayer* (Cincinnati: The Forward Movement, n.d.).

5. Springs Pre-Renovaré Conference, Camp Hill United Methodist Church, Camp Hill, PA, March 23, 2007.

6. Walter Brueggemann, *Isaiah 40-66* (Louisville: John Knox Press, 1998), 42.

7. Claus Westermann, *Isaiah 40-66* (Philadelphia: Westminster Press, 1969), 94.

8. Brueggemann, *Isaiah 40-66*, 42.

9. Greenleaf, *Servant Leadership*, 34. Greenleaf was instrumental in and subsequently participated in Yokefellow, a movement of small-group prayer for renewal of the church led by Elton Trueblood, based at Earlham College in Richmond, IN. See also Elton Trueblood, *While It Is Day* (Richmond, IN: Yokefellow Press, 1974), 113, 116, 117.

10. Greenleaf, *Servant Leadership*, 10.

Chapter 5:
Embarking on a Church's Spiritual Journey

1. James Bryan Smith with Lynda Graybeal, *A Spiritual Formation Workbook* (San Francisco: HarperSanFrancisco, 1991).

2. Nate Turner, *Leading Small Groups: Basic Skills for Church and Community Organizations* (Valley Forge, PA: Judson Press, 1996), 15. This book can be helpful for a wide range of small groups.

3. Richard J. Foster, *Celebration of Discipline* (New York: Harper & Row, 1978). Also see app. 3 of this book.

4. See Robert Mager, *Preparing Instructional Objectives* (Atlanta: Center for Effective Performance, 1997).

5. Go to http://www.bibles.com/page.php?id=113.

6. James Bryan Smith with Lynda Graybeal, *A Spiritual Formation Workbook: Small Group Resources for Nurturing Christian Growth* (San Francisco: HarperSanFrancisco, 1991).

7. M. Robert Mulholland Jr., *Shaped by the Word: The Power of Scripture in Spiritual Formation* (Nashville: Upper Room Books, 2000), 95.

8. Ibid.

Chapter 6:
Encountering Christ Through Prayer

1. See Merrill Abbey, *Communication in Pulpit and Parish* (Philadelphia: Westminster Press, 1973).

2. For helps on the discipline of meditation see Richard J. Foster, *Celebration of Discipline* (San Francisco: Harper & Row, 1978), 29ff.

3. You can begin with resources like Foster, *Celebration of Discipline* and the companion volume Richard J. Foster and Emilie Griffin, eds., *Spiritual Classics* (San Francisco: Harper, 2000). The latter has readings

in the classics for each of the twelve disciplines, Scripture lessons, and helpful guides to devotion.

4. See Phyllis Tickle, *The Divine Hours: A Manual for Prayer*, 3 vols. (New York: Doubleday, 2000).

5. Tilden Edwards, *Living Simply Through the Day* (Mahwah, NJ: Paulist Press, 1977), 86.

6. Tim Jones, *A Place for God* (New York: Doubleday, 2000), 52.

7. See M. Basil Pennington, *Centering Prayer* (New York: Doubleday, 1982), and for a unique perspective on examen, see George Ashenbrenner, *Consciousness Examen* (Wernersville, PA: The Jesuit Center, 1972).

8. Thomas Kelly, *Testament of Devotion* (New York: HarperOne, 1996), 30.

9. Julian of Norwich, *Showings*, trans. Edmund Colledge and James Walsh, in *The Classics of Western Spirituality* (Mahwah, NJ: Paulist Press, 1978).

10. Foster and Griffin, eds., *Spiritual Classics*. Also Richard J. Foster and James Bryan Smith, eds., *Devotional Classics* (San Francisco: HarperSanFrancisco, 1990), which is a companion to Foster's *Streams of Living Water: Celebrating the Great Traditions of Christian Faith* (New York, HarperOne, 1998).

11. See Thelma Hall, *Too Deep for Words: Rediscovering Lectio Divina* (Mahwah, NJ: Paulist Press, 1988), and Susan Muto, *Pathways of Christian Living* (Petersham, MA: St. Bede's Publications, 1984), 89ff.

12. The *lectio* process as passed through Dr. Jerry Flora from Fr. Keith McClellan OSB at St. Michael the Archangel Church, Schererville, IN.

13. Rueben Job and Norman Shawchuck, *A Guide to Prayer* (Nashville: Upper Room Books, 1983). See also Reuben Job and Norman Shawchuck, *A Guide to Prayer for All God's People* (Nashville: Upper Room Books, 1990).

14. This idea comes from Thomas Green, *A Vacation with the Lord* (Notre Dame: Ave Marie Press, 1986), 28. Green reminds us that the biblical day began in the evening of the night before.

15. Richard J. Foster, *Celebration of Discipline*.

Chapter 7:
Discovering the Gift of Spiritual Discernment

1. Suzanne Farnham, Stephanie Hall, and R. Taylor McLean,

Grounded in God: Listening Hearts Discernment for Group Deliberations (Harrisburg, PA: Morehouse Publishing, 1999), 8.

2. Thomas Green, *Weeds Among the Wheat, Discernment: Where Prayer and Action Meet* (Notre Dame: Ave Marie Press, 1984), 178.

3. Thomas Merton, *Thoughts in Solitude* (Boston: Shambhala, 1993), 116.

4. Green, *Weeds*, 168.

5. Thomas Kelly, *Testament of Devotion* (New York: Harper & Row, 1941), 29-30.

6. Materials are now in a format in which you can do the retreat over a period of months at home and incorporate the growth in your daily life. See H. Cornell Bradley, The 19th Annotation in 24 weeks for the 21st Century (Philadelphia: Saint Joseph's University Press).

7. See George J. Schemel, "Beyond Individuation to Discipleship: A Directory for Those Who Give the Spiritual Exercises of St. Ignatius," http://www.isecp.org/frontcover.html. Also credit to Rev. Edwin Saunders, SJ, spiritual director and former instructor on spirituality at Lancaster Theological Seminary, Lancaster, PA.

8. Saint Ignatius of Loyola, *The Spiritual Exercises* (New York: Catholic Publishing House, 1948), 157.

9. Ibid.

10. Thomas à Kempis, *Imitation of Christ*, trans. William Creasy (Notre Dame: Ave Marie Press, 1989), 80.

11. See David Fleming, *The Spiritual Exercises of Saint Ignatius: A Literal Translation and a Contemporary Reading* (St. Louis: The Institute of Jesuit Sources, 1978), 202-13.

12. See *Review for Religious* 51:3 (May-June 1992), 373-87. Also in *Ignatian Exercises: Contemporary Annotations*, ed. David Fleming (St. Louis: Review for Religious, 1996), 285-98.

13. Schemel, "Beyond Individuation," 3.

Chapter 8:
Discerning the Spiritual Movements of Renewal

1. David S. Young, "Lay Witness—Road to Renewal," in *Call the Witnesses*, ed. Paul M. Robinson (Elgin, IL: Brethren Press, 1974), 105-11.

2. Richard J. Foster, *Celebration of Discipline* (San Francisco: Harper & Row, 1978), 7.

3. David S. Young, *A New Heart and a New Spirit: A Plan for Renewing Your Church* (Valley Forge, PA: Judson Press), 73-74.

4. Bradley Holt, *Thirsty for God: A Brief History of Christian Spirituality* (Minneapolis: Augsburg, 1993), 1.

5. William A. Barry, *Paying Attention to God* (Notre Dame: Ave Maria Press, 1990), 34-35.

6. Dennis Linn, Sheila Fabricant Linn, and Matthew Linn, *Sleeping with Bread: Holding What Gives You Life* (Mahwah, NJ: Paulist Press, 1995), 20-21.

7. See S. Joan Hershey, *The First Thirty Seconds* (Fort Wayne, IN: New Life Ministries, 2000), and Fred Bernhard and Steve Clapp, *Widening the Welcome of Your Church: Biblical Hospitality and the Vital Congregation* (Elgin, IL: Brethren Press, 1996).

8. Roy Oswald and Speed Leas, *The Inviting Church* (Bethesda, MD: Alban Institute, 1987).

9. Ibid.

10. Ibid., 70

11. David S. Young, "Sunday Schools That Transform," in *Builder: An Educational Magazine for Congregational Leaders*, February 1989, 11-19.

12. The Pennsylvania State Sunday School Association, 5915 Fox Street, Harrisburg, PA 17112 or www.SundaySchoolHelp.Com.

13. Curriculum written by Teresa Eshbach.

14. One book in the series is David S. Young, *James: Faith in Action* (Elgin, IL: Brethren Press, 1992).

15. James Bryan Smith and Lynda Graybill, *A Spiritual Formation Workbook: Small-Group Resources for Nurturing Christian Growth* (San Francisco: Harper, 1991).

16. David S. Young, "Sunday Schools That Transform," 11-19.

Chapter 9:
Experiencing Transformation, New Life, and Motivation

1. David S. Young, "Hospitality, Andrew Style," *Messenger*, November 2005, 16-17.

2. David S. Young, "Foresight: The Lead that the Leader Has," in *Focus on Leadership: Servant-Leadership for the Twenty-First Century*, eds. Larry C. Spears and Michele Lawrence (New York: John Wiley & Sons, 2002), 245-57.

3. See ibid., which explains how foresight has been used over the years in the renewal process to help churches discern a vision and a plan.

4. Robert Greenleaf, *Servant Leadership: A Journey into the Nature of Legitimate Power and Greatness* (Mahwah, NJ: Paulist Press, 1977), 18.

5. Ibid., 16, 32.

6. Dietrich Bonhoeffer, *Life Together* (New York: Harper & Row, 1954), 26ff.

7. Eric H. Erikson, *Identity, Youth and Crisis* (New York: Norton, 1968), 165.

8. Ibid., 132.

Chapter 10:
Transforming Pastoral Leadership

1. Vernard Eller, *War and Peace: From Genesis to Revelation* (Eugene, OR: Wipf & Stock, 2003).

2. Thomas Kelly, *Testament of Devotion* (New York: HarperOne, 1996), 124.

3. See Marjorie Thompson, *Leading from the Center*, General Board of Discipleship of the United Methodist Church, 2.

4. From notes taken in classes on preaching given by James Forbes at Auburn Theological Seminary in New York.

5. John Westerhoff, *Spiritual Life and the Foundation for Preaching and Teaching* (Louisville: Westminster Press, 1994), 8.

6. Richard J. Foster, *Celebration of Discipline* (San Francisco: Harper & Row, 1978), 166.

7. Reuel Howe, *Partners in Preaching: Clergy and Laity in Dialogue* (New York: Seabury Press, 1967), 77.

8. In a personal letter from Rueul Howe, dated October 22, 1981.

9. James Forbes, *The Holy Spirit and Preaching* (Nashville: Abingdon Press, 1989), 83.

Chapter 11:
Developing Healthy Churches

1. Richard J. Foster, *Study Guide for Celebration of Discipline* (New York: Harper & Row, 1983).

2. Ronald Richardson, *Creating a Healthier Church* (Minneapolis: Fortress Press, 1996). This section relies on the excellent work of the above authors and persons like Serena Sellers, who presented this work

at Hatfield Church of the Brethren. Sellers credits Peter Steinke, Healthy Congregations (Bethesda, MD: Alban Institute, 1996).

3. George Parsons and Speed Leas, *Understanding Your Congregation as a System* (Bethesda, MD: Alban Institute, 1993), 19.

4. From notes of Serena Sellers, trainer for Hatfield Church of the Brethren, building on Steinke, Healthy Congregations.

5. Loren B. Mead, *A Change of Pastors and How It Affects Change in the Congregation* (Herdon, VA: Alban Institute, 2005), 22.

6. Peter Steinke, "The Balancing Act: The Congregation as an Emotional System," available from Seraphim Communications, 1568 Eustis Street, St. Paul, MN 55108; http://www.seracomm.com. See the DVD "Congregational Leadership in Anxious Times: Conversations and Reflections with Dr. Peter Steinke" from Seraphim Communications, which accompanies the book *Congregational Leadership in Anxious Times: Being Calm and Courageous No Matter What* (Herndon, VA: Alban Institute, 2006).

7. See Dietrich Bonhoeffer, *Life Together* (New York: Harper & Row, 1954), 29-30.

8. Ronald Richardson, *Creating a Healthier Church* (Minneapolis: Fortress Press, 1996), 121-28.

9. For a good treatment of family systems and the church, see Ronald W. Richardson, *Creating a Healthier Church: Family Systems Theory, Leadership, and Congregational Life* (Minneapolis: Fortress Press, 1996).

10. Roy Oswald and Speed Leas, *The Inviting Church* (Bethesda, MD: Alban Institute, 1987), 18.

11. Henry Cloud and John Townsend, *Boundaries* (Grand Rapids: Zondervan, 1992), 33.

12. Ibid., 32.

13. The Church of the Brethren has an ethics paper that could be used as a reference. It is available through the General Offices of the Church of the Brethren, 1451 Dundee Avenue, Elgin, IL 60120.

14. Martin Saarinen, *The Life Cycle of a Congregation* (Bethesda, MD: Alban Institute, 1986), 5.

15. See Ichak Adizes, "Organizational Passages—Diagnosing and Treating Lifecycle Problems of Organizations," *Organizational Dynamics*, Summer 1979, 5-6.

16. Saarinen, *Life Cycle*

Chapter 12:
Experiencing Deep Transformation

1. Credit for such principles is given to Donald Rowe, former district executive of the Mid-Atlantic District of the Church of the Brethren, who served on the professional advisory group for the doctor of ministry program at Bush Creek.

2. Robert Quinn, *Deep Change* (San Francisco: Jossey Bass, 1996), 3.

3. Adapted from David S. Young, "How the Pastor Can Help Motivate and Supervise Renewal in the Local Congregation" (doctor of ministry thesis, Bethany Theological Seminary, 1976), 47-48.

4. Foster, *Celebration of Discipline*, 144-45.

5. Richard J. Foster and Emilie Griffin, eds., *Spiritual Classics* (San Francisco: Harper, 2000), 247-48.

6. See Thomas Harris, *I'm OK–You're OK* (New York: Harper & Row, 1967), and wikipedia.org/wiki/Karpman_drama_triangle.

7. Saarinen, *Life Cycle*, 10.

8. See James M. Kouzes and Barry Z. Posner, *The Leadership Challenge* (San Francisco: Jossey-Bass, 2002).

Chapter 13:
Implementing a Renewal Plan

1. Craig Barnes, *Sacred Thirst: Meeting God in the Desert of Our Longings* (Grand Rapids: Zondervan, 2001), 195.

2. James M. Kouzes and Barry Z. Posner, *The Leadership Challenge* (San Francisco: Jossey-Bass, 2002), 14.

3. Richard J. Foster, *Celebration of Discipline* (San Francisco: Harper & Row, 1978), 145.

4. For more information on the center, go to www.cpyu.org.

5. Kendra Creasy Jones and Ron Foster, *The God Bearing Life: The Art of Soul Tending for Youth Ministry* (Nashville: Upper Room Books, 1998). See appendices C and D for professional development of people in youth ministry.

6. See Jeremiah 1:6 (NRSV): "Ah, Lord God! Truly I do not know how to speak, for I am only a boy." Overcoming the objections, God replies, "Do not be afraid of them, for I am with you to deliver you, says the Lord" (v. 8).

7. David S. Young, *A New Heart and a New Spirit: A Plan to Renew Your Church* (Valley Forge, PA: Judson Press, 1994), esp. chap. 5,

"Supervising Persons in Renewal," 45-56. Also, David S. Young, "Equipping the Saints through Supervision," in *The Calling of the Laity*, ed. Verna Dozier (Bethesda, MD: Alban Institute, 1988), 142-49.

Chapter 14:
Launching Servant Ministries
    1. Jean Vanier, *The Scandal of Service: Jesus Washes Our Feet* (Toronto: Novalis, 1996), 8-9.
    2. Ibid., 49, 37.
    3. Jean-Pierre De Caussade, *The Sacrament of the Present Moment* (New York: Harper and Row, 1982), 7.
    4. Roy Oswald and Speed Leas, *The Inviting Church* (Bethesda, MD: Alban Institute, 1987).
    5. Arlin Rothauge, "Sizing Up a Congregation for New Member Ministry," is available through Education for Mission and Ministry Office, Episcopal Church Center, 815 Second Avenue, New York, NY 10017. For each size, Rothauge gives the structure of the church, factors in attracting new members, characteristics of entry, basic needs of the newcomer, and suggestions for responding to basic needs.
    6. Alice Mann, *Can Our Church Live: Redeveloping Congregations in Decline* (Bethesda, MD: Alban Institute, 1999), 138-47.
    7. Ibid., 147.
    8. David S. Young, *Servant Leadership for Church Renewal* (Scottdale, PA: Herald Press, 1999), 120-21.
    9. For discussions on both servant leadership and handling hardship see ibid., 104ff., 119ff.
    10. Elizabeth O'Connor, *Servant Leaders, Servant Structures* (Washington, D.C.: The Servant Leadership School, n.d.), 11.
    11. Ibid., 15.

Chapter 15:
Nurturing Disciples
    1. Bishop Claude Payne, *Reclaiming the Great Commission: A Practical Model for Transforming Denominations and Congregations* (San Francisco: Jossey-Bass, 2000), 125.
    2. Dallas Willard, *The Great Omission: Reclaiming Jesus's Essential Teachings on Discipleship* (New York: HarperCollins, 2006), 53.
    3. For more information go to Alphana.org or call 1-888-WhyAlpha.

Materials include the student book, a guide with questions, and a handbook for directors, leaders, and helpers, along with videos of the lessons.

4. Nicky Gumbel, *Questions of Life* (East Sussex: Kingsway Publication, 1993). Lessons can be adapted to denominational preferences.

5. Bernhard Anderson, *The Unfolding Drama of the Bible* (New York: Association Press, 1971); Chris Wright, *The User's Guide to the Bible* (Oxford: A Lion Manual, 1993); David Ewert, *How to Understand the Bible* (Scottdale, PA: Herald Press, 2000).

6. David S. Young, *James: Faith in Action*, Covenant Bible Study Series (Elgin, IL: Brethren Press, 1992); George Peck and John Hoffman, ed., *Laity in Ministry* (Valley Forge, PA: Judson Press, 1984); Verna Dozier, *The Calling of the Laity* (Bethesda, MD: Alban Institute, 1988).

7. Michele Hershberger, *God's Story, Our Story: Exploring Christian Faith and Life* (Scottdale, PA: Herald Press, 2003); and Arthur Paul Boers, et al., eds., *Take Our Moments and Our Days: An Anabaptist Prayer Book* (Scottdale, PA: Herald Press, 2007).

8. Two good resources on marriage are Harvey Yoder, *Lasting Marriage: The Owner's Manual* (Scottdale, PA: Herald Press, 2007), and Gerald W. and L. Marlene Kaufman, *Monday Marriage: Celebrating the Ordinary* (Scottdale, PA: Herald Press, 2005).

9. Two books that are helpful in teaching peacemaking and pacifism are Myron S. Augsburger, *The Robe of God: Reconciliation, the Believers Church Essential* (Scottdale, PA: Herald Press, 2000), and Willard M. Swartley, *Send Forth Your Light: A Vision for Peace, Mission, and Worship* (Scottdale, PA: Herald Press, 2007).

10. Richard Armstrong, *Service Evangelism* (Philadelphia: Westminster Press, 1979).

11. Richard Armstrong, *Faithful Witnesses: A Course in Evangelism for Presbyterian Laity* (Louisville: Westminster John Knox Press, 1987), 32-33.

12. Ibid.

13. Several other resources on the theme of church building and mission are Stuart Murray, *Church Planting: Lay Foundations* (Scottdale, PA: Herald Press, 2001); David W. Shenk and Ervin R. Stutzman, *Creating Communities of the Kingdom: New Testament Models of Church Planting* (Scottdale, PA: Herald Press, 1988); Richard Showalter, *On the Way with Jesus: A Passion for Mission* (Scottdale, PA: Herald Press, 2008).

14. S. Joan Hershey, *The First Thirty Seconds* (Fort Wayne, IN: New Life Ministries, 2000).

15. Written and compiled by S. Joan Hershey in 2004, the packet is available through Life Quest at 6404 S. Calhoun Street, Fort Wayne, IN 46807, 1-800-774-3360.

16. From handouts by Lou George.

17. Stewardship University's email is education@mma-online.org.

18. All these titles are available from Herald Press, Scottdale, PA.

Chapter 16:
Claiming the Deeper Journey

1. *Springs of Living Water* DVD, produced by Kenneth and Beckie Bomberger as a training tool.

2. Phyllis Tickle, *The Divine Hours*, 3 vols. (New York: Doubleday, 2001). See viii-xii for a brief history of fixed-hour prayer.

3. Rufus Jones, *The Double Search* (Richmond, IN: Friends United Press, 1906), 14.

4. Douglas Steere, *Dimensions of Prayer: Cultivating a Relationship with God* (New York: The United Methodist Church, 1962), 51.

5. Ibid.

6. Karl Barth, "The Doctrine of Reconciliation," in *Church Dogmatics*, vol. 4, pt. 3 (Edinburgh: T & T Clark, 1962), 647-48.

7. Ibid., 899.

8. Lois Barrett, et al., *Treasure in Clay Jars: Patterns in Missional Faithfulness* (Grand Rapids: Eerdmans, 2004), ix-x.

9. David S. Young, *Servant Leadership for Church Renewal: Shepherds by the Living Streams* (Scottdale, PA: Herald Press, 1999).

10. Thomas Green, *When the Well Runs Dry: Prayer Beyond the Beginnings* (Notre Dame: Ave Maria Press, 1998), 123.

11. Dietrich Bonhoeffer, *Life Together* (New York: Harper & Row, 1954), 21.

12. Ibid., 22, 23, 24, 26, 27.

13. *A Guide to Prayer* and *A Guide to Prayer for All God's People* by Rueben Job and Norman Shawchuck are two very helpful resources from Upper Room Books.

14. Emilie Griffin, *Wilderness Time: A Guide for Spiritual Retreat* (New York: HarperCollins, 1997), 7.

15. Timothy Jones, *A Place for God* (New York: Doubleday, 2000). For information on preparing for retreat, see 3-86.

16. Tilden Edwards, *Sabbath Time* (Nashville: Upper Room Books, 1992).

17. Steven Ott, Center for Career Development and Ministry, gives four aspects of Sabbath rest: (1) rest—sleeping in, off schedule, napping, physical restoration; (2) mental—doing something enjoyable to grow in one's interests; (3) travel—having a change of scenery, culture, or country (budget dependent); (4) spiritual rest and nurture—can be done on retreat and with a spiritual director.

18. Robert Mulholland, *Invitation to a Journey: A Road Map for Spiritual Formation* (Downers Grove, IL: InterVarsity Press, 1993), 32.

Index

The Author

David S. Young is an ordained minister in the Church of the Brethren and has held permanent and interim positions in small and large churches since 1970. He has helped numerous churches facilitate renewal. He and his wife, Joan, have established the Springs of Living Water revitalization initiative for congregations desiring new life. David holds a Doctor of Ministry in church renewal from Bethany Theological Seminary. He is the author of *Servant Leadership for Church Renewal: Shepherds by the Living Springs* and *A New Heart and A New Spirit: A Plan for Renewing Your Church*. He lives in Ephrata, Pennsylvania.

Notes

Notes

Notes